LEGAL PHILOSOPHY

Other books from Automatic Press ♦ $\frac{V}{I}$P

Formal Philosophy
edited by Vincent F. Hendricks & John Symons
November 2005

Thought$_2$Talk: A Crash Course in Reflection and Expression
by Vincent F. Hendricks
September 2006

Masses of Formal Philosophy
edited by Vincent F. Hendricks & John Symons
October 2006

Political Questions: 5 Questions for Political Philosophers
edited by Morten Ebbe Juul Nielsen
December 2006

Philosophy of Technology: 5 Questions
edited by Jan-Kyrre Berg Olsen & Evan Selinger
February 2007

Game Theory: 5 Questions
edited by Vincent F. Hendricks & Pelle Guldborg Hansen
April 2007

Philosophy of Mathematics: 5 Questions
edited by Vincent F. Hendricks & Hannes Leitgeb
November 2007

Normative Ethics: 5 Questions
edited by Jesper Ryberg & Thomas S. Petersen
November 2007

Philosophy of Physics: 5 Questions
edited by Juan Ferret & John Symons
March 2008

Probability and Statistics: 5 Questions
edited by Alan Hájek & Vincent F. Hendricks
March 2008

LEGAL PHILOSOPHY
5 QUESTIONS

edited by

Morten Ebbe Juul Nielsen

Automatic Press ♦ $\frac{V}{I}$P

Automatic Press ♦ V|P

Information on this title: www.legalphilosophy.org

© Automatic Press / VIP 2007

This publication is in copyright. Subject to statuary exception
and to the provisions of relevant collective licensing agreements,
no reproduction of any part may take place without
the written permission of the publisher.

First published 2007

Printed in the United States of America
and the United Kingdom

ISBN-13   978-87-92130-01-3   paperback

The publisher has no responsibilities for
the persistence or accuracy of URLs for external or
third party Internet Web sites referred to in this publication
and does not guarantee that any content on such
Web sites is, or will remain, accurate or appropriate.

Typeset in $\LaTeX 2_\varepsilon$
Graphic design by Vincent F. Hendricks

Contents

Preface	iii
Acknowledgements	v
1 Robert Alexy	1
2 Tom Campbell	13
3 Jules L. Coleman	27
4 John Gardner	45
5 Ruth Gavison	59
6 Leslie Green	75
7 Andrew von Hirsch	89
8 Tony Honoré	101
9 Douglas Husak	113
10 Nicola Lacey	125
11 Brian Leiter	143
12 David Lyons	153
13 Sir Neil MacCormick	171
14 Stanley L. Paulson	187
15 Frederick Schauer	199
16 Scott J. Shapiro	209
About the Editor	227

About Legal Philosophy	229
Index	231

Preface

What is legal philosophy, or philosophy of law? It obviously concerns one of the most wondrous constructions of humankind: Law. One does not need a particularly philosophical frame of mind to be engrossed in wonder and puzzlement over the nature of law. Why and when does the law apply to me? By what (magic?) process do decisions or words commonly thought to be "law" hold "authority" over me? Is that authority unlimited, or somehow constrained, and if so, how and why? Why is it that the law suddenly becomes different, just because I cross some border? How do I know what laws apply to me? How do judges reach their decisions? What is it to "treat like cases alike?" Can there be unwritten laws? And so on.

Given the state of refinement and specialization in contemporary legal philosophy one might respond that some of these questions are contrived, or long since solved, or shown to be irrelevant, or perhaps just unnecessarily naïve. On the other hand, I expect that no one would say that we have a general consensus and a nice, clear picture about the nature of law. The same goes, *a fortiori*, for more applied questions regarding the law.

Philosophers from any philosophical discipline must from time to time engage in the meta-question about its identity. However, the question seems particularly pressing when legal philosophy is concerned; so much, in fact, that some its practitioners often refer to its "ongoing quest for identity". This must be an institutional question about how "legal philosophy" should fit into the established scholarly philosophical categories, or perhaps a question of methodology rather than a question of subject: for even though we have no clear cut picture about the nature of law, we all know that there is law; have a rough idea about what it is and how it works; and when it does not.

It is one of the main aims of this volume to engage and hopefully contribute to this quest for identity. The questions asked all relate more or less directly to that point. For example, when I ask the participants "for which of your contribution(s) to legal philosophy so far would you most like to be remembered, and why?", the (thinly veiled) agenda is not only to get them to comment retrospectively on their own most outstanding works, but also to get a glimpse of how these distinguished legal philosophers *think* legal philosophy and what they believe is important for that particular area. Most obviously, the question "what are the most important issues in legal philosophy, and why are they distinctively issues of legal philosophy rather than some other discipline?" goes right to the heart of the question of identity. For the optimist, the diversity of the answers given to that question, as well as for the rest, bears testimony to a field that is very much alive and kicking. The pessimist or skeptic might respond that this is a field of enquiry in deep crisis. I side with the optimist.

A couple of notes on the selection and format of *Legal Philosophy – Five Questions*. There are three evident constraints on the selection of contributors. First, all except Robert Alexy and Stanley Paulson are wholly or predominantly Anglophone, and second, they all belong more or less squarely within the analytic (or perhaps "post-analytic") approach. Thirdly, whereas a good deal of the contributors are, or have been, working "in the field" as lawyers etc., and have written material which belongs in law schools rather than in philosophy classes and journals, the reason they are included here is exclusively for their excellence and influence in *philosophy* of law.

Regarding the format of the essay/interviews, I decided from the outset that they should retain whatever "impromptu" feeling they might have – if any. Accordingly, the authors had almost free reins in answering the questions, and I have not attempted to standardize the format of the different essays. The lists of literature after each essay are provided by the contributors.

Thanks to: Ian Farrell, University of Wollongong, for helping out with the selection of authors and other kinds of invaluable advice and help.

Morten Ebbe Juul Nielsen
Frederiksberg
September 2007

Acknowledgements

Thanks to: Ian Farrell, University of Wollongong, for helping out with the selection of authors and other kinds of invaluable advice and help. In addition I would like to express my gratitude to Christopher M. Whalin and Elizabeth Pando for proof-reading the manuscript and to my publisher **Automatic Press ♦ $\frac{V}{I}$P**, in particular senior publishing editor V.J. Menshy for taking on this project

Morten Ebbe Juul Nielsen
Frederiksberg
September 2007

1
Robert Alexy

Professor of Public Law and Legal Philosophy
Christian Albrechts University, Kiel, Germany [1]

Why were you initially drawn to the philosophy of law?

I was interested in philosophy even before attending the university, and when I began my studies in Göttingen, in 1968, I signed up for courses in philosophy as well as in law. The combination quite naturally led me to the philosophy of law.

Interest does not necessarily bespeak a lasting commitment, of course. That my interest in legal philosophy remained constant throughout my student years is a tribute to my teachers. In my very first year in Göttingen, I had the good fortune of studying philosophy with Günther Patzig. He introduced me not only to Kant and Aristotle but also to analytic philosophy, especially the work of Gottlob Frege. And he taught me the value of the analytical approach to reading the great philosophers. Toward the end of my university studies, good fortune was once again mine. Ralf Dreier accepted a professorship in Göttingen. When, in 1973, I began writing my dissertation, *A Theory of Legal Argumentation*, under his supervision, I was – unbeknownst to me at the time, of course – taking up legal philosophy as my profession.

I have been happy with my decision to focus on legal philosophy. My work confronts me with worthy challenges, piques my curiosity, and gives me pleasure. It has never been boring.

---

[1]* I should like to thank Stanley L. Paulson and Bonnie Litschewski Paulson for suggestions and advice on matters of English style.

For which of your contribution(s) to legal philosophy so far would you like to be remembered, and why?

Most of my work has been devoted to three themes: first, legal reasoning or argumentation, second, human and constitutional rights, and, third, the concept and nature of law. The overarching idea is the institutionalization of practical reason. If the three themes can be united by means of this idea, the result may well be a system.

Legal reasoning is the subject of *A Theory of Legal Argumentation*, first published in German in 1978. The English translation by Ruth Adler and Neil MacCormick followed in 1989. The leitmotif of the book is the question of what 'rational legal argumentation' comes to and whether, indeed, it is possible. My answer, from the beginning, has been that legal argumentation or discourse can be established as a rational enterprise if one conceives of it as a special case of general practical discourse. This is the *special case thesis*. Two factors are of significance here.

First, legal discourse is a case of general practical discourse. This is the case because legal argumentation, like general practical argumentation, is, in the end, concerned with what is obligatory, prohibited, or permitted, that is to say, with practical questions. Second, it is a special case, for the claim to correctness raised in legal discourse refers not simply to what is correct in an ideal or absolute sense but to what is correct within the framework of a specific legal system. This is the real or relative dimension of legal discourse. What is correct in a legal system depends essentially on what is authoritatively or institutionally issued. The special character of legal discourse can be expressed by the formula that legal argumentation is bound, first, to statutes and, second, to precedent, and that it has, third, to proceed with the intention of rendering coherent the decisions of the legislator and the judiciary – proceeding, then, with a systematic intent.

This special character by no means implies, however, that legal argumentation has an exclusively authoritative or institutional character. The ideal or critical dimension of general practical discourse is at work, too, in the authoritative or institutional context. Two reasons serve to explain this fact. The first is the open texture of law that stems from such phenomena as the vagueness of the language of law, the indefiniteness of the intentions of the lawmaker, the possibility of conflict between norms and precedents, the appearance of new cases, the possibility of overruling precedent, and – albeit only in special circumstances – deciding contrary to the express text of a statute. In such cases the authoritative material does not suffice to decide the case. Where the authoritative reasons have run out, then, if legal decisions are to be based on reasons, as required by law's claim to correctness, the reasons for the decision must include non-authoritative reasons. These additional non-authoritative or non-institutional reasons can only be those of general practical discourse. General practical discourse comprises, first, moral arguments referring to what is just and unjust, second, ethical arguments relating to individual and collective self-understanding, and, third, pragmatic arguments based on considerations of welfare and utility. Law's claim to correctness requires that justice, that is, morality, be given priority in cases of conflict within the family of general practical arguments. In this sense, the special case thesis establishes a necessary connection between law and morality.

The second reason in explanation of the fact that the ideal or critical dimension is at work, too, in the authoritative or institutional context of law is that legal decisions claim not only that the open area of law is closed in a rational, well-reasoned way but also that it is rational to apply the existing authoritative material. Whoever decides a case claims not only that his decision is correct on the basis, and within the framework, of the legal system but also that it is rational or correct to apply the norm he is applying. This means that the officials of the legal system cannot escape a public responsibility for decisions that, although not made, are applied by them. In spite of the fact that these decisions are beyond their control, they must nevertheless claim that *their* decisions, *qua* legal decisions, are correct. This demonstrates that the rationality of legal argumentation is not a question confined to legal methodology but one that can only be answered in a theory of law that attempts to explain the structure and content of law's claim to correctness.

As an objection to the special case thesis, it might be said that any reasonable connection of law and moral argument has to presuppose the possibility of rational moral argument. This possibility, so the objection goes, does not, however, exist. Moral argument lacks rationality and, with it, objectivity and correctness or truth. For this reason, the theory of legal reasoning ought to be confined to a theory of authoritative or institutional reasons. My reply to this 'irrationality objection', as it might be called, is set out in the theory of rational practical discourse, in short, *discourse theory*.

Discourse theory is a procedural theory of practical correctness or truth. According to discourse theory, a practical proposition is correct if it can be the result of a rational discourse. In *A Theory of Legal Argumentation,* I attempted to make explicit the conditions of discursive rationality by means of a system of twenty-eight rules and forms of general practical discourse. This system comprises rules that demand non-contradiction, clarity of language, reliability of the empirical premises, and sincerity, as well as rules and forms that speak to the consequences, as well as to balancing, universalizability, and the analysis of the genesis of normative convictions. The procedural core consists of rules that guarantee freedom and equality in discourse by granting to everyone the right to participate in discourse and the right to question as well as to defend any assertion.

To be sure, discourse theory is confronted with a number of serious philosophical problems. I have discussed some of them in the article 'Problems of Discourse Theory' (1988). Two points are of interest here. The first concerns a problem of discourse theory that might be called the 'problem of knowledge'. This problem stems from the fact that discourse is not a procedure that always yields just one right answer. It may well be the case that a argues on behalf of the normative proposition p, b on behalf of non-p, and neither of them violates any discourse rule. In this case, p as well as non-p are discursively possible, and, in this sense, are relatively right or correct. In this instance, which is by no means exceptional, legally regulated procedures that guarantee a decision are necessary. The problem of knowledge inherent in discourse theory leads in this way to the necessity of law.

A second point is this. The connection between discourse and law is by no means a one-way street. Law requires discourse in order to be legitimate. For that reason, discourse cannot be completely replaced by decision; on the contrary, the two must be connected. In this way, the problem of the legitimacy of law might well be resolved.

The rules of discourse are the result of an attempt to make explicit what is implicit in our practice of asserting, asking, and arguing. The fact that the discourse rules give expression to the values of freedom and equality underscores the point that our discursive practice necessarily contains values. In the article 'Discourse Theory and Human Rights' (1996) I tried to establish that this may serve as a basis for the justification of human rights. Should this be true, there would then exist an intrinsic substantive connection between discourse theory and human and constitutional rights.

Constitutional rights are the subject of *A Theory of Constitutional Rights*, which first appeared, in German, in 1985. The English translation by Julian Rivers was published in 2002. The central thesis of this book is that the main problems of the theory of constitutional rights can be solved by means of a distinction between rules and principles, a distinction that is based, in turn, on the thesis that principles are optimization requirements. Optimization requirements are norms demanding that something be realized to the greatest extent possible, given the factual and legal possibilities. By contrast, rules are norms requiring something definitively. They are definitive commands.

The elaboration of this distinction yields what might be called *'principle theory'*. The significance of principle theory for constitutional rights stems, first of all, from the fact that this theory is the basis of proportionality analysis. Proportionality analysis is not only a theoretically well-founded test of whether or not a constitutional right has been violated by an infringement, it is also gaining international recognition in the practice of constitutional review.

Proportionality analysis consists in the application of the standard or principle of proportionality. Here 'principle' is being used in a general sense and not in the specific sense of principle theory. The principle of proportionality consists of three sub-principles: the principle of suitability, of necessity, and of proportionality in its narrower sense. The principles of suitability and necessity concern optimization relative to what is factually possible. In this respect, they are concerned not with balancing as such but with avoiding those interferences with constitutional rights that can be avoided without costs to other principles. These two principles are concerned, in other words, with Pareto-optimality. By contrast, the third sub-principle, the principle of proportionality in its narrower sense, concerns the optimization relative to the legal possibilities. The legal possibilities, rules aside, are essentially defined by competing principles. This is the proper field of balancing, for balancing consists in nothing other than optimisation relative to competing principles. Principle theory, therefore, is in essence a theory of balancing.

Whether balancing is rational is, to be sure, a highly contested matter. In my work I have attempted to show, first, that it is, and, second, that the method of balancing is indispensible if the definitive content of constitutional rights is to be determined in as rational a way as possible. This can be demonstrated by means of a *weight formula* that defines the concrete weight of a principle P_i relative to a colliding principle P_j as the quotient of, first, the product of the intensity of the interference with P_i times the abstract weight of P_i times the degree of reliability of the empirical assumptions concerning what the measure in question means for the non-realization of P_i, and, second, the product of the corresponding values with respect to P_j, now related to the realisation of P_j. All this can be elaborated in a mathematical model that, as such, employs numbers ('On Balancing and Subsumption' (2003)). This is not to say, however, that calculation is substituted for argument. The numbers – on the basis of a theory of scales in constitutional law – that have to be substituted for the variables of the weight formula represent judgments about intensity of interference, abstract weight, and degree of reliability. These judgments, as with judgments generally, require justification by means of argument. Thus, the weight formula turns out to be nothing other than an argument form of practical discourse. In this sense, argument or discourse is the basis of the theory of constitutional rights ('Balancing, constitutional review, and representation' (2005)).

My third main theme, the concept and the nature of law, is the subject of *The Argument from Injustice. A Reply to Legal Positivism*, first published, in German, in 1992 under the title *Begriff und Geltung des Rechts*. The English translation by Bonnie Litschewski Paulson and Stanley L. Paulson appeared in 2002. The aim of the book is to defend a non-positivistic theory of law. All positivistic theories defend some form of the separation thesis. The thesis maintains that what the law is does not necessarily depend on what the law ought to be, that is, on moral or other evaluative criteria. By contrast, all non-positivistic theories defend some form of the connection thesis. This thesis maintains, basically, that what the law is necessarily depends on what the law ought to be, that is, on moral or other evaluative criteria.

The connection thesis, as I defend it, by no means says that the real or institutional dimension of law is to be excluded from the concept of law. Rather, it maintains that the nature of law comprises a real or institutional dimension, defined by authoritative issuance and social efficacy, as well as an ideal or critical dimension, defined by substantial and procedural correctness, especially moral correctness. The version of the connection thesis that I defend might therefore be termed the '*dual-nature thesis*'. The dual-nature thesis maintains, in short, that what the law is necessarily depends both on social facts and moral values.

The mere fact that the debate over the concept and the nature of law reaches back over a period of more than two millennia, and without showing any sign of either agreement or exhaustion, gives rise to the conjecture that positivists and non-positivists are discussing different questions. In *The Argument from Injustice* I argue that the separation thesis is correct from the perspective of an observer but wrong from the perspective of a participant. From the latter perspective, the connection thesis alone is correct. The participant's perspective is to be distinguished from the observer's perspective in that the participant asks and argues on behalf of what he deems to be the correct answer to a legal question in his legal system, whereas the observer asks and argues on behalf of the question of how legal questions are actually decided in that legal system. Now the participant's perspective is necessary for the existence of a legal system. A legal system without participants is not conceivable. The question of whether, from the participant's perspective, the separation thesis is mistaken and the connection thesis correct speaks, therefore, to the question of the essence of law.

My argument for the connection thesis cannot be elaborated here. I will confine myself to two remarks. The first is that the basis of my argument consists in the thesis that law necessarily raises a claim to correctness, and that this claim comprises a claim to moral correctness. This is the *correctness thesis* ('Law and Correctness' (1998)). This is not to say, however, that morally incorrect legal decisions, simply in virtue of being morally incorrect, are thereby rendered legally invalid. They are, however, owing to the necessity of law's claim to correctness, not only morally defective but also legally defective. Moral incorrectness implies legal incorrectness, for law's own claim to correctness refers to moral correctness – and this reference is not tied to some extra-legal point of view. One may term this a 'qualifying' or 'ideal' connection between law and morality.

My second remark concerns what I have called the 'argument from injustice'. The argument from injustice, in its most compressed form, says that extreme injustice is not law. The *extreme injustice thesis* is a summary statement of Gustav Radbruch's formula ('A Defense of Radbruch's Formula' (2001)). It gives expression to the idea that the necessary connection between law and morality, established by the claim to correctness, does not imply, on the one hand, that each and every moral defect reaches to legal validity, which is not however to say, on the other hand, that legal validity remains untouched by all moral defects. Once the extremity threshold is crossed, legal validity is lost.

What are the most important issues in legal philosophy, and why are they distinctively issues of legal philosophy rather than some other discipline?

There are three main issues in legal philosophy: first, the concept and the nature of law, second, legal argumentation and interpretation, and, third, rights and justice.

The first issue is the main focus of legal philosophy. Philosophy is the field of general and systematic reflection about what there is, what ought to be done or is good, and how knowledge about both is possible. Legal philosophy raises these questions with respect to the law ('The Nature of Legal Philosophy' (2006)). In doing so, legal philosophy addresses first and foremost the question of what there is, if there is law. To enquire into this question is to be engaged in reasoning about the nature and the concept of law ('The Nature of Arguments about the Nature of Law' (2003)). No other discipline can do this. If it did, it would be legal philosophy and not some other discipline.

The second issue, legal argumentation and interpretation, is closely connected to the first issue. Or, more precisely, this is the case if legal argumentation and interpretation are a part of the law. The analysis of the structure of rational legal argumentation and interpretation is, on the other hand, a special case of the general philosophical analysis of sound argument and correct interpretation. This, again, underscores the close connection between law and philosophy.

The third issue, rights and justice, addresses to the general philosophical question of what ought to be done or is good. This suggests, correctly, that rights and justice are themes not only of legal philosophy but also of political and moral philosophy. It is not possible to draw a sharp line between the disciplines here.

1. Robert Alexy

What is the relationship between legal philosophy and legal practice? Should legal philosophers be more concerned about the effects of their scholarship on legal practice?

There are authors who claim that there exists no intrinsic relation between legal philosophy and legal practice. Just the opposite, I think, is the case. All jurists have a more or less clear and more or less coherent idea about what the law is, that is to say, a more or less clear and more or less coherent philosophy of law. This has to be the case, for without an idea of what the law is, one could not distinguish legal reasons from other reasons, but jurists do in fact make such distinctions, albeit incorrectly in some instances. The fact that the concept of law explicitly or implicitly used by jurists can be either correct or incorrect implies, when coupled with the claim to correctness necessarily raised in legal argumentation, that jurists are not only participants in a parochial enterprise, reflecting the real or authoritative dimension of law, but also in an universal enterprise ('On Two Juxtapositions: Concept and Nature, Law and Philosophy' (2007)). The latter is an expression of the ideal or critical dimension of law.

The relationship between legal philosophy and legal practice is not confined to general themes such as the concept and nature of law. Law and philosophy have other themes in common, too. Here a certain bit of give-and-take is possible. All of the fundamental concepts and principles of law are enhanced by philosophical analysis, and philosophy for its part can learn from an elaboration of the niceties of legal practice that has withstood the test of time. Examples include the concepts of human dignity, constitutional rights, proportionality, responsibility, and property, along with the principles of freedom, equality, and democracy.

The value of legal philosophy for legal practice consists not only in the elucidation of concepts and the perfection of theories. The enhancement of self-understanding and reflection that may be achieved by philosophical analysis is, I believe, equally important.

Should legal philosophers be more concerned about the effect of their scholarship on legal practice? The answer is: yes and no. Legal philosophy *qua* philosophy cannot be pursued with an eye to positive practical effects. Like basic research generally, it must be free. Still, legal philosophy *qua* reflection about law is by its nature addressed to legal problems. Thus, a relation to legal practice is not something imposed on legal philosophy from without.

Rather, it is an aspiration that stems from the very nature of the juridico-philosophical enterprise. In light of this background it seems advisable that legal philosophers also be experts in at least one area of substantive law. Needless to say, there are many other forms, too, for bringing together and reflecting on the relationship between legal philosophy and legal practice.

To which problem, issue or broad area of legal philosophy would you most like to see more attention paid in the future?

I would like to see more attention paid, in the future, to three areas of legal philosophy: first, conflicts of rights, second, relations between and among legal systems, and, third, theories of objectivity.

In the last decades, there has been a considerable extension of human and constitutional rights. This applies equally to their number, their kinds, their effects, and their scope. To extend rights, however, is, *inter alia*, to increase legal conflicts. These may be conflicts between different rights or between rights and collective goods. If conflicts of these sorts are not to endanger the very idea of rights, they have to be taken seriously. This leads to a broad spectrum of themes that stem from the issues of our day. The spectrum reaches from human embryo research to the protection of the environment and on to the struggle against terrorism.

It is a truism that in many parts of the world, the legal systems of very different countries are coming together. This phenomenon may be described as the globalization of law. It represents a great challenge for legal philosophy – from both an analytical standpoint and a normative point of view – and it is an area whose problems, if not resolved, may well threaten the future of mankind.

In recent years, considerable progress has been made on the issues clustered around the notion of objectivity in law. Still, many questions remain open. These issues address, for example, the relation between what one might term the 'members of the objectivity family', that is, the concepts of truth, correctness, justification, intersubjectivity, rationality, reality, knowledge, and the like. One would like to think that enquiries here will promote the self-confidence of reason.

Bibliography

Books

A Theory of Legal Argumentation (first published in 1978), trans. Ruth Adler and Neil MacCormick (Oxford: Clarendon Press, 1989).

A Theory of Constitutional Rights (first published in 1985), trans. Julian Rivers (Oxford: Oxford University Press, 2002).

The Argument from Injustice. A Reply to Legal Positivism (first published in 1992), trans. Bonnie Litschewski Paulson and Stanley L. Paulson (Oxford: Clarendon Press, 2002).

Articles

'Problems of Discourse Theory', *crítica*, 20 (1988), 43–65.

'Discourse Theory and Human Rights', *Ratio Juris*, 9 (1996), 209–35.

'Law and Correctness', *Current Legal Problems*, 51 (1998), 205–21.

'A Defense of Radbruch's Formula', in *Lloyd's Introduction to Jurisprudence*, 7nd edn., ed. M.D.A. Freeman (London: Sweet & Maxwell, 2001), 374–91.

'On Balancing and Subsumption', *Ratio Juris*, 16 (2003), 433–49.

'The Nature of Arguments about the Nature of Law', in *Rights, Culture, and Law. Themes from the Legal and Political Philosophy of Joseph Raz*, ed. Lukas H. Meyer, Stanley L. Paulson, and Thomas W. Pogge (Oxford: Oxford University Press, 2003), 3–16.

'Balancing, constitutional review, and representation', *International Journal of Constitutional Law'*, 3 (2005), 572–82.

'The Nature of Legal Philosophy', in *Philosophy of Law. Critical Concepts in Philosophy*, vol. 1, ed. Brian H. Bix (London and New York: Routledge, 2006), 21–32.

'On Two Juxtapositions: Concept and Nature, Law and Philosophy. Some Comments on Joseph Raz's "Can There Be a Theory of Law?"', *Ratio Juris*, 20 (2007), 162–9.

2
Tom Campbell

Professorial Fellow, Centre for Applied Philosophy and Public Ethics (CAPPE), Charles Sturt University, Australia

Visiting Professor, School of Law, King's College London, UK

Why were you initially drawn to the philosophy of law?

I came to legal philosophy as such rather late after specializing, as in a way I still do, in moral and political philosophy. At the University of Glasgow in the early 1960s, I studied philosophy as a compulsory part of the 'Ordinary MA' (a first degree, in Scotland) which I was doing as a preparation for going to qualify in divinity and become a minister of the Church of Scotland. As it turned out I never escaped from the fascination of philosophy, although my subsequent BA in Oxford was in Theology and my first university position was in the Department of Politics and Sociology at Glasgow University. Traditionally the ancient Scottish universities had a department of general philosophy (with names such as Logic and Rhetoric) and a separate department of Moral Philosophy and it was the professor of Moral Philosophy, W.G. Maclagan, whose inspiring introductory lectures to a class of over 300 students, had an enormous impact on me. I still have my carefully typed notes of these lectures today. Maclagan was a staunch defender of the 'a priori synthetic' (substantive knowledge acquired independently of empirical evidence), the sort of view that was ridiculed by the dominant and sometimes domineering 'ordinary language' philosophers of the period, whose views were well represented by the younger lecturers at Glasgow. This was an exciting mixture that exposed a small but enthusiastic group of Honours students to lively debates, largely in 'meta-ethics', the received wisdom being that philosophy did not engage in moral reasoning but only in reasoning about morality. These contemporary controversies were balanced by an emphasis on the history of philosophy, which constituted at least half of the curriculum and introduced us to the major figures in the history of philosophy, with a special emphasis on the Enlightenment, although not, rather curiously, with any specific emphasis on the Scottish Enlightenment, but plenty of Hume.

Much as I enjoyed and benefited from my philosophical studies, I found, and still find, the intellectual attitudes to be found in many philosophy departments rather arid and inward looking. For this reason, I sought a position a politics department which is I saw as being more directly concerned first order questions about issues, such as capital punishment and censorship, with meta-ethics providing no more than an important background to these practical debates. I was particularly keen to work with Glasgow University's first Professor of Politics, D.D. Raphael, whose engagement with matters of rights, justice and equality, in combination with a profound scholarly interest in the British Moralists, showed what political philosophy could be, well before the seismic impact of John Rawls, *A Theory of Justice* in the early 1970s. This proved to be a happy association, as David Raphael became my PhD supervisor (a good first degree was all that was needed for a lecturing appointment at the time) and pointed me in the direction of Adam Smith, a onetime Professor of Moral Philosophy at the University of Glasgow. This was prompted in part by the fact that a copy of a student's notes of Smith's Lectures in Jurisprudence, rather longer than the already published notes of another student who had attended the same lectures in another year, had been discovered in an Aberdeen bookshop and acquired by the University of Glasgow. I read the typescript of these notes only to have them withdrawn by a committee who took the view that such access prior to publication was, for some reason, inappropriate. That was no matter, I spent four rewarding years reading and rereading Smith's *The Theory of Moral Sentiments* and struggling to understand it in the light of Smith's economic, political, literary and jurisprudential work and the moral and social theory of his time and my own. Among the many things that I absorbed in this process was the interconnection in what we nowadays call 'applied philosophy' of social, political, economic and legal phenomena. Following in this tradition there was no time at which I saw myself in the study of Smith, or in my associated work on such topics as political obligation, rights, justice, equality, welfare, abortion, free speech, as moving from one branch of philosophy to another.

Nevertheless there are institutional boundaries in academia that affect career choices, and I moved on to the Department of Moral Philosophy, with Professor Robin Downie, a pioneer in bioethics, who had taught me as a student and influenced me by his writing, especially, *Respect for Persons* (with Elizabeth Telfer), and then to the Philosophy Department in the new University of Stirling, where I spent 5 years in a young and lively department, which included the now well-known philosopher of criminal law, Antony Duff. It was at this time that David Raphael and Neil MacCormick (a contemporary at Glasgow and Balliol), recently appointed to the Regius Chair of Public Law and the Law of Nations at the University of Edinburgh, were involved in establishing a branch of the IVR (The International Association of Social Philosophy and Philosophy of Law) in the UK. My participation in that group undoubtedly turned my attention further towards the legal philosophy I had got to know through the debates of Hart and Devlin on the enforcement of morals and Hart and Fuller on the impact of legal positivism in evil regimes. When the opportunity arose, therefore, it felt quite natural to move back to Glasgow, into the Faculty of Law and its Department of Jurisprudence which has the responsibility for teaching the compulsory class of Jurisprudence (variously called Legal Theory or Philosophy of Law elsewhere) to third year law students.

Familiar only with the work of H.L.A. Hart. Lon Fuller and some American Legal Realists, I had some work to do to catch up on more specialist work in the area of legal reasoning, to say nothing of the basic law that I had not directly confronted before. As a Professor of Jurisprudence at Glasgow and later as Professor of Law at The Australian National University, I welcomed the opportunity to work out my own philosophy of law, a project that resulted in *The Legal Theory of Ethical Positivism* (1996), which, although as much a work in political theory as legal philosophy, represents my rather late coming of age in legal philosophy.

For which of your contribution(s) to legal philosophy so far would you like to be remembered, and why?

I would liked to be seen as contributing to the resurgence of interest in the normative aspects of legal positivism, particularly the moral and political benefits of a model of law that focuses in developing and impartially following and applying a body of rules that can routinely be understood and adjudicated without recourse to adopting a particular position on controversial moral and factual matters. Within legal positivism, I suggest, the important conceptual issues regarding law, legal reasoning and legal obligation, are best tackled in the framework of either normative or empirical studies, rather than as a purely analytical exercise. In the jargon of the time, I described my position as 'prescriptive exclusive legal positivism' as that seemed to capture the thesis that much of the legal positivist tradition can be read as recommending that moral criteria should not be included in the 'rule of recognition', whereby citizens and officials can identify what is the law of a particular jurisdiction. 'Prescriptive exclusive legal positivism' is a bit of a mouthful, so I now tend to speak of 'prescriptive legal positivism' (PLP for short) to distinguish it from the alternatives of 'conceptual legal positivism (undesirable!) and empirical legal positivism (under-developed!).

I have not been able to settle on what is the best label to put on this approach to legal positivism. I rejected the term 'normative positivism' because this was already used for those who understood law as a set of norms rather than commands. In *The Legal Theory of Ethical Positivism* I adopted the term 'ethical positivism' because I wanted to emphasize that the legal positivist ideal requires a certain type of role morality (rule-commitment) on the part of judges, legislators, public servants and citizens. However, this term generated expectations of a theory of ethics rather of law. Also 'ethical positivism' does not stress sufficiently the fact that many of the important moral arguments for legal positivism are based on its commitment to the rule of positive law as a crucial part of democracy. Indeed, I toyed with the label 'democratic legal positivism' at one stage, but that seems too narrow to capture the full flavour of the theory which also promotes the benefits of rule-governance in non-democratic systems. So I am back with 'PLP', the title I gave to a recent collection of my previously published work.

All this is slightly ironic since it amounts to a non-lawyer urging that the study and practice of law should focus more on what is (now dismissively) referred to as 'black letter law' and recognize that the social and political value of legal institutions, and in particular lawyers, depends on them being focussed on the distinctively legal enterprise rather than merging it with methods and attitudes of the democratic political process that does (or should) inform the process of law-making. This is not to say that Law Schools should not include a concern with moral and political critiques of existing law and legal process and proposals for law reform. It is much to be welcomed that study and research concerning law involves an appreciation of the ingredients of policy making and the legal aspects of its implementation. Moreover, lawyers, as citizens have as much right and perhaps more duty than as other citizen to engage in such debates and decision-making about what the law ought to be. This should not, however, displace the distinctively legal skill and concern of maintaining a system of law in which it is possible to ask and answer the question 'what is the law on this matter' without engaging in a substantive moral exercise concerning what the law ought to be.

While one of the main practical issues to which PLP is particularly relevant is the controversy over the role of courts in substantive judicial review on the basis of an entrenched or legislated bill of rights, this was not an issue of particular concern at the time I came to lay the groundwork of the theory. The book which, as a cheap paperback, was widely read at the time, *The Left and Rights: A Conceptual Analysis of the Idea of Socialist Rights* (1983), focuses on the alleged problems of utilizing the apparently liberal notion of rights within political programs that were 'socialist' to the extent of supporting universal welfare provision, promoting public goods above individual property rights and exercising democratic control, directly or indirectly, over economic systems. The excitement of the Civil Rights movement in the US, dismay over the evident discrimination that led to the renewal of 'the troubles' in Northern Ireland, enthusiasm over the (successful) political campaigns for the abolition of capital punishment and the modernization of abortion law, and later the irresistible case for equal rights for women, and the inhumanities of the war in Vietnam—on all these issues rights talk was on the progressive side. Yet there was an understandable reluctance on the part of those who were aware of the history of reactionary utilization of the idea of individual rights to bolster an unfair and inefficient form of capitalism. It was in this context that I sought to present a theory of rights around a form of democratic rule governance which could form a consensual framework for debate and decision-making about the laws we ought to have, without committing us to the rampant individualism of some rights discourse or the coerciveness that was argued to be the defining characteristic of legal rights. This proved to be timely during the emergence of a 'third way' in politics in the UK, and may have contributed to a reconceptualization of one area of political ideology. This position enabled me to remain a human rights enthusiast. Only later did I realize that most of my fellow travellers took this to involve a transfer of political authority from Parliaments to Courts with the consequent diminution of political rights, a short-cut to social progress of which I was, and remain, profoundly sceptical.

Encouraging 'reconceptualization' in the service of moral goals, was, perhaps, a rebellion against the limitations of 'ordinary language philosophy' which sought philosophical truth and social understanding through a detailed analysis of 'our' use of words. When working on Adam Smith I quickly became aware of the now familiar fact that the founder of free market economics had an intensely social theory of human nature and commended egalitarian and interventionist policies well in advance of his time. Going beyond that, I realized that, despite the natural law terminology in which the his social theory of moral sentiments is based, and his forceful rejection of social engineering as a dangerous form of political domination, there is ultimately a (somewhat theological) utilitarian basis to his theory, which, although largely 'contemplative' rather than activist, enables us to regard Smith as a community oriented welfare theorist (*Adam Smith's Science of Morals* 1971).

This triggered in me a penchant for conceptual reform as to the ideological affiliations of particular discourses. This is evident not only in articulating 'socialist rights' but also in my work on justice where I challenge the view, almost universally followed post-Rawls, that 'justice' is the prime or overriding political (and legal) value. An advantage of dispensing with this dogma (which, in Rawls's case was perhaps no more than a stipulation made for the purpose of identifying the parameters of his theory), is that it enables us to acknowledge the fact that the actual discourse of justice is closely tied to ideas of merit and desert, criteria of distribution that few reflective persons would wish to be socially and politically overriding. This set the scene for asking the question: which concept (or conception) of justice ought we to adopt? My answer was: the one which is particularly useful in the development and application of political policy. To this end, the preferred conceptual analysis should identify what is distinctive about the characteristic terminology in actual discourse, and best enables us to makes clear, beyond the confines of academia, the value judgments that have to be made in making personal and political decisions.

I suggested that material 'justice' should be defined in terms of desert and formal 'justice' as conformity to authoritative rules.

This does not mean, however, that material justice, and therefore desert, should be the overriding consideration in political decision-making, or that rule-conformity is beyond moral challenge. Reconceptualization is, of course, no more than one useful strategy amongst others, with much depending on the normative or other purpose of the philosopher in question. Reconceptualisation is, however, particularly germane to legal philosophy which, in my view, ought to be deeply concerned with conceptual developments that promote the articulation of alternative positions that are intelligible and therefore more transparent to the voting public as well as to the professionals whose role it is to erect a publicly understandable and accessible legal system. In this way legal philosophy can make some sort of contribution to the promotion of a common conceptual framework without which a well-functioning democratic legal system is scarcely feasible.

Moving to more concrete examples of the sort of endeavour with which I would like to be associated, I would point primarily to the work, co-authored with the then Director of MIND (the UK mental health association, not the philosophical journal) Chris Heginbotham: *Mental Illness: Prejudice, Discrimination and the Law*, 1991, in which we seek to make out the case that public fear of mental illness has led to systematic discrimination against persons with mental illnesses when it comes to such matters as detention in the interests of other people and the provision of health and welfare services. In my case, this work grew out of my experience as a lay person on The Mental Welfare Commission for Scotland which involved me in decision-making concerning the review of civil detention and in visiting the many large residential mental health facilities that have since been greatly reduced in number and size. This experience brought me to a sharp realisation of the relevance of legal philosophy to the righting of contemporary wrongs. Other issues with which I have engaged include abortion law, euthanasia, free speech, juvenile justice, and gender discrimination. While these contributions are all marginal and ephemeral in themselves, cumulatively they make an important point as to the role of legal philosophers in society and the interrelationship of theory and practice.

Recently I have become somewhat preoccupied with critiquing the movement towards promoting human rights through bills of rights, partly because of I think this will eventually bring the human rights movement into disrepute, and partly because I am aware of the often rather poor quality of argument or affirmation in which this bill of rights case is presented. I do not, however, want to be remembered as someone who became obsessively concerned with negating the arguments for adopting constitutional style bills of rights or using such bills for creative adjudication. Making such criticisms may help to hold in check 'judicial activism', but it is a rather negative image to project. I still regret going along with the title *Sceptical Essays on Human Rights* (2001) when the book is in fact sceptical about the UK Human Rights Act 1988, not about human rights. I am currently seeking to turn this around by adopting a more positive approach to alternative ways of promoting human rights, emphasizing a political rather than a narrowly legal theory of human rights, which is more in line with the motivation of my earlier work and the thesis expounded in *The Left and Rights*.

What are the most important issues in legal philosophy, and why are they distinctively issues of legal philosophy rather than some other discipline?

The most important (but not necessarily the most interesting) issues in legal philosophy relate to the part that law should play in a good society. While these issues cannot be detached from an appreciation of the standard content of laws, they are relatively independent of what is thought to be the best law in substance, rather than form. The sort of question that needs to be answered is : why go about pursuing the morally justifiable objectives of social life in a law-governed way? This, of course, requires us to be very clear about what constitutes a law-governed way of doing things. As my answer to the previous questions indicates I do not see this principally as a conceptual question but as a moral and practical issue about what concepts we should adopt, something which has pragmatic (general intelligibility) as well as intellectual (clarity and consistency) goals. What is involved here is the capacity for understanding law as it actually operates and then developing a more specific model of law that encapsulates the more desirable aspects of the wide range of legal phenomena (here 'legal' is being used in a broad and open-ended way for the purpose of identifying the subject-matter in question).

My model here would be Lon Fuller, *The Morality of Law* (1969), excluding the later parts where he (mistakenly in my view) goes on to assert a closer connection than can be established between the aspirational 'internal' morality of law and the limitations this imposes on its content. Fuller graphically illustrates his approach by illustrating both the efficiency and the injustice or a ruler (King Rex) who, by neglecting such formalities as clarity, prospectivity, publicity and consistency, ends up simply failing to make law at all and thereby showing himself to be unjust and incompetent. This has much more in common with H.L.A. Hart's more famous *Concept of Law* (1962) than either he or Fuller were prepared to admit, for Hart in effect explains the benefits in efficiency and fairness that derive from the transition of a first order system of social norms, that apply directly to ordinary conduct, into a more complex system in which there are second order rules (that is rules that affect first order rules) which serve for the identification and implementation of a set of authoritative first order rules, a model that is morally acceptable and sociologically effective.

Inevitably this approach leads on to the centrality of judicial method in adjudicating cases on the basis of positive law. The possibilities, options and recommendations involved here are both distinctive and central to legal philosophy. This impacts, in turn on current debates about the rule of law, where I would say the most significant (or do I mean 'the most acceptable'?) contributions are made by Fred Schauer, Joseph Raz and Jeremy Waldron. This debate has a particular importance because of the (challengeable) assumption that such matters as are classified under 'the rule of law' should, thereby, be for purely judicial determination, so that including substantive values with the requirements of the rule of law has the effect of shifting the domain of decision-making to courts.

Distinctiveness here comes down to subject matter not method. While disagreeing with him on many issues I think Ronald Dworkin is right in so far as he sees legal philosophizing as a form of normative political philosophy and that this needs to be explicitly recognized to liberate us from the bounded intellectual circle of ostensibly pure conceptual theorizing. Evidently such normative theorizing has to take account of all the epistemological and ontological issues that a rise within philosophy more generally but there is no peculiar epistemology or ontology of law. It is a matter of subjective preference whether to the boundaries of legal philosophy should be extended to cover the explanation of law as a social phenomenon. There is a danger that work of this sort done by philosophers not trained in empirical method are rather amateurish and unconvincing and there are good reasons to distinguish between the empirical study of social phenomena and their normative assessment. Yet there is clearly a substantial overlap here, not only with respect to common subject matter, but to also with respect to the need to explain social phenomena partly in the light of values and the requirement of most normative approaches to consider the empirical consequences of implementing their recommendations.

What is the relationship between legal philosophy and legal practice? Should legal philosophers be more concerned about the effects of their scholarship on legal practice?

Principles of the division of labour suggest that legal philosophers should neither seek to sell their wares to practitioners nor seek to outdo practitioners in their knowledge of everyday legal practice. However, the logic of my answers to the previous questions must result in the view that legal philosophy should have important implications for legal practice and indeed for the function of law in society more generally. It is a matter of regret and concern that not only legal philosophy but much scholarly work undertaken generally in laws schools is not now of much interest to practitioners, so the question is not confined to the role of philosophers within the legal academy. There is certainly work to be done within legal philosophy surrounding the more abstract and metaphysical questions that must be taken into account as part the general enterprise of arriving at an acceptable model of what law ought to be, work that no practitioner in their right mind would spend billable hours mastering.

Nevertheless, a core ingredient of legal philosophy focuses on the proper role of lawyers in society and has enormous implications for the profession in its various manifestations. This can be presented as part of legal ethics, the ethics not only of how lawyers should conduct themselves in advising and representing clients, but how they should conduct themselves as prosecutors, administrators, and as judges. It is particularly interesting that judicial ethics generally neglects the core issue of how judges ought to reason in determining the law and deciding cases. We know and insist that judges should not take bribes, or fall asleep on the bench, but appropriate legal method is simply left to them to sort out for themselves, a matter of their collective discretion rather than their collective morality. This situation that has resulted in part from the liberation of judges form the 'declaratory theory' according to which they discover, but do not make, and the encouragement to be purposive and 'liberal' in their reading of law which has been the dominant message of legal philosophy over the past few decades. Now that there is greater realization of the need for laws which make it more feasible for judges to apply the law with minimal creativity, the long run effects of legal philosophy on judicial practice may change, although this can and should be something that is mediated through the democratic process. Nevertheless, legal philosophy is not a branch of practice and should be less concerned with its effect than its truth, if that is not too strong a word to use for expressing the goal of? a value-oriented study.

To which problem, issue or broad area of legal philosophy would you most like to see more attention paid in the future?

One gaping hole in the current practice of legal philosophy is the relative neglect of legislation in favour of case-law. To be sure, much case-law is statutory interpretation. Nevertheless, insufficient attention is given to what goes into making formally 'good' law, which in terms of PLP, means law that is capable of being understood and applied without recourse to the moral choices and empirical decisions that ought to have gone in to the making of that law in the first place. Very little attention is given in legal education and legal scholarship to legislative drafting, and I would like to see legal philosophers taking the lead in remedying this neglect. This would require more engagement with the legislative process tracing it back in to the political debate and decision-making that leads up to it, and the delegated legislation and administrative application that follows.

In the constitutional area, currently a major source of interest in legal philosophy, I would like to see more attention paid to the problem of what I have called constitutional constipation, namely the difficulty that political systems with entrenched written constitutions have in bringing forth constitutional change in a democratic manner in normal times without the laxative of revolution. This blockage is one of the factors giving rise to the asserted necessity for judicial creativity in constitutional interpretation. To move from metaphor to simile, more work needs to be done in combating the 'living tree' approach to constitutionalism which, in my view, provides a false legitimation for activist judicial 'interpretation' While it is historically clear that constitutions do not need to be entrenched (although they can scarcely do their job if they are subject to frequent changes) we need to work out a principled basis for routinizing democratic constitutional change as an important element in the right of self-determination.

Finally, legal philosophers should be, and are, turning their attention the legal aspects of the 'war on terror' which many civil rights advocates see as a involving a 'war on the rule of law'. These events have led some legal scholars to lose faith in the capacity of courts to defend human rights under severe threat, and others to look elsewhere for the decisive action that some view as required to combat terrorism and which others see as a gross overreaction to events that are, in the grand scheme of things, relatively minor and quite normal harms. This opens up fertile ground for examining the interaction of political constitutionalism and legal constitutionalism, a distinction that is lost in much contemporary legal philosophy.

Selected Bibliography

Adam Smith's Science of Morals, London: Allen & Unwin, 1971.

The Left and Rights: A Conceptual Analysis of the Idea of Socialist Rights, London: Routledge and Kegan Paul, 1983.

Mental Illness: Prejudice, Discrimination and the Law, Aldershot: Dartmouth, 1991. With C Heginbotham.

The Legal Theory of Ethical Positivism, Aldershot: Dartmouth, 1996.

Judicial Power, Democracy and Legal Positivism, Aldershot: Dartmouth, 2000. Edited with J. Goldsworthy.

Justice, 2nd edn, London: PalgraveMacmillan, 2001.

Sceptical Essays on Human Rights, Oxford University Press, 2001. Edited with Keith Ewing and Adam Tomkins.

Legal Interpretation in Democratic States, Aldershot: Dartmouth, 2001. Edited with J Goldsworthy.

Protecting Human Rights: Instruments and Institutions, Oxford University Press, 2003, edited with J Goldsworthy and A Stone.

Prescriptive Legal Positivism: Law, Rights and Democracy, London: UCL-Cavendish, 2004.

Protecting Rights without a Bill of Rights, Aldershot: Ashgate, 2006, Edited with J. Goldsworthy and A. Stone.

Rights: A Critical Introduction, Abingdon: Routledge, 2006.

3

Jules L. Coleman

Wesley Newcomb Hohfeld Professor of Jurisprudence and Professor of Philosophy
Yale Law School, USA

Why were you initially drawn to the philosophy of law?
One could be drawn to a subject for a variety of different kinds of reasons. I was drawn to the philosophy of law for both intellectual and personal reasons. I was also drawn to different areas within the philosophy of law for very different reasons.

I distinguish among three areas within the philosophy of law. The first of these is jurisprudence – that is, inquiry into the nature of law. The second of these is the political philosophy of law – that is, the set of principles to which the ideal legislator would appeal in designing law; or the set of ideals that are likely to expressed in the law of a liberal society. The third of these is the philosophy of particular areas of the law – for example, the philosophy of criminal law, tort law, contract, property, constitutional law, and so on. Other legal philosophers might well partition the field differently. Others might note more distinctions than I do; and others still might emphasize fewer distinctions than I have, or formulate the projects within various subfields of legal philosophy differently than I have. I do not claim either uniqueness or originality for the way I have come to partition the field. My claim is simply that this is the way I have to think about the philosophy of law and I have approached my various research agendas within legal philosophy in this way. This partition – jurisprudence, the political philosophy of law, and the philosophy of this or that area of law – is reflected in the way I have put together the materials in Feinberg and Coleman, *The Philosophy of Law*, (Westview, 8th Edition) reader. In addition, I have pursued research projects in all three of these areas of legal philosophy.

I took my first course in philosophy of law with Michael Bayles while I was an undergraduate student in philosophy and economics at Brooklyn College. Brooklyn College had a long tradition of excellence in philosophy and four students from my class went on to become academic philosophers: a fifth, Barry Shapiro, was the best of us and he was admitted to Harvard. He died tragically in 1968 after being brutally attacked while marching in protest at the Democratic National Convention in Chicago. His death made philosophy real for me in ways I only came to appreciate much later.

While an undergraduate at Brooklyn College I was drawn to philosophy as much by the quality of the instruction in the department as by the nature of philosophical inquiry itself. My family had belonged to an Orthodox Temple and my grandfather had anointed me the child who was to go on to become a rabbi. I took my religious training seriously, but my chief interests were in sports and science. I abandoned my religion soon after my Bar Mitzvah, but I was never ever to shake completely its influence. Philosophy combined science with religion: both in subject matter and methodology. The entirety of philosophy excited me. I was influenced to pursue normative issues in philosophy by three of my instructors: Paul Taylor, Paul Edwards and Michael Bayles. I worked a bit as a research assistant for Edwards who was the Editor of the first edition of the *MacMillan Encyclopedia of Philosophy*. I did not get to know Taylor personally but he was a model of calm and precision in his work and a masterful instructor. Bayles was a young Assistant Professor and he was happy to find such an enthusiastic student with interests very similar to his. We became life-long friends in time. Sadly he took his life twenty or so years later, and I don't think I will ever forget receiving the phone call from his wife informing me of his suicide.

The Vietnam War was in full force as I neared graduation and I applied to graduate school in philosophy, physics and to both law and medical school. I hated the sight of blood and really didn't have the skills to be a physicist. I was looking for a way out of the army. My family imagined me a lawyer and so did I. However, no one in my family had the money to help me pay for law school and they possessed even less imagination as to how I might be able to fund my education otherwise. Several graduate departments in philosophy offered me full fellowships under the then National Defense Education Act and nearly by default I decided to pursue a Ph.D in philosophy. The question was where to go:

Bayles and Taylor encouraged me to go to graduate school at Michigan to study with the great ethicists: Brandt, Stevenson and

Frankena. All were far on in their career when I arrived and only Brandt was an active member of the department. None taught any ethics to speak of during my one and only year at Michigan. Instead, I discussed normative philosophy with two other first years: Greg Kavka and Don Regan, both of whom went on to distinguished careers in philosophy, Greg's of course tragically cut short by terminal cancer.

My expectations that Michigan thwarted, I ended working primarily in the philosophy of science with Larry Sklar and Jaegwon Kim. The other important event during this year – other than a disastrous relationship with an older woman – was my involvement in a terrible car accident that nearly took my life. With so much turmoil and pain, I was pretty much committed to returning to NYC to be close to family. Sklar and Kim both encouraged me to apply to The Rockefeller University, which had only recently started a Ph.D program in philosophy. The program was naturally conceived so that it would emphasize the philosophy of science since Rockefeller itself was a graduate school with a near total emphasis on the biological and life sciences. There were no social sciences to speak of but for some psychology and no humanities at all other than philosophy.

I applied, was interviewed and accepted into the program. The program was tiny by any standards. At its largest there were about 15 graduate students and a similar number of professors, post-docs and lecturers. Normally no more than two students per year were admitted into the program, but in the year I applied the program was expanded and four of us were admitted. I joke that I was admitted to Rockefeller when there was a total decline in standards for admission. I mean for it to be a joke, but I am certain there is a good deal of truth in it nonetheless.

The excellent philosopher of physics, John Earman joined the Rockefeller faculty the same year I came as a graduate student. I imagined that he would be my mentor and advisor, and during my first year, I did work with him on a few topics in the philosophy of physics. I worked with other faculty members in the context of the distinctive Rockefeller system of tutorials.

It was in this context that I had my first sustained and serious encounter with philosophy of law. I took a tutorial with Robert Nozick as soon as I arrived on campus. Nozick had already committed to leaving to become the youngest full professor at Harvard, but he was nevertheless very generous to me with whatever time he had left at Rockefeller. Nozick had a profound but largely indirect influence on my scholarly development. We discussed two topics quite a bit: coercion, on the one hand, and game and decision theory on the other. The former was important ultimately to my thinking about the nature of law in its relationship both to its emphasis on sanctioning and its claims to legitimacy. The latter was crucial to my work both on the foundations of the economic analysis of law and to my research on rational choice political philosophy.

After Nozick's departure, I still fancied myself a potential philosopher of physics – at least until I took a seminar given by John Earman that was attended by every philosopher of physics in the greater New York area. I could follow the arguments, but I had nothing original to offer. I had found my ceiling and it was too close to the top of my head. I figured that I might do better using some of the technical skills I had both in the philosophy of science and in game and decision theory elsewhere. I rediscovered my original love for issues in Ethics. Ironically, Rockefeller University turned out to be much stronger in social and political philosophy than advertised. In the same way that Michigan surprised with its strength in philosophy of science – Sklar and Kim in particular – Rockefeller surprised with its strengths in normative philosophy – especially Joel Feinberg, Donald Davidson, Harry Frankfurt, and Marshall Cohen and Robert Nozick (both only briefly however).

In short order I became the primary graduate student of Joel Feinberg's. Virtually everything I have become as a philosopher of law I owe to him. Donald Davidson joined with Feinberg to constitute my dissertation committee, but Davidson had little impact on my early work in legal philosophy. Ironically, perhaps, I felt his influence much later when I turned attention to the relationship of the philosophy of law to the philosophies of language, mind and action theory.

I never would have imagined that my work would ultimately take this turn and much of my time spent with Davidson during my formative years was more unpleasant than anything else. I never felt up to snuff in his presence – a kind of relationship of inadequacy that he nurtured in others, and sometimes I think one that he enjoyed. To the best of my recollection, not once did he apply anything remotely resembling any version of the principle of charity to his interpretation of my work – oral or written (the principle of charity in interpretation of course being one of the ideas most closely associated with him).

I was quite certain that he took me to be an idiot whose one saving grace was his beautiful, intelligent and charming wife. Years later – when I had already become an established philosopher in my own right – Feinberg reported that during a chance meeting with him Davidson allowed that he was quite proud of my accomplishments, and was certain early on of my likely success – were I driven hard enough. I must report that in all the years I knew him, I was never treated to anything that would count as evidence either of his pride in my success or of his confidence in its eventuality – other than his willingness to drive me hard, and his apparent joy in doing so. Only recently did I learn after sharing a series of email exchanges with the excellent philosopher, Tyler Burge, that he too had the same experience as a student of Davidson's. My view in retrospect is that if it was good enough for Burge – who is a truly exceptional philosopher – it is good enough for me; so I can't complain.

During the period when he was my teacher and advisor, Feinberg had already completed the essays that were collected in *Doing and Deserving*, a book that contains what I regard as among his best and least appreciated essays. Having put this body of work to one side, he turned his attention to what he came to call the moral limits of the criminal law – one central set of questions in what I referred to at the outset of this answer as the political philosophy of law. Philosophically, Feinberg was interested in three parts of criminal law theory: (1) what can be punished? (2) What are the conditions of responsibility that must be satisfied in order for someone to be justifiably punished? (3) What justifies punishment? His massive four volume work on the moral limits of the criminal law focuses on the first of these, but I am partial to his work on the latter two – especially his essays on responsibility and the expressive function of punishment. I have never been drawn to the broadly speaking Millian approach to justifying state authority: not just because of its reliance on the harm principle as somehow basic, but more importantly because it conceives of the problem in the wrong way – that is, in terms of a presumption in favor of liberty as well as its assuming that coercion calls for a special kind of justification. Feinberg works squarely within this tradition and I do not.

In any event, when the time came for me to present a dissertation proposal to him, I offered up what must have struck him as a lame, dull and altogether unpromising prospectus on the philosophy of punishment. With all the kindness he could muster, Feinberg suggested that the philosophy of punishment was such well-trodden ground that whatever my considerable talents might be (Joel was always generous to a fault – so much so that sometimes his kindnesses undermined his intentions) I would find it more barren than rich. He thought I would find pursuing such a project frustrating and ultimately unsatisfying.

He presented me with a gift that proved to be the defining moment of my academic career: a copy of Guido Calabresi's recently published, *The Costs of Accidents*. Feinberg had not yet read it, but expressed the view that there was likely more fruitful areas of research in the rather unchartered territory of tort law than I would find in the criminal law. I took the book home and read it with great interest. A few weeks later, I returned to Feinberg's office filled with excitement about this area of the law I had never before encountered. I had searched the libraries for philosophical articles on tort law and found almost none. This made me even more excited, but left me uncertain as to how to go about finding a particularly important philosophical problem in tort law. The absence of other articles meant I would be entering a field with a lot of potentially low hanging fruit. On the other hand, no articles meant no guidance, and I was pretty much left on my own to figure out what might be the most interesting philosophical issues in tort law. I was more full of excitement than concrete ideas.

Joel and I discussed how to proceed and we thought it would make sense for me to sit in on a torts class in law school if that could be arranged. Joel's friend and co-author, Hy Gross, arranged for me to audit a torts course at NYU Law School and so my interest in the philosophy of tort law began in earnest.

I don't often claim originality, and I do think of myself as modest – and for the good reason that I have, as they say, a lot to be modest about. Still, I think I hit upon a pretty original way into the philosophy of tort law. It struck me that a very good question of genuine philosophical interest would be: does justice require that liability in torts be based upon the fault of the injurer? And in one year I was able to complete a draft of my dissertation: Justice in the *Allocation of Accident Costs*. I have been working on issues pertaining to the philosophy of tort law ever since, for which I offer no apology. After all, I went into a field that was largely unshaped by philosophical reflection, and what I take myself to be doing over the years is to continuously exploring different ways of approaching it philosophically. I have been reworking and reshaping it – in time along with many others, some of whom are probably better at it than I am – in an effort to identify its central features and philosophically most interesting and important dimensions.

In my earliest works on tort law I was in the grip of two paradigms that I ultimately came to abandon – but not easily. The first was to focus on tort law from the point of view of principles of justice that seemed appropriate to the imposition of liability based on desert – i.e. retributive justice. And so I asked whether principles of retributive justice required imposing the liability on the basis of fault. This was the focus of my very first paper on tort law published in the *Journal of Philosophy*. The second paradigm stood in stark contrast with the first. It was marked by two important elements: the problem of tort law is the problem of 'accidents;' the normatively important property of accidents is their 'costs.' The problem is how to allocate the costs of accidents? According to this paradigm, tort law is a potential solution to that problem: I came to see this view of tort law as kind of social technology.

Whereas economists and economically minded academic lawyers like Calabresi approached this problem by asking, how ought we allocate accident costs to optimize the sum of the costs of accidents and the costs of avoiding them, I took the question to be: what does fairness require in the distribution of accident costs? This meant that the relevant principles of justice in tort law would be those of distributive justice. In addition, whereas the focus on retributive justice conceptualized tort law on an individual case basis, the focus on the just distribution of accident costs conceptualized tort law as a tool for solving a social problem – that of accidents and their costs.

In time I came to see that there were serious but different problems with both of these frameworks. The concept of fault in torts does not mirror that of moral fault and so the reliance on desert and its connection to retributive justice is inapt. I saw this pretty quickly and thus abandoned any effort to think about tort law and tort liability along the lines of criminal law and criminal punishment. The problems with the 'costs of accidents' approach run deeper still, and it took me much longer to figure them out and to shed this approach entirely.

In the first place, an accident may be the most prevalent kind of tort, but it is not the paradigmatic tort. If torts are wrongs, the paradigm torts are wrongs to persons and property: e.g. battery, assault, trespass and conversion. Secondly, accidents may be a social problem, but a tort is a wrong between parties. Tort is not an instrument for solving a social problem; its conceptual foundation is a deontic relation between individuals – not a form of societal wrongdoing or misfortune. What defines the normative relationship between plaintiff and defendant is the notion of a duty of care one owes the other, not the causal relationship between (as I like to say) mischief and misfortune. Finally, the key normative notion is not that of a cost – which invites the 'allocation' question – but 'wrong' which invites questions of duty, right and redress.

Neither the retributive nor the distributive paradigms of tort law recognize the fundamental relational character of tort law; and so in time – and in some ways, not soon enough– I came to see that the relevant principles of justice regulating tort law were those of corrective not distributive justice or retributive justice.

This is the line of argument I have pressed ever since – in one form or another. And the problem I have been emphasizing in my work has been that of offering a conception of corrective justice and of its relationship to tort law. Having been in the grip of other ways of conceiving of tort law the process of coming around to a coherent version of corrective justice was some time in the making. Indeed, certain elements of my earlier views, especially the reliance on the notion of cost and its sibling, loss, as well as my inclination to see a tort as raising two different kinds of questions – one pertaining to a claim to compensation for loss, and the other pertaining to a duty to provide it understood as a species of a duty to come to the aid of others – filled me with interesting ideas (and gave rise to a number of articles as well as my book Risks and Wrongs), but kept me from getting to the core of both tort law and the principle of corrective justice. To be honest, several of my philosophical friends, from Jeff McMahan to Jerry Postema, were more influenced and persuaded by the arguments of *Risks and Wrongs* and its conception of the relationship between corrective justice and tort law than they have been by my subsequent views – which, by my lights, anyway, are closer to the truth of the matter. This shows I think that some false ideas can be pretty influential in a positive way, and can be stimulating and valuable. At least I hope so, since I have so many of them.

I noted above that I had personal as well as intellectual grounds for my particular interests in legal philosophy. My personal reasons for being drawn to tort law and corrective justice are far more revealing, and very likely, more interesting. Unfortunately for me, I was not aware of what they were and only came to understand them during many years later while undergoing psychoanalysis.

My original formulations of the principle of corrective justice were based on several distinctions I had drawn. The first of these was between the grounds of a claim to compensation and the grounds of a duty of provide it: a distinction to which I have already alluded above. The second distinction was between the grounds of compensation or liability to repair on the one hand and what I called the 'mode of rectification' on the other. These distinctions were central to the conception of corrective justice as requiring that 'wrongful gains and losses' be annulled. This conception dominated my early work on corrective justice and was perhaps the most interesting yet mistaken view I have ever been associated with – by which I mean to suggest not that it is the only mistaken view I have endorsed, but simply that it is likely the most interesting and valuable of the many mistaken ones that I have advanced.

The key feature of my view then was that someone could have a right to recover in corrective justice (having satisfied the grounds of repair) yet it remain open as to what mode of rectification is called for. This meant that on my view, it was not necessarily the case that the person who caused the victim to suffer a wrongful loss has the duty to repair it. The victim's claim in justice is satisfied provided her loss is repaired and while one mode of addressing her claim is to have the injurer pay it is not the only one. The fact that a victim suffers a wrongful loss, that is, one occasioned by the wrongdoing of another, grounds her claim to repair; it does not yet tell us who has a duty of repair. That depends on what the relevant considerations and principles of the duty of repair are: what principles in other words guide us in determining appropriate modes of rectification.

This conception of corrective justice was novel, controversial and the source of considerable discussion. Of all the objections raised to it, the ones I found the most persuasive were offered by Stephen Perry who argued that so understood, my account lacked the resources to distinguish adequately distributive from corrective justice. Over time, I have found this way of putting the point less convincing, but the underlying objection has always struck me as correct: namely, that those who are responsible for the wrong stand in a relationship to it that others – even those who might have other reasons to come to the aid of the wronged party – do not. And though for quite some time, I tried to accommodate this insight in some other ways, I ultimately came to the view that it was this feature of the reciprocal normativity of corrective justice, and not annulment of gains and losses, that was at the core of it. As I say, it took me just about as long if not longer to come around to the idea that the central normative concept in corrective justice was 'wrong,' not 'loss' or 'cost.'

The interesting point I want to share about my views here is how personal they were to me. After years of psychoanalysis it dawned on me that both my interest in corrective justice (not in tort law itself) and my particular account of corrective justice could be traced to my childhood. Without revealing too much personal history, my mother always struck me (and her) as a person who had been the victim of a good deal of bad luck: a victim of life's misfortunes that were at once caused by human agency but not by culpable fault.

In her mind, she suffered a great deal of misfortune that causally was my father's doing. Still, there was no sense in which my father had acted culpably. He did the best he could and his failures to provide for her in ways that she had reason to believe were her due were not the result of any defect in his character or motivation. Beyond that, he secured no gains at my mother's expense; quite the contrary—this was a lose/lose situation.

For a variety of reasons, it was easy for me to distinguish the legitimacy of my mother's claim to repair from any judgment about my father's moral responsibility for it. Psychologically, I came to take my mother's misfortune as a wrong to her, but one I had as good a reason to help rectify as my father had. He was morally blameless, and even if he were to blame for her loss, we could impose other hardships and suffering on him to respond to that fact about him. The moral concern my mother's situation presented was what to do to rectify her wrongful loss; not what costs should be imposed upon a blameless person whose conduct contributed to that loss. And, of course, given my natural instinct as a son to identify with my father's plight, I took up the burden of repair – as best I could – as a way of solidifying my bond with him while making my mother better.

Those who know me well know that this 'responsiveness to the wrongful misfortunes of others' has been a fundamental motivation in my life, but not one that has always produced more good than harm. It had its roots in the home – that can hardly come as a surprise – and it is as responsible for what I have come to think about and do as it is for who I have become.

In time I came to abandon aspects of this conception of corrective justice, but giving it up was hard in part because of how close to home it struck – and continues to. Believe me, from time to time, I toy with various ways of reformulating the basic insight to preserve not just the position, but my conception of my early family life ϑ

My interests in other areas of the philosophy of law had more innocent origins (at least I think so). My interest in jurisprudence had two immediate sources. The first is that Joel Feinberg had often confided in me that Hart was the person who had the greatest intellectual influence on him. Still, while Feinberg's work touched on every other area of legal philosophy that Hart's did, he wrote nothing of significance on Hart's jurisprudence. This left an opening for me to carry on the lineage but to do so by taking up some issues that Feinberg, my mentor, had not already taken up.

Because Feinberg had no real interest in jurisprudence, I had no guidance in pursuing the field during my graduate school education. The key moment for me came during my second year at Rockefeller. Ronald Dworkin came from Oxford where he had recently taken up the Chair in Jurisprudence upon Hart's retirement to spend a week giving lectures to the students and faculty at Rockefeller. All lectures and seminars at Rockefeller drew large audiences from the greater New York area and Dworkin's were no exception. Dworkin presented lectures on judicial discretion and provided early formulations of some of the central ideas that were to characterize the stances in jurisprudence with which he has long been associated.

I found one lecture especially interesting and powerful. I can't recall exactly how Dworkin put the point then, but in retrospect it seems to me that his point was that legal positivists see law as autonomous and self contained by rules that determine what is in and what is outside law; and that this view of law which made it more like baseball say than morality is precisely what is most deeply mistaken about it.

Ultimately I came to reformulate Dworkin's concern in a number of different ways. One way of understanding his objection is that positivists see law in terms of its ultimately having a conventional foundation or source. He and I have had our share of disagreements about the conventionality of law ever since. It began a few years after Dworkin's lectures at Rockefeller when I junior professor in the Jurisprudence and Philosophy Program at Berkeley. The *California Law Review* invited me to review his book, Dworkin's *Taking Rights Seriously*. This provided me with an opportunity to think about how Hart might respond to Dworkin's objections and my review formed the basis of what was to become "Negative and Positive Positivism." That essay is often taken as staking out what has come to be called, Inclusive Legal Positivism, the version of positivism arguably that Hart himself ultimately came to endorse. The review of TRS set the stage for my formulations of positivism: what I first called Incorporationism and which others have labeled Inclusive Legal Positivism.

In both my review of TRS and "Negative and Positive Positivism," I did not see myself as staking out or developing a new version of legal positivism. In all honesty, I simply saw myself as providing an interpretation of Hart's legal positivism. Only much later, and only in retrospect, did it appear plausible to treat either of these essays as setting out a distinctive jurisprudential account. Even though a great deal of the literature on legal positivism since the mid 1980s has focused on the differences between inclusive and exclusive legal positivism, I confess that I have never been particularly drawn to this debate. Instead, I was always much more interested in the point that Dworkin had made in those early lectures at Rockefeller University. He put the point in terms of positivism as a closed system, a domain defined by rules with a more or less well defined boundary. I saw it more as a question not about the boundaries but about the foundations.

This is the objection to positivism that has really preoccupied me. Over the years I have formulated it in at least two ways: the first is the so-called conventionality of law that I have been alluding to. The second way of formulating Dworkin's concern may be even more interesting. I think we can interpret Dworkin as asking an even better question: Is law the sort of activity that defines what counts as a valid move within the game. Does law define all the legitimate moves within law?

There are very personal features of my interest in jurisprudence no doubt. The central features of law include its claim to authority and the fact that the reasons it purports to provide are content-independent. These are of course features of authority more generally, and anyone who has grown up Orthodox has this concern about religious authority. I experienced much the same view of authority at home. No more needs to be said on that front!

The two people who have been most influential on my work in jurisprudence have been H.L.A. Hart and Ronald Dworkin. I hardly knew Hart, but I did meet him on a couple of occasions in Oxford and he was very generous and encouraging to me. Several years ago, Wil Waluchow, who was Hart's last doctoral student, told me the following story, and it has been the greatest source of pride and comfort to me in the face of some very mean spirited treatment that I have experienced.

According to Wil, when he went to Hart with a prospectus to write a dissertation on jurisprudence, Hart gave him a copy of my essay, "Negative and Positive Positivism," and told him to come back to him on the same topic only if he thought that he could add anything beyond what I had already written. I never knew that Hart felt so strongly about my piece. As it happens of course, Wil has had a good deal of importance to say well beyond what I wrote in that piece, but I will never forget Wil for sharing that with me, and I find that I often turn to that story and Hart's appreciation of my work when facing some of the harsh criticisms I have received.

And most of those have come from Dworkin who to my mind anyway is the most significant legal philosopher of our time. I have my share of disagreements with him of course, but he is by far the most creative and original thinker in our field. I have spent a great deal of time trying to present his arguments in ways that make them persuasive and valuable to other legal positivists who are inclined often to dismiss them as resting on tricks and unfair characterizations of positivism. One would be hard pressed to defend Dworkin as a fair interpreter sometimes of the work of those he criticizes (I know this from personal experience), but it would be a mistake to take too lightly his criticisms and insights in jurisprudence – almost all of which have strongly influenced my own thinking. That he dismisses my work and treats me with so much apparent disdain in print is a source of constant pain and disappointment to me. That I continue nevertheless to engage his work and try to interpret it as sympathetically as I can may call for psychological explanation beyond my current understanding of myself; but until then I just see it as part of what it means to be a philosopher and someone committed to the field of jurisprudence and open to the possibility that others see things that you don't.

For which of your contribution(s) to legal philosophy so far would you like to be remembered, and why?

Who knows if I will be remembered for anything, and if so for how long and by whom? I worry that I will be best remembered in jurisprudence for inclusive legal positivism. In the past several years I have traveled throughout Europe a great deal – especially in Italy and Spain – and it seems that inclusive legal positivism has been extremely influential there. I have always thought of inclusive legal positivism as a position that needed to be articulated and shown to be compatible both with positivism more generally and with law's claim to authority. I never meant to defend it as the best explanation of actual legal practice; and I think I have been pretty open about that from the outset. I am agnostic about that. Others are more sanguine about inclusive legal positivism as an account of actual legal practice.

If it were up to me, I would like to be remembered as much for the way I have conducted myself as a legal philosopher and for the role I have played within the profession as for any particular substantive contributions I have made. As regards the first of these categories, I hope to be remembered as an extremely careful and precise philosopher, a sympathetic interpreter of the works of others and completely open-minded, willing to follow the argument wherever it leads. I also want to be remembered for my role along with Terry Moore in creating the *Cambridge Studies in Law and Philosophy* and along with Larry Alexander and Fred Schauer in creating the journal, *Legal Theory*. Above all else, I want to be remembered as an excellent mentor to younger philosophers of law – not just to my students, none of whom share my substantive views in jurisprudence.

When I joined the faculty in philosophy at Arizona, Joel Feinberg, who was then the Chair of the Department, shared that when he was my advisor he had real concerns about my future. As he reported it to me, he had no doubts about my talents (if so, he was unique in this regard), but he worried that I would not find my own way – that I would follow too closely the paths he had chosen: that I would work on the same problems he did, approach them in the ways he did, and that I might even come to share his views on the substance of the issues he pursued. I thought that his fear was that I lacked an independent mind – and maybe it was. But in telling me the story that is not the fear he expressed. Rather as he tells the story, he feared most that he had not given me enough room or encouraged me enough to find my own way. I will of course never know the truth, but if he feared that I lacked an independent mind, I would have completely understood. The truth is I lacked confidence and knowledge more than anything else.

As things turned out, Joel had little to worry about. We have always worked on very different problems, approached them in almost completely different ways; and I doubt that we share many substantive views. To be honest, I wish I shared his appreciation of the human condition and his elegance in expressing the complexity of the distinctly human capacity to respond to it.

I have been mindful ever since of Joel's concerns. I have taken pains as a teacher and advisor to instill in my students a sense of responsibility to the profession and its standards, and respect for the problems of legal philosophy and especially for those philosophers who have preceded them and devoted their considerable talents and energies to grappling with those problems. I have encouraged scholarly commitment and independence of thought – and intellectual modesty above all else.

I have had the great good fortune of being a professor at the Yale Law School for over twenty years now, but there are two things about my experience at Yale that I have not been nearly so fond of. First, I cannot abide the arrogance and unjustified self-confidence that too many of my colleagues have: a disease that has spread among law faculties everywhere in the United States. It seems to me that law professors confuse monetary reward with academic achievement. How sad – and frankly, frustrating. The arrogance and self-confidence is too often matched only by pretense.

More importantly, I have missed teaching real graduate students. Law students are really undergraduates and the depth of their knowledge is thin. The skill of the lawyer is synthesis and breadth, not depth. Fortunately, Yale Law School attracts a number of students each year who have secured advanced degrees before coming to law school and I have been fortunate to have more than my fair share of such students.

To be honest, I want real students for the same reason I want philosophical colleagues – to learn, and not merely to teach. I want to be remembered as a teacher who never stopped being a student: a student of my colleagues and my students: a student of philosophy.

With regard to substantive matters in legal philosophy, I hope to be remembered for my work on corrective justice including its relationship to tort law. I want people to recall that I played a nontrivial role in shaping a field that had not existed prior to my taking a stab at it (along with others) – that field being the philosophy of tort law. I would hope to be remembered for also adding to the discussion of the relationship between corrective and distributive justice beyond what Aristotle and others had to say. In jurisprudence, while I am less excited about inclusive legal positivism, I don't want to run away from my contributions to its development. But I would prefer to be remembered for making the case for the view that the fundamental problems in jurisprudence are not unique to jurisprudence: they are the same problems that arise everywhere in philosophy. This is one of the points I have tried to make in my work on law and language and the methodology of jurisprudence.

What are the most important issues in legal philosophy, and why are they distinctively issues of legal philosophy rather than some other discipline?

In an obvious way the major problem of jurisprudence – what is the nature of law – is unique to legal philosophy. But my entire career has been devoted to rejecting the idea that the problems of legal philosophy are distinctive; they are the problems of philosophy – it's just that they take on a particular character in the legal context.

What is the relationship between legal philosophy and legal practice? Should legal philosophers be more concerned about the effects of their scholarship on legal practice?

Competent performance in legal practice involves reflection on the theory of law in ways in which competent performance in other large-scale coordinative activities does not require comparable theoretical reflection. Those who participate in markets don't have to have theories of markets in order to participate successfully in a market. Being a competent speaker of a natural language does not require that one have a theory of language – a semantics or a syntax. Arguably, law is different. At least some important legal actors have to reflect on what they are doing and even on what law is in order to participate successfully in law. In a sense that needs to be developed legal theory is part of legal practice, or at least, the line between legal theory and practice is not as sharp as that between language and the theory of language or that between market behavior and the theory of markets. I have more to say about the relationship of legal theory to legal practice in the research that I am currently engaged in – and those interested in what I have to say can find it in my new book on jurisprudence for Oxford University Press. (*Law and Reason*: Oxford University Press, forthcoming).

To which problem, issue or broad area of legal philosophy would you most like to see more attention paid in the future?

I think of myself as a philosopher first, and a philosopher of law second. In the past twenty or so years, philosophers in other areas have become increasingly more reflective about the methods appropriate to their areas of inquiry. Methodologically speaking, the philosophy of law has lagged far behind. So I am quite committed to bringing philosophical reflection of method to legal philosophy. This is part of my view that the problems and methods of legal philosophy are the problems and methods of philosophy more broadly.

Selected Book Publications

Analytic Jurisprudence (forthcoming from Oxford University Press – New York, 2008).

Philosophy of the Law (forthcoming from Oxford University Press, 2008).

The Practice of Principle: In Defense of a Pragmatist Approach to Legal Theory (Oxford University Press, 2000. Translated into Italian in 2006, Chinese in 2008, Spanish and Portuguese,2008).

Risks and Wrongs (Cambridge University Press, 1992. Reissued by Oxford University Press, 2002).

Markets, Morals and the Law (Cambridge University Press, 1988. Reissued by Oxford University Press, 2002).

Philosophy of Law: An Introduction to Jurisprudence (with Jeffrie Murphy) (Rowman and Allenheld, 1984, Revised. Westview 1990 and thereafter).

4
John Gardner

Professor of Jurisprudence
University of Oxford, UK

Why were you initially drawn to the philosophy of law?

I don't really know why, so let me tell you how. My parents were both Germanists. As a schoolboy, languages were my forte. In 1982 I was admitted to study French and German at New College, Oxford. But I got cold feet within days of the offer. The other linguists I had met at my Oxford interview all seemed to be native speakers of more than one language, and racy cosmopolites, whereas I was a notably unracy Glaswegian who had laboured his way to the respectable standard of grammatical accuracy needed to impress jaded A-level examiners. I began to think that I might be more comfortable studying a subject in which my peers and I would all be clumsy beginners in the same boat, so that I would have none of the dispiriting experience of starting my university education at a disadvantage. I flirted with Philosophy, Politics and Economics but in the end I chose Law. I was cheeky enough to ask New College to switch me over into the undergraduate Law intake for 1983, and New College was unbureaucratic enough to oblige.

I turned out to be good at law, and soon lived comfortably enough on a diet of cases and statutes. In my first year I was lucky to be taught by outstanding academic lawyers, and I quickly picked up the dark arts. I was a natural advocate with a contrarian taste in arguments and I saw myself becoming a barrister. I only started to acquire a rival, more scholarly self-image about a year later, when Nicola Lacey arrived from London to take over as my main law tutor and mentor at New College. Niki's multidisciplinary interests and wide-ranging contributions to academic life had a lasting positive impact on me. As my jurisprudence teacher, she encouraged me to experiment with ideas. She introduced me enthrallingly to analytical philosophy of law, of which she had a formidable grasp, but she also served up tasty morsels from other philosophical traditions and indeed from other disciplines. At the start of my third year, she encouraged me to defect for a term from the Law Faculty to the Philosophy Faculty, taking a course of ethics tutorials with Jonathan Glover. Jonathan in turn worked his magic on me. Like many law students I was a card-carrying moral relativist. I thought law was somehow (how?) more real than morality. In four weeks Jonathan took me and my moral relativism to the edge of a nihilistic precipice, pointing out down below the hell that awaited me: unobjectionable mass-murderers, unimpeachable rapists, unchallengeable racists. Then he spent four weeks bringing me back from the edge, a reformed character. Never again would I flirt with any kind of relativism. Eight tutorials with Jonathan Glover is the law student's equivalent of eight weeks in rehab.

When I started graduate study in 1986 – on the Oxford BCL degree – I still took it for granted that I would head off to train as a legal practitioner the following year. Yet it seemed equally obvious that in the meantime I needed to do as much philosophy as possible, while I still had the chance. I registered to take seminar courses with Joseph Raz, John Finnis, Tony Honoré and various other jurisprudential giants of the Law Faculty. I also sat in on philosophical seminars in neighboring faculties, such as those of Derek Parfit, Jerry Cohen, and Amartya Sen. This was a fabulous era in which to embark on a training in legal, moral and political philosophy in Oxford. The mountain was high and the climb was steep, but the views were breathtaking and the guides were unbeatable. The atmosphere was also electric. Parfit's *Reasons and Persons*[1] and Raz's *The Morality of Freedom*[2] were recently published and there were so many new ideas to discuss. I was lucky enough to present my first real philosophical paper in Raz's class, and to enjoy (if that is the right word) his always eye-opening and sometimes eye-watering criticisms. Suitably revamped, this short seminar paper was to appear in 1988 as my first philosophical publication.[3] I also presented a paper on causation in Honoré's class, inaugurating an enduring collaboration and friendship: Honoré and I have now co-taught legal philosophy seminars on the BCL

---

[1] Oxford: Oxford University Press 1984.
[2] Oxford: Clarendon Press 1986.
[3] 'Concerning Permissive Sources and Gaps', *Oxford Journal of Legal Studies* 8 (1988), 457.

for 18 years.

Perhaps most formatively, during my BCL year I won a Prize Fellowship at All Souls College. I was astounded. These Fellowships – lasting seven years – are awarded on the strength of comically wide-ranging examination papers set and blind-marked by the college. To succeed in these papers, what one knows is less important than how one thinks. I didn't know whether I thought well, but I certainly thought a lot. With the arrogance of youth I found the idea of being asked to write about football and Frenchness alongside family law and Frege enticing. It was all a bit of a wheeze. I certainly never thought of it as a career move. Yet it turned out to be one. My unexpected and arguably unintended success in the competition put pressure on me to do well on the BCL, but it also required me, more generally, to hold myself to high standards of scholarly self-evaluation. Cohen, Honoré, Parfit and Sen were now my colleagues as well as my teachers, and to make matters worse they treated me as such. They and other senior Fellows talked to me with enthusiasm about intellectual puzzles and listened to me as if I knew what I was talking about. The only way to return the compliment was to know what I was talking about—to professionalize myself as quickly as possible.

So I worked like a demon late into the night to broaden and deepen my philosophical education, at the same time as keeping up with the official BCL curriculum in jurisprudence and related subjects. These were complementary pursuits and I did well on the BCL as well as starting to develop some research ideas of my own. Although I did go on to qualify as a barrister the following year – still with a vague plan of practising – I was then inevitably drawn back to Oxford where I started doctoral work on legal and moral responsibility, still based at All Souls. With the support of Honoré and then Raz as my university supervisors, Parfit as my college advisor, and Bernard Williams and Antony Duff as my DPhil examiners, I gradually and somewhat accidentally turned into a professional philosopher of law.

I think my work shows the influence of all the people I have mentioned. Let me pick out four. Tony Honoré helped me to be a philosopher of law who is read and appreciated by law teachers and law students. He nurtured my respect and affection for law as a discipline and my continuing interest in its technical workings. Derek Parfit helped me to see that philosophy is also a discipline with technical workings, and he taught me not to be afraid of counterintuitive propositions or unexpected inferences. Nicola Lacey helped me to engage with problems that caught the eye of people from other disciplines, especially in the social sciences. Thanks to her I have always looked for philosophical subtexts in the work of economists, psychologists, and sociologists, as well as lawyers. Intellectually, Joseph Raz has probably influenced me most of all. I have tried to follow his example in not leaving hostages to fortune, and in tackling each subject with only the degree of precision that it can bear (so that my work ranges in style from rather formal to rather narrative). I have also learnt from him not to be too locked into established ways of framing or demarcating philosophical puzzles.

For which of your contribution(s) to legal philosophy so far would you like to be remembered, and why?

I have worked on quite a wide range of topics. Some of my work has been in what is known as 'general jurisprudence'. It concerns the nature of law, the nature of legal reasoning, the nature of adjudication, and so forth. This work mainly spins off from my undergraduate lectures. I do not regard it as particularly original. It aims to tackle gaps in understanding caused by a mismatch between the preoccupations of professional philosophers and the preoccupations of law students. I find it by turns amusing and alarming that this work is so widely cited.

My more original work has focused on philosophical issues that underlie particular areas of law, especially but not only in Anglo-American legal systems. Some people who theorize about particular areas of law are interested in accounting for (or criticizing) the outcomes of particular cases. Why did the plaintiff win in case A but lose in case B? As a lawyer I am interested in this question but as a philosopher it is not my main preoccupation. In many appellate cases, the court might reasonably have decided for either side. The dissenting judges have as much to recommend their conclusion as do the judges in the majority. The philosophical interest does not lie in backing a winner. It lies in the way that the arguments are conducted: the classifications and distinctions used by the judges, the assumptions that they make, and the logic of their inferences. Focusing on such matters, I have written about various areas of law, including anti-discrimination law, criminal law, and the law of torts. I suppose my most extensive body of work concerns criminal law, about which I have written maybe twenty papers over fifteen years. Here my most distinctive contribution has been to the theory of justification and excuse. I have done my bit (along with Jeremy Horder and others) to revive a broadly Aristotelian way of thinking about excuses, and how they differ from (but are related to) justifications. This work has attracted a lot of criticism and resistance from all sides, which (ever the contrarian) I regard as evidence of its being broadly right!

However I think my most valuable work, philosophically speaking, is not this work in criminal law but some work focused ostensibly on the law of torts. I say 'ostensibly' because really it uses the law of torts as a vehicle for exploring some much broader and older puzzles in moral philosophy. I am thinking of my twin papers 'Obligations and Outcomes in the Law of Torts'[4] and 'The Wrongdoing that Gets Results'[5], in which I explore some aspects of the problem that has come to be known as the problem of 'moral luck'. Actually, in both papers, I object to that *arriviste* way of conceptualizing the problem, which dates back only thirty years.[6] I conceptualize it less question-beggingly as a problem about the rational salience of the way that our actions turn out. These papers are the only ones I have written where I feel that I have come close to proposing an original solution to an ancient puzzle. The first of the papers, inspired by Tony Honoré's work[7] on the subject, makes an affirmative argument for the counterintuitive proposal that the basic or paradigmatic reasons for action are reasons to succeed, i.e. reasons to perform actions partly constituted by their results. The second paper argues that these reasons can also be reasons of duty, so that there can be duties to succeed, and hence wrongs that are partly defined by the way they turn out. In this second paper I proceed negatively, by criticizing Kant's influential but under-scrutinized argument for the contrary view.

There is some of my work that I am particularly proud of for a different reason. I have been lucky enough to collaborate in print with various friends and colleagues over the years. My repeated collaborations with Stephen Shute and more recently with Timothy Macklem have, I think, proved particularly fruitful. When I have worked with Stephen or with Timothy the approach has been

---

[4] In Peter Cane and John Gardner (eds), *Relating to Responsibility: Essays for Tony Honoré on his Eightieth Birthday* (Oxford: Hart Publishing 2001).

[5] In *Philosophical Perspectives* 18 (2004), 53.

[6] It stems from the eponymous debate between Bernard Williams and Thomas Nagel in *Proceedings of the Aristotelian Society Supplementary Volume* 50 (1976), 115.

[7] Especially the papers collected in Honoré, *Responsibility and Fault* (Oxford: Hart Publishing 1999).

to stew over every word together, huddled side-by-side at the computer for days on end. I am not someone who likes to draft roughly, and then to improve the work gradually through successive drafts. So not for me the traditional process of exchanging drafts with a co-author. Rather I like to get each sentence right before moving on to the next one. Stephen and Timothy are like-minded in this respect, so collaboration with them has been organizationally simple as well as intellectually demanding. But they are each also a foil to me in their different ways. Stephen resists my flights of fancy. Timothy dislikes my flirtations with philosophical formality, being a more literary person. All in all, I think my work with both of them has been highly profitable. So I would like to be remembered for my ability to collaborate with scholars of this calibre, as much as for the achievements, such as they are, of my solo work.

What are the most important issues in legal philosophy, and why are they distinctively issues of legal philosophy rather than some other discipline?

I should begin by expressing my doubts about the distinctiveness of legal philosophy. It is best to think of legal philosophy as part of political philosophy, which in turn is part of moral philosophy, which in turn is part of the philosophy of practical rationality, which in turn is part of the philosophy of rationality in general (to which philosophical aesthetics and epistemology also belong). The partitioning involved in this nested structure is, however, somewhat arbitrary. Except for the purposes of designing courses, recruiting students, and hiring colleagues, it doesn't really matter which issues are classified as belonging to the philosophy of law or to any other branch of philosophy. What matters is that good philosophers do interesting work on deep puzzles in a way which shows sufficient sensitivity to their interrelations with other deep puzzles. One of the pitfalls of attempting to demarcate different areas of philosophy (or different areas of any discipline, or indeed different disciplines) is that it encourages a bureaucratic approach to academic life: those who do primary work in moral philosophy, for example, may feel that it is legitimate to borrow ready-to-wear theories from the 'epistemology' rack, rather than tackling epistemic problems for themselves. They may look comical dressed in these borrowed theories, since they lack an original creator's sense of how the theories are supposed to be used and developed. The philosophy of law is not immune from this comedy.

When I suggested that the philosophy of law is part of political philosophy, you may have heard echoes of Ronald Dworkin. Dworkin criticizes those (including me) who try to tackle conceptual problems about law in a way that leaves open what political actors, including judges, should do. He protests that we are guilty of presenting the philosophy of law as too autonomous, too divorced from political philosophy.[8] Dworkin is right to insist that the philosophy of law cannot be autonomous of political philosophy, for it is part of it. His mistake lies in his view of political philosophy itself. Political philosophy is not exhausted or even dominated by questions about what political actors should do. Just as epistemology includes the conceptual question 'what is belief?', the answer to which does not determine or even suggest what beliefs anyone should hold, so political philosophy includes numerous conceptual questions (what is legislation? what is a state? what is an election?), the answers to which do not determine or even suggest what anyone should do. We need to answer these questions if we are to make sense of the proposed political principles in which the concepts in question figure (e.g. 'legislation should be a last resort', 'state power should be exercised for the common good', 'all should vote in general elections'). And we need to make sense of these proposed political principles before we can judge which of them, if any, is sound, and hence what any political actors should do. In that sense the conceptual questions are prior to the normative ones. By denying that there are any such prior conceptual questions, or at least that there are any such prior conceptual questions about law, Dworkin is not campaigning for a greater integration of legal philosophy into political philosophy. He is campaigning for those of us who already regard legal philosophy as part of political philosophy to change our understanding of political philosophy, maybe indeed philosophy as a whole.

This is an object lesson in why we should avoid demarcation disputes about what belongs to the philosophy of law. Which subdiscipline of philosophy a problem belongs to has no bearing at all on what counts as a successful solution to it. So I resist the second half of the question ('why are they distinctively issues of legal philosophy rather than some other discipline?'). I also have trouble with the first half of the question ('what are the most important issues in legal philosophy?'). I'm not sure how to judge

---

[8] *Justice in Robes* (Cambridge, Mass: Harvard University Press 2006), 213-4.

philosophical importance, and in any event I'm not sure that it's a healthy thing to be pursuing. Personally, I'm on the lookout for interesting issues more than important ones (although I can see that interestingness is one possible criterion of importance). So once again let me answer a different question from the one set. Let me answer the more agreeable question: What are the most interesting issues in legal philosophy?

My answer to this question changes, of course, depending on what I am currently working on. But two sets of puzzles I find perennially intriguing. I encountered them as a graduate student and have struggled with them ever since—without conspicuous success. One set of puzzles concerns the moral and legal importance of blame, and connected with that the moral and legal importance of fault. You may think that, since I have worked extensively on the theory of justifications and excuses, which are denials of fault, I would know why fault matters. But I am not sure that I do. I am not sure that I know why I should care that such-and-such a disaster was my fault, as opposed to just being my doing (with or without fault). This reverses the puzzle as it strikes many lawyers. Many lawyers think that it is obvious why I should care that such-and-such a disaster was my fault, but baffling why I should care that it was just my doing (in the absence of fault). They think that 'fault liability' is morally easy to defend while 'strict liability' is morally problematic. I learnt from the work of Bernard Williams that this is the opposite of the truth.[9] Lawyers are happier with fault liability mainly for institutional reasons. It is easier to square fault liability with the demand for 'fair warning' that is part of the ideal of the rule of law. But morality is not bound by the rule of law. It need not and does not give fair warning. So the lawyer's gut instinct that fault liability is somehow fairer doesn't help to solve the underlying question of why, apart from questions of institutional fairness, our being at fault matters. (You may say that once it is phrased this way, it is not clear in what sense the problem belongs to legal philosophy. I reply: Who cares?)

The other cluster of puzzles that I find perennially intriguing concern what counts as my doing. I have already made clear that the most basic reasons, to my mind, are reasons to succeed. They

---

[9] See particularly 'Moral Luck', above note [], and 'Internal Reasons and the Obscurity of Blame' in Williams, *Making Sense of Humanity* (Cambridge: Cambridge University Press 1995).

are reasons for actions that are partly constituted by their results. But which of the many turns of events to which my actions make a causal contributions count as the results of my actions? How far down the line of repercussions should we go? This is the problem of causal responsibility and it has often been tackled with overconfident oversimplifications. For example, it has often been assumed that a certain turn of events should not be regarded as the result of my actions if it is the result of someone else's actions. But if this were so, there would be no complicity. I am influenced by the work of Hart and Honoré to think that there is more than one mode of causal responsibility, more than one kind of causal connection that I may have to a turn of events that may, on occasions, be morally or legally salient. In particular there is a basic moral difference, I think, between principalship and complicity as modes of causal involvement. I have tried to sketch out the explanation for this in a recent paper called 'Complicity and Causality'.[10] But I must confess that the paper only makes the first few halting steps. The wider problem of causal responsibility is still very much on my mind. It is one of the deepest and most difficult puzzles of moral philosophy, and it has pervasive implications for every legal system. Maybe it is important as well as interesting? I would not like to say.

What is the relationship between legal philosophy and legal practice? Should legal philosophers be more concerned about the effects of their scholarship on legal practice?

The second part of this question might be asked with two quite different subtexts. Some might think that philosophers of law should be putting more effort into influencing or assisting judges, lawyers, legislators, etc. Some might think, on the contrary, that they should be putting more effort into avoiding such influence or assistance (for it will inevitably involve gross misunderstanding or misuse of ideas). Although I agree with those who say that philosophical ideas are doomed to be mangled or bowdlerized by lawyers and policymakers who try to use them, I tend to think that trying to influence the world for the better and trying to avoid influencing it for the worse are both equally misguided forms of vanity in an academic. I take an austere view of the political re-

---

[10] *Criminal Law and Philosophy* 1 (2007), 127.

sponsibility of intellectuals according to which we answer mainly to intellectual values in our work, barring an imminent, foreseeable and dangerous abuse of our work by others. As an intellectual, it seems to me, Marx should be more embarrassed by his frequent nonsequiturs than by the many immoralities that were later committed in his name.

Another way to put this is to say that, while I dislike the bureaucratic partitioning of academic endeavours from each other, I happily embrace a bureaucratic conception of academic life as a whole. Those who want academics to be intentionally and extensively engaged with public life are insufficiently aware, it seems to me, of the problem of counterproductivity. Of course scholars, like journalists and lawyers, have an important role in exposing political doublespeak, judicial humbug, and so on. They can be an important check on excesses of public and private power. But scholars play this role best, as a rule, when they do not try to play it. For the most part, in their academic work, they should aim at true premises, valid arguments, clear thinking, attention to detail, avoidance of banality, and so forth, without regard to the consequences of their work, if any, for the development of public policy, world peace, human flourishing, etc. In particular, they should not confuse themselves with campaigners, pundits, advocates, or government advisers. Sticking to purely intellectual objectives is usually the best way (and is certainly the distinctive way) for them to avoid becoming corrupted by the system that they help to check.

Having said that, I have occasionally done a bit of campaigning or reforming work myself. Like anyone else I am occasionally outraged by government policies or by decisions of the courts and I do not deny myself the chance to attack them or propose improvements merely because I am also a philosopher. But I think it is important not to confuse the two roles in one's own mind. There are some political topics on which, in the course of my academic work, I have become reasonably well-versed. As an academic, I also have access to reasonably good channels for publication of contributions to political debate. But when I write this stuff I am obviously not writing as a philosopher. If you wanted policy advice, would you look up 'philosophers' in the Yellow Pages? I certainly wouldn't. I would be interested in talking to someone with concrete policy expertise. On some issues I might choose to talk to someone with legal expertise. And of course I have a bit of that expertise myself. If I make contributions to public debate, it is my legal more than my philosophical wisdom that comes to the fore.

In short: it is not my job, as a philosopher of law, to act as a consultant or a conscience for the law industry, or for any other part of the machinery of public power. Rather, I am engaged in the scholarly study of some relatively abstract aspects of that industry and of that machinery. I am interested in understanding its nature (good or bad) and the logic of its discourse (precise or muddled). Meanwhile my main way of influencing its future development, it seems to me, should be and is indirect. I teach philosophy to many talented law students. In the process I help them (I hope) to sharpen their analytical skills, to widen their horizons, to become more thoughtful about their lives and work, and to value humanity. Many of them will later go into legal practice or other jobs carrying public responsibilities. If they take even some of their philosophical sensitivities with them, they are likely to exert a benign collective influence on public culture well beyond what I could or should hope to exert by my own clumsy public interventions.

To which problem, issue or broad area of legal philosophy would you most like to see more attention paid in the future?

I have a special interest in reparation, apology, the offering of explanations, and other reactions to wrongdoing by wrongdoers, together with the attitudes that accompany them. I do not think that the justification for such reactions and attitudes is at all well understood, and with few exceptions I do not think that recent philosophers have really appreciated how complex and difficult they are. Partly this is because of an excessive preoccupation with the special case of punishment. Punishment is a special case because it involves deliberately adding extra suffering to the world in response to a supposed wrong. I do not underestimate how hard that is to justify. Philosophers have not made much progress with this problem either. But the extra difficulty of justifying such an apparently perverse reaction to wrongdoing has often led philosophers to underestimate the difficulty of justifying reactions that do not include this feature. I always marvel at the ease with which reparation, in particular, is portrayed as simply and basically just, without further ado. Much of the modern writing about corrective justice in the law of torts and the law of contract tends to exemplify this tendency, in spite of its highfalutin technical apparatus.

Many theorists of private law seem to think that showing reparative principles to be principles of corrective justice is the same as showing them to be defensible. This is mystifying. Even when we know that reparative principles are principles of corrective justice, we still need to know what justifies the relevant principles of corrective justice. For all we know, until shown otherwise, all principles of corrective justice are indefensible.

So I would like to see more work on this topic, and I would like to do more work on this topic. It is a topic that brings the philosophy of law into direct engagement with some of the deepest problems of moral philosophy more generally. It raises in sharp relief the vexed and ancient question of what kind of attitude we should be taking to our own pasts, and why. Shouldn't we be getting on with improving the future rather than dwelling on the past? Isn't regret (and hence apology, and hence reparation) fundamentally irrational, a kind of crying over spilt milk? I don't think I yet have satisfying answers to these questions but I would like to think that further and better answers are available, and that philosophers of law in my generation and the next will help to uncover them.

Selected publications

'Liberals and Unlawful Discrimination', *Oxford Journal of Legal Studies* 9 (1989), 1.

'Rationality and the Rule of Law in Offences Against the Person', *Cambridge Law Journal* 53 (1994), 502.

'Justifications and Reasons', in Andrew Simester and A.T.H. Smith (eds), *Harm and Culpability* (Oxford: Clarendon Press 1996).

'On the Ground of her Sex(uality)', *Oxford Journal of Legal Studies* 18 (1998), 167.

'The Gist of Excuses', *Buffalo Criminal Law Journal* 1 (1997), 575.

'The Wrongness of Rape' (co-author: Stephen Shute), in Jeremy Horder (ed), *Oxford Essays in Jurisprudence, Fourth Series* (Oxford: Clarendon Press, 2000).

'Obligations and Outcomes in the Law of Torts' in Peter Cane and John Gardner (eds), *Relating to Responsibility: Essays for Tony Honoré* (Oxford: Hart Publishing, 2001).

'Reasons' (co-author: Timothy Macklem) in Jules Coleman and Scott Shapiro (eds), *The Oxford Handbook of Jurisprudence and Philosophy of Law* (Oxford: Oxford University Press 2002).

'Legal Positivism: 5 Myths', *American Journal of Jurisprudence* 46 (2001), 199.

'The Wrongdoing that Gets Results', *Philosophical Perspectives* 18 (2004), 53.

'Value, Interest, and Well-Being' (co-author:Timothy Macklem), *Utilitas* 18 (2006), 362.

5
Ruth Gavison

Haim H. Cohn Professor of Human Rights
Faculty of Law, Hebrew University, Jerusalem, Israel

Why were you initially drawn to the philosophy of law?

My initial attraction to the philosophy of law was quick, strong and came very naturally. Unlike some of my friends in legal philosophy, I have always liked the law both as an academic discipline and as a professional calling. I enjoyed its intellectual challenges and the fact that it could be a tool for changing society for the better. Philosophy on the other hand was the way to make sense of things, to explore their meaning and presuppositions. Straight thinking is not a guarantee of quality and truth, but it helps. In addition, the broader conception of philosophy as a guide to the good and meaningful life was very enticing. I grew up in a tradition in which analytical philosophy and grander visions of the discipline had an uneasy coexistence. I was initiated into a great respect for logic, truth, and analysis, tempered by the understanding that what really mattered were the good life and our contribution to it.

So the inclination was natural. I got the last push in that direction by a course in legal philosophy offered by Joseph Raz who had just returned to the Hebrew University after completing his doctoral thesis on "The Concept of a Legal System" under the supervision of H.L.A. Hart in Oxford. I have found the way Raz taught us to think about law, its nature and its functions, truly transformative. I had a feeling I finally discovered the attitude and the tools needed to think about the law. Defining my field as that of legal philosophy seemed an obvious choice. When I acquired a degree in philosophy my feeling of homecoming was complete.

However, I soon realized that the philosophy of law proper – thinking hard about the nature of law – was not the exclusive center of my interest. I retained my sense that clarity of thought and attention to arguments and the avoidance of muddles were critical. I kept teaching legal theory and I still believe that it is a course of great importance to all lawyers. But I moved towards thinking and writing about issues in which law and its nature always featured, but never exhausted the thrust of the work. As time passed, it became harder for me to see myself as a philosopher of law (or to see myself as a clear player in any other field of legal academics).

In fact, the doubt started with my DPhil dissertation. My plan was to write about the relationships between validity and existence of legal norms (an issue which I still find intriguing, at the heart of legal philosophy). I recall coming to H.L.A. Hart's messy room in University College for the first of many meetings. He listened carefully to my presentation, and said this was indeed an important subject; he himself had written a bit about it; but did I really think it could capture my interest and imagination for the length of time it would take to write a dissertation? I was slightly puzzled, but (too quickly) replied in the affirmative. I went off happily to read Austin and Kelsen and Hart and Raz on validity and existence, writing short papers and trying to structure a decent thesis. At the same time I was taking courses. Oxford was unbelievably exciting, and I enjoyed sampling the very rich diet of courses in philosophy which was offered there. In addition to Hart and Dworkin and Raz and Finnis and MacCormick on philosophy of law, there was a lot to listen to. Among other things I attended an eye-opening seminar by John Plamenatz on political philosophy. Towards the end of the term he was talking about the idea of privacy and the private-public distinction. Only then I finally understood what Hart had been trying to tell me. I was totally captivated by the richness and the depth of the subject. It intrigued me in many ways. I liked the fact that it raised issues from politics, philosophy, social theory, law and psychology all at once; that privacy was challenging at the level of conceptual analysis, but that it also had a relevant history and diverse functions.

I went back to Hart and asked to change my subject. Hart was very gracious. He in fact encouraged me and agreed that the new subject sounded richer and more satisfying. But, he said, he could not really supervise me on that one, because he knew nothing about it. I do not remember how I persuaded him to take the road with me, but he did. I will remain forever grateful for the model supervision he gave me, and for the generous way in which he introduced me to thinking about the law within broader perspectives.

In addition, while struggling to define my 'field' in academics, I have always invested a lot of time, energy, and thought to activities in the public sphere. I have been a human rights activist (spent 25 years helping to found and build Israel's Association for Civil Rights in Israel (ACRI)), and was engaged in various initiatives in Israel's civil society.

For which of your contribution(s) to legal philosophy so far would you like to be remembered, and why?

I like my work on various aspects of the idea of privacy and its justification, the private-public distinction and the legal protection of privacy. I am glad these works are cited and hope they will be read in the future as well. I believe privacy is a rich, complex and important idea(1), which is misunderstood and under-rated in some western democracies. These works do raise some very central questions of legal philosophy, such as the limits of law and the need to distinguish the question whether some conduct or value is desirable and the very different question whether the conduct should be regulated, or the value be promoted, by law; and if so – should legislatures or courts be the ones making the primary decisions. The answer to these last questions does presuppose familiarity with the nature of law and its special features.

Closer to classic legal philosophy is my work on theories of adjudication, the role of courts, constitutionalism and the relationships of law and 'other things that matter', like morals, religion, politics and social change. I have been teaching these subjects and writing about them throughout my working life, with changing emphases. All of these presuppose some understanding of law, its nature and functions and unique characteristics, as compared to other social forces or normative systems. They further require a good grasp of the distinctions between law as a social practice characterized by a claimed normativity and a monopoly over the justified use of force in society on the one hand, and reflecting and theorizing about law as theoretical pursuits on the other.

But another sense of importance comes into the picture here. In my own country the contribution of these writings is on a different level. Israel (like some other countries) has been going in the last three decades through a process of 'legalization'. Law and the courts have become the remedies to all social ills and the last arbiters of all controversies. They, through an expansive reading of the ideal of the 'rule of law', are seen as the last hope of enlightenment and decency. All issues of public importance end up in the courts. Many controversial issues are couched in terms of rights discourse and consequently are brought to the court so they can be decided by the 'forum of principle'.

The fascinating story of Israel's constitutional journey is too long to be told here. It must be read against the background of the tormented history of Israel and the challenges it has to face. What is relevant to our concerns here is that the struggle for the constitution and judicial review came to be seen as a struggle for liberalism and human rights against religion, Jewish particularism, and corrupt government. Some have even claimed that arguing against the necessity of a constitution and judicial review, or against judicial activism, was an attack on the very independence and the legitimacy of the court, the notions of democracy, and human rights.

Many of my works on these subjects have been written in the general context of these debates. I took a position against judicial activism, but in particular against the view that such activism was an inevitable consequence of an adequate analysis of law and adjudication. I sought to explain the central importance of human rights and judicial independence while at the same time stressing the dangers of expanding human rights and the role of courts and thereby impoverishing politics and threatening a central element of democracy. I insisted that we discuss the issues of Israel's constitutionalism on the merits, and not through slogans.

I do not expect a knock-out in these debates. They are eternal and immanent. I do hope that in Israel we can have a serious discussion of these issues that will go beyond claims that the very idea(l) of democracy, human rights and the rule of law either require or prohibit an entrenched constitution with judicial review.

Of special importance to me are the competing claims of law and religion(s). I have written extensively on the subject, in many contexts. Here, too, there is a tendency to argue that the only possible relationship between law and religion in a liberal democracy is that of American-type separation. I am pleased this view is losing some of its hegemony. I am even more pleased that the subjects connect with the distinction between 'private' and 'public'. Strong separation is in fact a claim that religion should be 'privatized'. I do not believe that religion (or ethnic affiliations) can or should be privatized, even if liberal democracies should indeed stress the difference between the civic commitment to the constitution shared by all citizens, and the various affiliations that give individuals and communities their richer sense of identity. Both elements are essential for a stable liberal democracy. It must have a strong sense of a civic nation, one whose cementing 'public religion' is a civic solidarity. But a nation exhausted by its civic bonds will not last if all non-civic nature are privatized, in part because its members will be forced to come into the public sphere in an impoverished form. A civic constitution is critical precisely because we expect our society to recognize a public aspect to all aspects of our identities, including the ones in which we differ from each other. The public recognition of the differences – together with some basic culture and values shared by all citizens, including a commitment to democracy and human rights – is what gives strength and meaning to the shared civic framework which we all accept and within which we live.

Last, and related—my work on various aspects of the legal protection of human rights. I share the belief that the broad recognition of the idea(l) of human rights is one of the great achievements of the 20th century. However, in both my academic writings and in my public involvements I have insisted on distinguishing the promotion of human rights from partisan politics, and on the implication of this view—stressing the importance of giving human rights a 'thin' interpretation. I helped ACRI start an extensive litigation program, which has secured impressive achievements from Israel's Supreme Court. At the same time I have fought against the tendency of human rights groups to endorse one set of rights, or the rights of one group, and seek to promote them while ignoring the way this struggle affected conflicting rights, or the rights of others. My concern with this issue started with the conflict between privacy and free speech, went through the willingness of feminist activists to ignore rights of due process of men accused of abuse, and is now centered on the tragic conflict between Jews and Palestinians in which many on both sides claim their own right to national self-determination, while denying it to the other party. These stands resulted from a combination of my political commitments and my academic research. I developed them both in my academic writings and in my non-academic public statements. Working on both levels at the same time limited my contribution to each of them, but I hope it also made it more integrated. For me personally the constant feed back between academic work and public involvement was both challenging and enriching.

In sum, I hope these works will be read as contributions to the particular subjects with which they deal. I also hope that there will be a more general message that comes out of their totality: Law is an important public institution. A commitment to academic writing about the philosophy of law need not come with total detachment from one's society and its issues; one's commitment to academics, and to philosophy, should inspire both one's academic work and one's other pursuits. In one's public work, the academic virtues of knowledge, care, clear thinking and fair and valid reasoning should not be left aside. 'Politics' in the broad sense is a different vocation from 'science' in the same sense. But politics is better and deeper when it is inspired by the fruits and virtues of science. Philosophy is of course on the 'science' side of this divide. Less obvious but as important to me: Involvement with public issues is not only a burden in an academic commitment to thinking about law. It may inspire academic work and make it not only more relevant but also deeper and richer.

What are the most important issues in legal philosophy, and why are they distinctively issues of legal philosophy rather than some other discipline?

Let me put the question on its head, and start with the core of the philosophy of law in the strict sense. The basic question of the *nature of law* is the starting point of legal philosophy (I in fact prefer labeling the discipline 'philosophy of law', as in 'philosophy of science' or 'philosophy of history'. We would not call these fields 'historical' or 'scientific philosophy'?) I take it all will agree that this is a paradigmatic question for the philosophy of law, but some may argue that it is not in fact a very *important* issue in the field. They may say that dealing with definitions or conceptual analyses of law is just the kind of hairsplitting that gives analytical philosophy a bad name. I beg to differ.

True, I do not think any immediate theoretical or practical question depends on one's understanding of the nature of law. I also share Kelsen's view that there will never be a knock-out between positivism and natural law theories of law. Law is indeed both a social institution, with a strong factual element of power, and a system that claims authority and has a normative import built into it. Law is thus a complex phenomenon and any attempt to reduce conceptions of law in a way that will base it on just one of these tenets will fail. Which of these features we should emphasize in a given context is not something we can 'prove'. It has to do with context, temperament and general outlook more than it has to do with the 'truth' of one's conception of law. It may also change for any one person with the context of her enquiry.

Nonetheless, here we return to one of the basic claims of both analytical and political philosophy: The very fact of the plurality of language, systems of meaning and conceptualizations, as well as of interests and deep visions of the good life mean that we must share both a conceptual framework and a political framework in order to advance our ability to discuss, understand, and act together without just talking and being past each other as strangers in the dark. This is true for law as well: understanding the debate about the nature of law and appreciating the different perspectives, their strengths and their deficiencies, is critical to our ability to form a community that shares some understandings and presuppositions and can thus discuss central issues while creating a shared basis of understanding from which we can negotiate our differences. This ability is also critical to a useful construction of the central ideal of the rule of law. The history of the philosophy of law is full of instances of debates in which people use different conceptions of law and thus cannot make progress in any serious conversation. Familiarity with the debates about the nature of law therefore permits moving beyond them to meaningful discussions about the law, its functions and its evaluation.

The closer an issue is to that basic question of the nature of law – the closer it is to the core of the *philosophy of law*. However, most of the questions discussed by people in the philosophy of law are not 'pure'. They tend to be related to other branches of philosophy (in fact, insights of all other branches have been used in works within the philosophy of law), and to look at the law and at legal practices from disciplinary perspectives other than that of philosophy (such as sociology, history or psychology), or both. Since law is a complex social institution, which is designed to affect human behavior and perform social functions, the richness of perspectives is anything but surprising. It is necessary to give us a better understanding of law, which is the purpose of the philosophy of law itself.

Take the question of political obligation or the moral authority of law: To know if there is an obligation to obey the law we do need to know what laws are and how we identify the law. But we need to know a lot more about societies, and what keeps them cohesive and stable, and about the functions of law as an institution, irrespective of its content. It is trivial to say that we should obey good laws. The question of political obligation is meaningful if the obligation holds concerning all laws, as such. We just should know whether, and in what ways, law is, other things being equal, better than anarchy. Assuming we want to inculcate in people a healthy balance between an attitude of respect to law and an attitude of critical evaluation of its desirability that might alert one to the fact that there may be a liberty – or even a duty – to disobey some laws under certain circumstances, a lot may depend on our assessment of the natural tendencies of most people. If we believe that most people tend to obey authority, as Milgram's experiments have suggested, we may want to stress more the need to evaluate laws before obeying them. If we think people tend to be anarchists – we may emphasize the elements justifying a general *prima facie* obligation to obey in a well-ordered society. Philosophy of law itself thus cannot provide us with tools and knowledge necessary to respond to all these concerns. But its insights are critical if we want to think about them well.

Many may complain that the account I just gave of political obligation presupposes an approach identifying legal obligations by social facts and institutional procedures, without 'assuming' that all laws have moral value or that immoral 'laws' are not laws. Thus, I am not using the philosophy of law to advance clear thinking. Rather, I choose one theory of law over another. The account presupposes positivism and thus its validity and appeal depend on the endorsement of a controversial legal theory. A Natural Law approach – it may be argued – gives a better account of the law, it reflects the deep connections between law and morality, and thus connects law with a duty to obey and deals with immoral commands by the powerful theoretical and practical tool of denying them the status of law.

There is truth in this claim. It illustrates that the debate about the relative merits of these theories of law is itself a complex matter. Theories (not only about the law) may be evaluated by their theoretical coherence, elegance, adequacy or fruitfulness. But the nature of law as a *social* institution means that an important element in the evaluation of theories of law is the effect that these theories may have on the thinking and the behavior of individuals and groups when faced with situations which may call for a decision not to obey laws. And most of the factors relevant to this possible impact of theories on behavior are not, themselves, matters of legal philosophy at all. Yet we cannot think straight about issues like this without presupposing a conception of law.

Some argue for positivism because it alerts people to the fact that laws are a matter of power, so that moral evaluation of laws is necessary. They further point out that it is easier for judges to reach just results in unjust regimes because often general laws may support just results against the wishes of a bad ruler, and the judges can 'hide' behind the rule of law. Others criticize positivism because it induces obedience when it is wrong to obey. This only shows that the debate about obedience relates to moral and social facts about individuals and state orders called 'laws', and not to theories about the law. Often, both natural lawyers and positivists want people to obey commands that should be obeyed and not obey those that should not. The question is how to distinguish between the two. It is not clear that rules about identifying a command as 'law' will do the trick. This is the fact we need to understand to think straight about political obligation. It requires understanding the nature and the history of the enterprise of elucidating the nature of law. It requires seeing the philosophy of law itself in context. The natural lawyers' critique of positivism is based on their belief that the pre-theoretical understanding of law is a natural-law conception. People believe *law* should be obeyed. Therefore, describing something as law suggests a duty to obey. But positivists deny just that. For them, describing something as 'law' is a matter of fact, and the question of obedience is left distinct and separate... The only way to make progress here is to transcend the debate about what should be called 'law'. We can only do that effectively if we know why the meaning game is so important.

Legal philosophy should prepare the tools – conceptual and theoretical – to conduct important debates about law in the best way. Players in legal philosophy should each seek to either make a contribution to the tools, to use them well in contexts which will often go beyond legal philosophy itself, or to do both. Most people do the latter.

What is the relationship between legal philosophy and legal practice? Should legal philosophers be more concerned about the effects of their scholarship on legal practice?

I do not think most legal practitioners – be they lawyers or judges – are usually familiar with the literature of legal philosophy or legal theory, or affected by it. It is curious and illuminating to see that the latter is also true at some level even for practitioners who have themselves been legal philosophers. To take one obvious example: when Jerome Frank became a judge it was not easy to see how his legal philosophy background was reflected in his judicial decisions. Same with Richard Posner. The relationship is easier to see with scholars-cum-judges such as Holmes.

One might conclude that people doing legal philosophy should not be overly concerned with their impact on legal practice. I do not share this view.

Let me start with a story. One of the most gratifying experiences in my teaching career has been a National Endowment for the Humanities (NEH) seminar to (mostly lower courts) American judges on theories of adjudication. They started with great skepticism concerning the relevance of all these high theories to their practice. They did not see a serious theoretical depth to the task of hearing disputes and deciding them. Issues such as tensions between application of the law and adjudication that goes beyond the law, with the resulting issues of legitimacy and legality, seemed of no practical import. They felt the same way about the endless debates about the implications to adjudication of the indeterminacy of legal language or intent. Yet at the end most of them acknowledged that gaining insight into theories of adjudication helped them in understanding what they were doing and being better at it. True, they said, awareness of these theories mostly would not change the decision they would make. But it made it possible for them to think about what they were doing and should be doing in a more integrated way. They had acquired a better sense of what kinds of decisions and skills good adjudication required. They could now give a name, and a theoretical context, to what they have been struggling with. The distinction between what judges can do, tend to do, and should do, helped them think of their role differently. It structured their activity for them. They felt it made them better practitioners.

This is the kind of beneficial effect legal theory should have to legal practice, in all its various genres. Familiarity with legal theories and clear thinking about the law, its strengths and its limits, will make people better practitioners, because it means that they know their tools better and may therefore use them more effectively.

I am more ambitious than the interviewers, however. I do not think the only – or even primary – relevant audiences for the insights of legal philosophy are legal practitioners, be they advocates, state lawyers, or judges. Law is a social institution of critical functions. It seeks to affect and guide the lives and the activities of all those living in its 'jurisdiction'. Law, and especially the constitution and the expressive parts of the law, should be known to all. People should be initiated into the basic legal norms just as they are raised to internalize the basic moral norms in their society or sub-society. The ideal of the rule of law and its meaning, as well as the strengths and limits of law and its relations to other social and normative systems, are important elements in the kit of tools of individuals in modern democracies.

I return to the cluster of questions surrounding the (alleged) obligation to obey the law. Legal philosophy clarifies important issues such as the relevant differences between revolution, civil disobedience and conscientious objection. It helps us identify the law, understand reasons for obeying it, but alert us to the need to evaluate it critically. This knowledge alone will not make people decide well. But if it is available to them, they are likely to be less confused, and act in ways that are more effective. It is not an accident that interest in legal theory grows when societies face urgent debates concerning the legitimacy of government. We saw it around the Nuremberg Trials, then again in the US around Vietnam, and in Israel when issues of serving in the territories, participating in targeted killings or in the disengagement from Gaza were central.

To which problem, issue or broad area of legal philosophy would you most like to see more attention paid in the future?

My 'favorite' subject concerns the nature of rights, and includes such questions as the relationships between rights and other claims and interests, the special nature of legal rights, their relations with human rights, and the institutional implications of all of these. This subject is of the greatest theoretical and practical importance in our time. This is because it sets the discourse and the framework of thinking within which much of political philosophy and international relations are couched; and in it the special force of law is used to structure the very borders of the political.

Some legal philosophers hoped that the social, positive, element in law might make the analysis of legal rights and duties more straightforward than that of moral ones. Indeed, the fact that legal norms are often anchored in texts that are relatively easy to identify, and which can be further identified by reference to the actual practices of final and authoritative legal organs, and that often they may be vindicated by courts, yielded attempts to grant legal duties and rights a more solid basis than that of moral rights. Indeed, the institutional nature of law and the fact that it has sources often mean that claims of legal rights are made in courts of law. If successful, they may be enforced in a way different than claims of moral rights. Nonetheless, the normative strength of legal rights does not stem from these features. It is shared by moral rights. It stems from the fact that rights indicate that someone else is under a duty to act. Respecting rights – be they moral or legal – is not discretionary. The right-holder is entitled to it. Legal rights may be more enforceable than moral rights. They are not logically or normatively different from them.

This analysis makes it critical to identify the rights people have, because this may indicate the scope of the duties people (and governments) have. What I can claim as a matter of rights is removed from the world of politics, mercy, generosity, or love. In some sense, the broader the realm of rights – the narrower the world of striving to do the good or the meaningful becomes. When the rights are legal rights, constraining the work of the state and the political order, rights and rights discourse may impoverish the world of politics.

Human rights discourse has reached a critical stage. On the one hand, it is a very powerful agent of promoting justice and human rights in the world, within countries and in international relations. Bills of rights and independent courts or bodies have been very central in this important process. On the other hand, expansive readings of the discourse, in both contexts, often seek to promote political goals through the special preemptive power of rights discourse. These processes may weaken the rights discourse. They may also weaken the ability of courts – when they are perceived to be imposing their own political vision of the good – to protect core rights.

This is a serious and complex political and social issue of far-reaching importance. Today, the classical issues of politics are often discussed within the (human) rights discourse. The passage from a claim that there is such a right to the claim that it should be recognized by courts is quick. Social struggles are often fought primarily through litigation in national courts or through declarations of human rights by international NGOs, who then proceed to promote these alleged rights within international arenas.

Despite the enormous literature on these subjects, legal philosophy has not yet contributed its full share. Although we do not have a single ruling theory of law, and are unlikely to have one in the future, the range of the debate and its meaning have been clarified. We know the pros and cons of the available theories. It will be good if we can be in the same place when we are thinking and talking about the distinctive nature of claims of rights, the relationships between law and legal rights, the role of courts in developing rights and enforcing them, and the relationships between legal, constitutional, moral and human rights. Having good conceptual and theoretical tools to deal with these questions is critical for a good understanding of the idea of law itself. They are critical for understanding the way political and legal systems work and should work. They are critical for seeing the ways in which thinking about legal philosophy may help us understand the world and act effectively within it.

This is so because the special nature of right-talk has important structural theoretical and practical manifestations. If rights are indeed 'trumps', it becomes critical to identify the scope of rights and the identity of those who have the power to authoritatively decide it. In moral theory, powers to decide and interpret are not that central, because the discussion is based on persuasion, not power. Moral ideas and ideals have great importance in our lives, as they should. But the processes through which such idea(l)s affect us are indirect. All societies, especially societies with deep rifts, require an agreed-upon power-structure to legitimate political decisions. These structures are constitutional and legal. Human rights have the special power of being an element that is supposed to be shared by all, irrespective of opinion or group affiliation. They should form a part of the constitutional framework that is shared and gives groups the power to pursue, within it, their distinctive visions of the good. But if human rights are read expansively, they may fail to function in this way.

Thus the debate over rights has turned in part to a debate over who decides. With the rise of international human rights law, this is not only a question within states but also a question affecting relationships among them, and imposing on the less powerful states a set of external constraints not effective on stronger nations.

This in turn has far reaching implications for all of political theory, because it structures the relationships between *visions of the good* and the *rules of the political game*. If human rights are the final arbiters of political decisions, and if courts are the final and authoritative interpreters of human rights, and if courts tend to expand their power and jurisdiction so that they regularly decide ideological and political questions as matters of law and rights—this may indeed result in a serious weakening of the political branches of government and of the structures of political legitimacy which underlie all stable governments.

Legal philosophy can and should give us the conceptual, theoretical and normative tools to think well about these issues. This in itself is a very worthy cause. In addition, if we think well – this may increase the chance that we shall act well.

The knowledge that my academic work can do such things, even if indirectly, makes my work an integral part of my life. It is always a great joy when this happens. With law, the pleasure of integrating thinking and doing is central, natural and inevitable. I am grateful that it has been that way for me.

Bibliography

1. R. Gavison (ed.), *Issues in Contemporary Legal Philosophy: The Influence of H.L.A. Hart*, Oxford 1986.

2. 'Privacy and the Limits of Law', (1980) 89 *Yale L.J.* 421–471.

3. 'Natural Law, Positivism and the Limits of Jurisprudence: A Modern Round', 91 *Yale L.J.* 1250–1285 (1982).

4. 'Information Control: Availability and Exclusion', ch. 5 in Public and Private in *Social Life* (eds S.I. Benn and G.F. Gaus) Croom Helm 1983, 113–134.

5. 'The Controversy over Israel's Bill of Rights', 15 *I.Y.H.R.* 113–154 (1985)

6. 'The Implications of Jurisprudential Theories For Judicial Election, Selection and Accountability', 61 *U.S.C.L.Rev.* 2701–2746 (1988).

7. 'Too Early for a Requiem: Warren and Brandeis Were Right About Privacy vs. Free Speech', 43 S. *Carolina L.Rev.* 437–471, 1992.

8. 'Feminism and the Private-Public Distinction', 45 *Stan.L.Rev.* 1–45 (1992).

9. '(Public) Law and (Private?) Religion', in John Tasioulas (ed.), *Laws, Values and Social Practices*, Dartmouth, 165–190 1997.

10. 'The Role of Courts in Rifted Democracies', 33 *Isr. L.Rev.* 216–258, 1999.

11. 'Can Separate Be Equal: A Case Study', *Democratic Culture*, 3 (2000) 37.

12. 'A Constitution For Israel? Lessons from the American Experiment', 12 *Azure* (2002), 133–192.

13. 'The Jews' Right to Statehood – A defense', *Azure* 15, 2003, 70–108

14. 'The Relationships between Civil and Political and Social and Economic Rights', in Coicaud et al (eds.), *Globalization of Human Rights*, UNU Press 2003, 23–55.

15. 'Legislatures and the Quest for a Constitution: The Case of Israel', 11:2 *Review of Constitutional Studies*, 345–400 (2006).

6

Leslie Green

Professor of the Philosophy of Law
Fellow of Balliol College, University of Oxford, UK

Why were you initially drawn to the philosophy of law?

I came to the philosophy of law when I discovered that the problems of political philosophy I most wanted to explore required understanding the nature of law.

My philosophical interests developed gradually. The subject was not taught in my high school, though I had a dedicated history teacher who pushed various books my way, among them Ayer's *Language, Truth and Logic*. It was the first philosophy book I read. Although parts of it seemed obscure and others unappealing, I admired its tough-mindedness and its brio, and it probably inoculated me against the malarkey that a beginner is still likely to encounter on the 'philosophy' shelves in a bookstore or public library. As an undergraduate, I studied politics as well as philosophy, but they ran in parallel for my work in politics was mostly institutional and empirical. My first student essay in political philosophy was on the question of whether Rousseau was a totalitarian or a liberal. I can't remember what I argued—I hope I had the good sense to resist the alternatives. Shortly after that, I read Robert Paul Wolff's essay *In Defense of Anarchism*, which had a very unsettling effect: its conclusions seemed both irresistible and unpalatable.

I was increasingly drawn to these questions and, on finishing my degree, applied to graduate schools where I might pursue them further, and also to law schools, in case I needed a job. When I was offered a scholarship to go to Oxford, the decision was easy.

I left Canada for England before the first Québec referendum on independence and the period of intense debate over constitutional reform that followed it. Even from a distance it was impossible not to be caught up in all this, including question of whether Canada should have an entrenched bill of rights, and if so what should be in it. (In the end, Canada adopted a solution that sat well with my own ambivalence: an entrenched bill of rights supervised by the courts but subject to temporary derogation by the legislature.) These issues were very much on my mind, though I was not yet writing about them. At that stage, my intellectual formation was more influenced by the extraordinary community of scholars around me than by my reactions to political events at home or abroad. Hart, Honoré, Raz, Dworkin and Finnis were all active in the philosophy of law, as were Taylor, Sen, Parfit, Mackie and MacDowell in moral and political philosophy.

I was very lucky with my first teachers, especially Jonathan Glover, Joseph Raz and Charles Taylor, who could not have been better, or less alike. I first studied jurisprudence with Raz in 1980 and recall many of those early tutorials. One was about the individuation of laws—the question, as Bentham put it, of what constitutes one whole and complete law. This was a matter into which Raz had put prodigious effort; but I knew from my reading that others, including Dworkin, mocked the very idea of individuating laws—what were we trying to do, *count* them? (It is therefore interesting to read, in *Justice in Robes*, that Dworkin has now managed to individuate *concepts* of law, and has counted to four.) I struggled to understand the significance of the problem and to say something useful about it. What I came up with was a far-fetched analogy to Chomsky's idea of a deep structure in language, thus flaunting my ignorance of two subjects. Raz demolished it – quietly but utterly – in a few minutes. My late nights had produced little more than a metaphorical restatement of the problem. It was a humbling, and educating, experience.

Outside tutorials, I launched into a close reading of Kelsen's *General Theory* and *Pure Theory*, Fuller's *The Morality of Law* and, of course, Hart's *The Concept of Law*. Other books now on the canon were then still quite fresh; so as graduate students do we scoured the new works by Dworkin, Raz and Finnis, hoping to find both insights and errors. In seminars, Raz was already beginning to present the leading ideas of *Morality of Freedom* and Dworkin was talking about material from what would become *Law's Empire*. We could see that big things were happening, and it was exciting to be involved even as spectators. I also learned a lot from the other students. Jeremy Waldron and I worked through Hegel's *Philosophy of Right* over breakfasts; Denise Réaume forced me to take seriously feminist theory, which later influenced my work on gender and sexuality; Anthony Teasdale insisted I not lose sight of the empirical and institutional realities of politics. As we had complete freedom to attend lectures, in addition to my work for the courses I attended various lectures in general philosophy and in substantive law, which I now had to teach myself.

Having somehow survived the grueling examinations, I decided to begin a doctorate. Taylor supervised the initial stages of my work, about communitarian views of authority, but my interests and approach drifted from his own and when Taylor was about to resign the Chichele Chair I asked Raz if he would be willing to take me on as a research student. Thankfully, he had forgiven (or more probably forgotten) my essay on the individuation of laws, and agreed to become my supervisor. For me at any rate, those were enormously enjoyable years. On the strength of my examination results and several chapters of a thesis, I got a job at Lincoln College, Oxford, where I discovered how much I liked teaching and began to hope that there might be some prospect of making a living at it. Though my period *in statu pupillari* had come to an end, my education continued when I joined a discussion group that met in Tony Honoré's rooms at All Souls'. My debut paper criticized one of Finnis's central doctrines. His evident puzzlement did nothing for my self-confidence, but to compound my anxiety Hart fell asleep about three minutes into my talk, though he awakened towards the end with a searching question which he followed up the next day with a letter vigorously pursuing the point. I couldn't understand why Hart was so concerned about my objections to Finnis. I hadn't yet seen the drafts of what would become the *Postscript* to *The Concept of Law* where, in effort to evade Dworkin's telling criticisms of his theory of obligations, Hart took a conventionalist turn that was vulnerable to the very objections that I was now pressing against Finnis. Sometime around then I realized that I was settling into a career as a legal philosopher.

What are the most important issues in legal philosophy, and why are they distinctively issues of legal philosophy rather than some other discipline?

I am dubious about the desire to be remembered for one's work, or for that matter at all. Marcus Aurelius rightly says that all fame ultimately ends in oblivion, and I share Seneca's view that this life is long enough, provided we keep our cool and don't waste our time. Moreover, the desire to be remembered can become a vice if it fosters a disposition to write *in order* to be remembered. So I struggle to keep faith with the old view that philosophers ought to be oriented not to the memorable, or even the original, but only to the true and the illuminating. Needless to say, that is a standard unlikely to inspire lasting satisfaction with one's own writings, or those of most others. This is not to deny that I take a special pride in some of my work, but that has less to do with any supposed memorability than with the intellectual (and sometimes personal) challenges that writing them posed. Some things that were terribly difficult to get right seemed to attract limited attention; others came easily yet ended up reprinted, anthologized, translated, and so on. So even if I wanted to be remembered for my contributions to legal philosophy, I'm not sure how I would go about it. Still, any moderately optimistic philosopher of middle age or younger is entitled to hope that his best work still lies ahead of him, so perhaps I shall eventually find out.

But we might take the question more broadly, to include also one's contributions to the formation of other legal *philosophers*. I have always had a special admiration for those teachers who, whether by mission or irresistible example, shaped the next generation of thinkers in their field, who made them see why a subject matters and is worth taking risks to pursue. I fondly remember those who did that for me, and I hope that some of my own students might come to feel that way too. In that measure I suppose I depart from my Stoic forbears.

What are the most important issues in legal philosophy, and why are they distinctively issues of legal philosophy rather than some other discipline?

The notion of "importance" is interest-dependent and the relation "more important than" is not connected over the domain of relevant issues, so there *are* no "most important" issues in legal philosophy. As far as distinctiveness is concerned, several disciplines, including various branches of philosophy, have joint custody over the subject's central issues.

An issue is important when it is the site of some serious puzzlement, and what puzzles us depends as much on things external to philosophy as on things internal to it. In the 1960s, the independence of former British colonies made vivid many puzzles about the continuity of law through time; now it is hard to get students to see why these issues are (or were) so important. In the 1970s and '80s there was enormous interest in justice, rights and equality, many of which were cast aside when the commitment to social justice in rich capitalist states waned. Now we are in the midst of a period of intense interest in the rule of law, constitutionalism, and globalization, and these reflections will also prove productive and then, very probably, will also pass. Such shifts in philosophical attention are mostly benign and are in any case inevitable. But they too should make us leery about declaring anything to be "the most important" issue in legal philosophy.

That said, I regard the attempt to provide an explanation of the nature of law (and related problems) as of some importance. This betrays my view about the way other problems in legal philosophy, including normative problems, need to be approached. Consider the old question of whether there is a general obligation to obey the law. Does the fact that something is legally required add a *further* moral consideration in favour of compliance, one that strengthens or replaces our ordinary reasons that depend on the content of the law, and that binds all of law's subjects on all occasions on which their obedience is required? Put that way you probably see why it is an uphill battle to show that there is any such obligation. (On *all* occasions? Applying to *all* people?) So why not just lower the bar, and say that there is an obligation to obey the law provided there is a moral reason to do so, say, seven times out of ten, or one that applies to the average person? Why insist on universality? Because that is what the law asks of us. *It* purports to determine the scope of our obligation to obey; *it* fixes the line between lawful non-compliance and civil disobedience, etc. Now that is a thesis in general jurisprudence. Whether it makes sense to think of the law making any demands of us, and what content its demands are taken to have, are matters of the nature of law. Similar issues crop up with respect to other important problems, including the nature of legal reasoning, and the value of the rule of law.

Also important are the branches of special jurisprudence—the attempts to find philosophically satisfying accounts of the foundations of tort, contract, criminal law, human rights, and so on. Some issues in the area, such as causation, responsibility, and consent, run through many of these, others are limited to a particular doctrinal field. Here the work of the legal philosopher needs to cooperate most fully with that of the academic lawyer, for it is an embarrassment to a theory of tort, for example, that what it declares to be the very essence of tort law is something that is in fact marginal to the law actually in force, or that something a theory of contract declares to be a borderline case is regarded by the courts as a perfectly normal contract.

Apart from their subject matter, I'm not sure how far any of these are *distinctively* issues of legal philosophy, if that means issues on which other branches of philosophy or the social studies can cast no important light. My own view is that legal philosophy is a branch of political philosophy in both its institutional and normative aspects, and that there is only a rough demarcation between political philosophy and the other aspects of practical philosophy. Unlike Kelsen, I therefore expect a sound legal philosophy to be very "impure". But even if it makes sense to think of some of these problems as legal philosophy's private property, we still need to understand the relation between them and other issues: as Hart insisted, a large part of legal philosophy consists in explaining the relations between law and other forms of social order and between law and morality; and no one has a monopoly on those problems.

What is the relationship between legal philosophy and legal practice? Should legal philosophers be more concerned about the effect of their scholarship on legal practice?

I am tempted to answer "nothing" and "not at all," and those are almost the correct answers. Of course it depends on what one understands by "legal practice." If that simply means those practices that are legal ones, then the relationship is that legal philosophy offers a philosophical *explanation* of them, in general and special jurisprudence. But most people who ask this question are interested in a different issue: what is the relationship between legal philosophy and *the practice of law*, i.e. lawyering? Here the difficulty is that the latter is in fact a very complex set of practices, not all of which have much to do with the law or are fruitful objects of philosophical inquiry. They include not only litigation and adjudication, but also (and more often) interviewing, counseling, negotiating, bargaining, accounting, and so on. (I have even heard of a law school that hires people to teach its students how to dress for success. I suppose this too is part of legal practice.) Every practicing lawyer knows that skill in the profession has as much to do with mastery of these things as it does with anything we might consider legal acumen in the normal sense, and every law professor knows 'C' students who went on to become brilliant and wealthy advocates. This suggests that Aristotle was right to see inquiry and advocacy as radically different enterprises, which may be why he addressed the main problems of legal philosophy in the *Ethics* and *Politics* while confining advocacy to the *Rhetoric*. The advocate above all wants to *win* an argument and therefore needs to be exquisitely attentive to the predispositions of his actual audience; the philosopher above all wants to *have* an argument and aims to persuade only the reasonable.

Those who shape their legal philosophy in the hope that it will prove useful to some practitioner or other therefore need to adapt it to the parochial features of the legal system in question. If you are the sort of philosopher who aspires to a large and influential audience, you will be tempted to adapt it to the predispositions of the courts of large and influential countries. I don't see much good coming of this. It can sometimes lead to intellectual dishonesty; it always leads to trimming.

Let me give an example. Americans live under an eighteenth-century constitution, in a country with weak political parties and a popular culture influenced by decadent forms of Christianity that are practically extinct in western democracies. Those are not promising circumstances for many minority groups, and especially not for lesbians and gay men. Its federal courts are therefore very tolerant of sexual orientation discrimination, though they do purport to frown on sex discrimination. So liberal American advocates argue that sexual orientation discrimination just *is* sex discrimination. You can guess how the story goes: sex plays a role in defining sexual orientation because a homosexual is attracted to a person of the same *sex*, and sexual orientation discrimination overlaps with gender discrimination to the extent that it harms people who fail to conform to accepted norms (including norms of sexual conduct) for people of that *sex*. Unless there is a radical cultural shift in America, an argument along these lines is probably your best bet in an American court. But it would be very queer to offer that as an explanation of the *nature* of sexual orientation discrimination. Prohibitions on same-sex marriage or on gay adoption do not advantage one sex over the other; they do not restrict people's options on account of their sex; they encourage an obliteration of gay people from the law that has no parallel in the law's bias against women. To focus on the fact that they *employ* a sex classification – as if anti-discrimination was only a taboo on certain classifications – is to miss what is wrong with it.

Moreover, were we pleading such a case before a South African or Canadian court, we would never offer anything as far-fetched as the sex-reductivist theory that constitutes the American lawyer's last and best hope; but then the constitutions of those countries actually prohibit discrimination on grounds of sexual orientation. This shows that the American constitution needs to be amended but, as my American colleagues continually remind me, that idea and $3.50 might get you a chai-soy-latte, if you are lucky enough to live in Austin or Berkeley.

Advocates have little choice but to work with or around what the sources deal them and what the politics of the day allows; but why would a philosopher choose to labour in that harness? I can't help feeling the willingness to do so betrays a failure to absorb an important truth about the nature of law. The strength of a legal argument depends on the sources; the strength of a philosophical argument does not. The courts may laugh at you and yet you may be exactly right. The courts may fawn over you and you may for all that be completely wrong (and may, like Kelsen, come to rue the day they even cited you.)

For these reasons I don't think we need to worry too much about the effect of our scholarship on legal practices. Lawyers no more need the help of legal philosophers than working scientists need the help of philosophers of science or artists need the help of philosophers of aesthetics. When courts do cite legal philosophers, it is usually for decorative rather than functional reasons—everything the most extreme legal realists said about the courts' use of authorities is true in spades about their rare forays into legal philosophy. Admittedly, legal philosophy contributes in indirect ways to our legal and political culture, but it is only one vector of influence, and its net effect is both small and hard to predict.

To which problem, issue or broad area of legal philosophy would you most like to see more attention paid in the future?

First, we need a *lot* more work on the familiar problems, which constantly get reformulated in response to developments in general philosophy and shifts in our intellectual and political culture. Here are two examples. Whatever law is it includes legal rules, and in every legal system there are some legal rules that were not created by any act intended to create a rule. So we are not going to get very far without a theory of *customary* rules. Now think of all the different ways we have approached them: the practice theory of rules, game-theoretical accounts, interpretivist accounts, practical reasoning accounts, etc. We made significant advances here, showing that some theories are not even plausible candidates; but at the same time we keep coming back to the problem as new philosophical tools present themselves or new perspectives seem to demand it. Owing to the centrality of rules to many areas of philosophy and social theory, we can be confident that will only continue. Another example: for a long time legal realism seemed as dead as any legal theory could be. Like the imperatival account of law, it was part of the pre-history of our subject. It is true that a naïve form of realism remained popular in some law schools and political science departments, though not because it had any answer to the objections of Kelsen or Hart. It just operated in ignorance of their writings or in indifference to the concerns that made their objections pertinent. But when philosophical naturalism reached legal philosophy through Brian Leiter's important work, realism got a new lease on life as a proto-science of judicial decision—a primitive one but, it was argued, on the right methodological track and more likely to produce reliable knowledge of the nature of law than any sort of conceptual or interpretive analysis. This argument is far from over; it is scarcely beginning. My point is that we now need to reframe and reformulate our understanding of the strengths and weaknesses of legal realism. The same thing goes on in other areas of legal philosophy. Change almost always deepens our understanding of the issues and, when we are lucky it brings us nearer to the truth about them.

I do, however, think that we have also neglected certain important issues. The first is substantive. I would like legal philosophers, and not only historians and sociologists, to pay a good deal more attention to the role of *power* in law. (And by 'power' here I mean *social* power, not normative powers, such as the power to legislate or to contract—we already pay enough attention to those.) This comes up in all sorts of ways. First, a legal system does not exist unless it is broadly efficacious, which means that it can actually influence conduct and through it people's interests. Second, social power is relevant to the ascription of legal responsibility. Third, legal systems depend on centralized institutions that give some people power over others, as Hart famously argued, by untethering the existence of legal norms from any broad social acceptance of social norms.

I think there are two reasons that contemporary legal philosophers shy away from these issues. The first is the complete success of Hart and Raz's attack on coercion-based theories of the *normativity* of law. It is almost as if, having refuted the reductivist views that every law or every legal system necessarily deploys coercive power, legal philosophers decided there was nothing more that needed to be said about power in law: right is not might, and that is the end of it. I'm aware, of course, that Foucault-inspired scholars remained interested in power. But I don't anticipate much coming of that approach, at least in its present form. When it touches on law, it deploys a terribly dated view of what legal theory is like, illiterately repeating old arguments against sovereignty and command theories that Hart already made a generation ago. The Foucauldian conception of power is also far too broad, counting nearly all social causation as a form a power, and thus encouraging the striking but empty ideas that power is everywhere, that speech is "censored" by the rules of grammar, and so on. If that were all power amounts to, we could safely forget about it. But that is a defective account of power, and good work remains to be done to replace it.

A second reason for our neglect of power is the reluctance of legal philosophers to engage as fully as they should with empirical and institutional questions. Here we see the residue of a certain style of philosophy. G.A. Cohen recounts a story about his Oxford days in the 'sixties, when it was *de rigeur* to pounce on cloudy argument with the question of whether it proposed a conceptual claim or (merely) an empirical one. To the tiresome objection "But that's just an *empirical* point", Cohen remembers one of his colleagues pleading, "Can't we make empirical points *sometimes?*"[1] I have lots of sympathy for that plea, for I think that serious legal philosophy depends on empirical claims about political institutions and human psychology, albeit at a fairly general level. But even Hart occasionally succumbed to an anti-empirical ethos, once declaring the fact that homo sapiens need *food* to survive to be a "merely contingent" fact. In his more careful moods, however, he saw that we need also to attend to truths that, while neither conceptually necessary nor not merely contingent are, as we might say, *no accident.* That is, given the nature of people and of law, some things are to be expected in the normal course

---

[1] G.A. Cohen, *If You're An Egalitarian, How Come You're so Rich?* (Cambridge MA: Harvard University Press, 2000), pp. 185-86, n.13.

of events unless something very unusual intervenes. Thus, while it is not necessarily true that legal systems should incorporate ordinary understandings of responsibility, it is no accident that they do so. Nor is it an accident that law is a hierarchical form of social organization that, in addition to being a normative system, is a system of social power. Should we exclude these from the province of jurisprudence on the grounds that they are not conceptually necessary? Hart would not have done so. He was interested in necessary truths about law, but his idea of what those comprise was very catholic, including not only conceptual necessities, but also natural ones, and even what we might call culturally-dependent necessities. We can of course, repeat the empty mantra that necessary truths must be true of all possible legal systems, and in a way that is right. The difficulty is that it is hard to get a fix on all possible legal systems, unless that means all imaginable legal systems, which leaves legal philosophy hostage to people's variable powers of imagination. (Some say they can't imagine a sanctionless legal system—to me that is child's play compared with trying to imagine a legal system in which all the truth conditions of legal propositions are also justification conditions for legal coercion—on which see further below.) I think we should pay more attention than we now do to the 'soft' necessities of law, to what I've been calling the "non-accidental" truths, and I've a feeling that among them we will find many important conceptual and empirical truths about power that might help bring us back to a profitable conversation with the rest of social and political theory.

The second issue is methodological, perhaps sub-methodological. What are the adequacy criteria for a theory of law? It needs to be intelligible and coherent; but there is a difference between a theory of law that is merely consistent and one that is correct. One can consistently represent a legal system as if it were an incentive system. (I know some legal philosophers deny this—I wish them luck in proving it.) Notice that I do not say that a legal system actually *is* an incentive system, or that it can be so represented *without loss*. Nonetheless, one can consistently represent legal systems in a variety of ways: as a set of commands issued by a unitary sovereign, as a set orders to judges to apply sanctions when people misbehave, as ordinances of reason for the common good, and so forth. None of these saves all of the appearances, but then every legal theory does some squashing and scrunching. As Robert Nozick memorably put it, philosophical explanation is like pushing and shoving random objects into a fixed perimeter of specified shape, sometimes clipping corners and even jettisoning things in time for a quick photograph of the orderly arrangement—subject to later retouching.

Some possible claims about law do succumb to semantics: law is not an organism or an element. Others are epistemically irresponsible: we can no longer entertain theories that require reference to non-existent spirits and entities, or that rest on any methods that would warrant their existence. And we surely want to avoid patently silly theories, such as those that commit us to the view that the law is indifferent between its subjects refraining from murder, and murdering but suffering the penalty. But among theories free of such gross errors, we still face choices that can be justified only in light of the criteria of adequacy for a legal theory, and here we have not yet done enough.

Kelsen thought a theory of law had to be "pure", independent of any claims about morality, sociology or the empirical sciences. Hart said it had to? faithfully capture the "internal point of view" and thus understand the functions of law and legal rules from the point of view of those who actually use them. Finnis said it must show how law is prima facie moral obligatory; Dworkin how every true proposition of law at the same time functions as a justification for official coercion. Raz said that legal philosophy must consist only of propositions about law that are necessarily true, explanatory, and that conform to the sources theses. Such criteria of adequacy are much invoked but insufficiently defended. To take only one example, Dworkin's argument for the non-neutrality of legal philosophy hinges on his view that legal argument must show how what it takes to be law offers a prima facie moral reason for coercion and that no such reason would be valid unless permitted by standards laid down *in advance*. (Under a rather special interpretation of "laid down" and a special interpretation of "in advance"). But lots of people reject that adequacy condition. Not everyone thinks that people have a right to win a law suit only they have a right laid down in advance, and lots of people think that what makes a proposition of law true need not bear on the question whether anyone has a right to coerce people to conform to that law, let a lone whether they have a duty to obey. This is not the place to explore the issues, but only to say that we are long past the stage in legal philosophy where any of us can take such claims for granted, let alone as some kind of plateau of agreement. Our period of methodological innocence is over and we need explicit defense of these views, and preferably a defense that does not make an explanation of the nature of law utterly foreign from an explanation of the nature of other important social institutions such political parties, jails, or families. At any rate, these are among the issues that I think it would be fruitful to explore further.

Selected Works

Books

The Authority of the State, Oxford: Clarendon Press, 1990.

Law and the Community: The End of Individualism? Toronto: Carswell, 1989 (edited with A. Hutchinson).

Articles

"General Jurisprudence," 25 *Oxford Journal of Legal Studies* (2005), pp.565–580.

"Associative Obligations and the State," in J. Burley, ed. *Dworkin and his Critics* (Oxford: Blackwell, 2004), pp. 267–284.

"Law and Obligations," in J. Coleman and S. Shapiro, eds. *Oxford Handbook of Jurisprudence and Legal Philosophy* (Oxford: Clarendon Press, 2002), pp.514–547.

"Pluralism, Social Conflict, and Tolerance," in A. Soeteman, ed., *Pluralism and Law* (Dordrecht: Kluwer, 2001), pp. 85–105.

"Pornographies", 8 *Journal of Political Philosophy*, (2000), pp. 27–52.

"Positivism and Conventionalism," 12 *Canadian Journal of Law and Jurisprudence* (1999), pp. 35–52.

"Sexuality, Authenticity, and Modernity," in J. Feinberg and J. Coleman (eds.) *Philosophy of Law*, (Belmont, CA: Wadsworth, 1999), pp. 538–48.

"Who Believes in Political Obligation?" in W. Edmundson, ed., *The Duty to Obey the Law* (Totowa, NJ: Rowman and Littlefield, 1999), pp.301–17.

"Rights of Exit," 4 *Legal Theory* (1998), pp.165–85.

"Pornographizing, Subordinating, and Silencing," in R. Post, ed., *Censorship and Silencing: Practices of Cultural Regulation* (Los Angeles: Getty Research Institute, 1998), pp.285–311.

"The Concept of Law Revisited," 94 *Michigan Law Review* (1996), pp.1687–1717.

"Internal Minorities and their Rights," in W. Kymlicka, ed., *Rights of Cultural Minorities* (Oxford: Oxford University Press, 1995), pp. 257–272.

"Two Views of Collective Rights," 4 *Canadian Journal of Law and Jurisprudence* (1991), pp.315–327.

7
Andrew von Hirsch

Professor at the Institute of Criminology
University of Cambridge, UK

I. Beginnings of my interest in legal philosophy

Why was I drawn to philosophy? The subject has fascinated me ever since I began having intellectual interests. Moral issues particularly held my attention, especially those regarding individual rights and fair treatment – perhaps, in part, because of childhood experiences as a German refugee, just before World War II.

At school, I began reading philosophical texts, starting with Plato and Hume. I studied philosophy as an undergraduate at Harvard, and then enrolled in the B. Phil. programme in philosophy at Oxford. That was in the late 1950's—during the heyday of the Oxford analytical school. I had tutorials with John Austin, and attended lectures and seminars given by Austin himself, Peter Strawson, Stuart Hampshire and R.M. Hare. The time at Oxford was enormously stimulating.

However, the American conscription authorities eventually compelled me to return to the US, and I became a law student at the Harvard Law School. My intention was to pursue a career combining law with philosophy. However, Harvard's legal-education style proved to be of a markedly technical nature, and less stimulating than I had expected. Nevertheless, I took up a variety of law-related jobs: as an associate with a Wall Street law firm; as a staff member of a New York State regulatory agency; and finally (more interestingly) as a senior staff member in a US Senator's office. When the Senator was voted out of office in 1970, I found myself (at age 36) jobless, and without much sense of direction for my career.

At that point, good fortune intervened. My former boss, now the ex-Senator, was named chairman of a foundation-funded study committee on incarceration, and I was appointed the committee's executive director. Initially, a study of prison conditions had been contemplated; but I persuaded the project's sponsors that criminal sentencing and its aims should be addressed, instead. Sentencing reformers of the time had tended to favour rehabilitation as the paramount goal. I soon became convinced, however, that this rehabilitative emphasis should not be taken for granted, and that we should try, instead, to reconceptualize the rationale for sentencing. This approach raised a variety of normative issues concerning justice and fair punishment. I had (partly by happenstance) found myself dealing with questions that long had interested me: philosophical issues concerning justice, and legal-policy issues concerning the limits of the state's power to intervene in individuals' lives.

I spent the next five years developing the arguments for, and writing the committee's report. What eventually emerged was a sketch of a desert-based model for sentencing – constituting a substantial departure from the crime-prevention models that had dominated penological thinking. The volume appeared in 1976, under my authorship and the title, *Doing Justice: The Choice of Punishments.*

At that time, I was 42 years of age – not young for beginning an academic career. However, the book attracted considerable attention, and I was able to move into academic life. My first permanent academic post was at a criminological faculty, the School of Criminal Justice at Rutgers University; and I worked there for the next two decades. My intellectual contacts, however, came increasingly to be with British and Continental colleagues. Being European by origin and upbringing, I also had personal reasons (including my son and other family members living in Munich) for moving back across the Atlantic. In 1994, I was fortunate enough to be invited to join the academic staff at the Institute of Criminology at the University of Cambridge, where I remain a professor to this day.

By the time of my arrival in Cambridge, I had done much of my sentencing-theory work, and wished to explore other areas of punishment theory. I established, at the Institute, a small research centre – the Centre for Penal Theory and Penal Ethics. The Centre has undertaken a series of projects, including volumes on the ethics of situational crime prevention, restorative justice, and legal regulation of offensive behavior. I have also written on German criminal-law theory and doctrine.

II. My contributions to penal theory

Within penal theory, there exist four principal issues: (i) why the institution of the criminal sanction should exist at all; (ii) criminalization – i.e., the scope of the criminal prohibitions; (iii) the substantive criminal law and its moral underpinnings; and (iv) the rationale for sentencing. Of these four topics, it is the third (the criteria of the substantive criminal law) that has drawn the most attention among legal philosophers. By contrast, my work has dealt with the other three topics.

1. **Sentencing Theory.** When I began writing on sentencing theory in the mid-70's, legal philosophers showed scant interest in how the quantum of punishment should be decided. From the mid-70's to the early 90's, I devoted myself to this subject, writing three volumes on it: *Doing Justice* (1976); *Past or Future Crimes* (1985); and *Censure and Sanctions* (1993). A fourth book, co-authored with Andrew Ashworth, has appeared recently: *Proportionate Sentencing: Exploring the Principles* (2005). These volumes address a range of sentencing-theory issues, including the following:

(a) *The role of desert.* Before the 1970's, writers on sentencing (mostly, social scientists and legal scholars) assumed that the of sentence should principally be determined by crime-preventive considerations. Debates over sentencing theory addressed the relative merits of deterrent, incapacitative, or rehabilitative strategies. Desert, to the extent discussed at all, was thought to have a marginal role.

This emphasis appeared to me to be misplaced. According to ordinary people's sense of justice, a just punishment is one that fairly reflects the degree of reprehensibleness of the actor's offence. The emphasis thus should be on what the offender has done and how blameworthy it was – and not on what crimes that he or others might do in future. This pointed to a retributive conception of punishment – one in which the seriousness of the crime should be the principal determinant of the penalty. The task, as I saw it, was to re-conceptualize this perspective, in a manner reflecting liberal assumptions.

(b) *Reconceptualizing deserved punishment: censure and proportionality.* Although philosophers had debated retributive punishment for centuries, modern penologists had become sceptical of any such approach. There were, principally, two objections. One was that the notion of deserved punishment was incomprehensible: that it rested on obscure notions of requital of evil for evil, or the like. But perhaps, an alternative and less problematic account could be formulated. In an important 1970 essay, "The Expressive Functions of Punishment", Joel Feinberg had pointed out how punishment serves as a blaming institution. The implications of Feinberg's punishment-as-blaming thesis – namely, those concerning the criteria for allocating punishments – had not been much examined, and I turned my attention to these. If punishment involves censure of the actor for his criminal conduct, then *penalties should be allocated consistently with their blaming implications.* That supplies the basis of the principle of proportionality: that severity of the punishment (and thereby its degree of implied censure) should fairly reflect the degree of blameworthiness (that is, the seriousness) of the defendant's criminal conduct. Disproportionate or disparate punishments are unjust – not because they fail to 'fit' the punishment to the crime – but because they impose degrees of penal censure that are not warranted by the comparative reprehensibleness of offenders' wrongful behavior.

The other common objection to traditional retributivism related to its harshness: its supposed demand of an eye for an eye. However, a censure-based rationale for desert does not presuppose such a talionic criterion. Proportionate punishments may be imposed without increasing (indeed, while substantially *decreasing*) prevailing severity levels, so long as penalties are ranked in the order of crimes' seriousness, and comparably reprehensible criminal acts are penalized with approximately equivalent severity.

Penal censure, on this perspective, should not be viewed as mere denunciation of crime and criminals. It should be understood, rather, as a normative communication addressing the actor as an agent capable of moral deliberation. High overall severity levels, such as those involved in talionic punishments, would therefore be unacceptable—because they would effectively operate *in terrorem,* and fail to recognize actors' moral agency (see § II.2 below).

The central principle of sentencing, according to this desert-based model, is the principle of proportionality: that sentences should be scaled in their severity according to the degree of seriousness of the defendant's criminal conduct. The basis for deciding quanta of punishments should thus be retrospective: the seriousness of the law-violation the defendant has committed. On this approach, imprisonment (because of its severity) should be visited only on those convicted of seriously reprehensible conduct; for less serious criminal acts, a variety of non-custodial penalties should be employed, that also are graded according to the degree of gravity of the criminal conduct.

(c) *A micro-jurisprudence of penal desert?* The desert-oriented perspective came to be adopted in a number of jurisdictions: Finland, Sweden, England (during the 1990's), Oregon and Minnesota. Implementation of the desert model in these places did not tend to generate harsher sentencing policies, notwithstanding claims to the contrary by some critics. The Swedish and Finnish sentencing norms, for example, remain among the most moderate in Europe. Tough sentencing policies tend either to be rationalized on deterrent or incapacitative grounds, or else (as with California's notorious 'three strikes' law) primarily serve political aims, of expressing and exploiting popular resentment against criminals.

These developments made it important to devise criteria for deciding how much punishment is deserved. I thus tried to sketch a 'micro-jurisprudence' of sentence proportionality. Amongst the particular issues requiring attention were:

(i) *Ordinal vs. cardinal proportionality.* Should desert be treated as a 'determining' or only as a 'limiting' principle? While the idea of proportionality calls for grading penalties according to the seriousness of offenders' crimes, there seems to be no definite quanta of severity associated with these desert judgements. Armed robbers have committed a serious offence, deserving of substantial punishment; but no particular amount of sentence suggests itself as uniquely appropriate for this offence.

The solution to this difficulty, I suggested, lies in recognizing a distinction between *ordinal* and *cardinal* proportionality. A desert model imposes not one but two kinds of requirements. One requirement, ordinal proportionality, is addressed to comparative severities of punishment; here, desert does provide considerable guidance. Persons convicted of similar crimes should receive punishments of approximately comparable severity (save in special circumstances altering the harmfulness or culpability of the conduct). Those convicted of crimes of differing gravity should receive punishments correspondingly graded in onerousness. These requirements of ordinal proportionality are no mere limits; they are violated, for example, when offenders guilty of equally reprehensible conduct are punished substantially unequally – say, in order to enhance the deterrent or incapacitative effect of the penalty.

The other desert requirement, cardinal proportionality, deals with the penalty scale's overall magnitude and anchoring points. Once one has decided the penalty for some other crimes, one can fix the penalty for (say) armed robbery by comparing its seriousness with theirs'. These comparative judgements require a starting point, however; and there seems to be no specific quantum of punishment that can be identified as providing that point. This is because the extent of censure expressed through penal deprivation is, to some degree, a matter of convention. Hence, cardinal proportionality, unlike ordinal, provides only certain general constraints. The penalty scale should not, for example be inflated so much as to visit substantial deprivations on lesser criminal conduct—for a variety of reasons that I endeavoured to explain.

This leeway in deciding the penalty scale's anchoring points accounts for why we cannot perceive a uniquely right or fitting penalty for a crime. However, once the anchoring points of the scale have been decided (within the broad constraints of cardinal proportionality), the more restrictive requirements of ordinal proportionality begin to apply. These explain why it would be wrong to give short prison terms to some robbers and long ones to other robbers, on the basis, say, of predictive factors not reflecting differences in the harmfulness or culpability of their conduct.

(ii) *Gauging crimes' seriousness.* Since a desert model makes the sanction depend on the crime's seriousness, a method for gauging crime-seriousness is also needed. The gravity of a crime depends, ordinarily, upon the degree of harmfulness (or potential harmfulness) of the conduct, and the extent of the actor's culpability. Culpability can be gauged with the aid of clues from substantive criminal-law doctrine. The criminal law already distinguishes intentional conduct from reckless conduct and from criminally negligent behavior; for purposes of sentencing theory, more refined distinctions could be made. However, the harm dimension seems more puzzling: why, for example, should robbery be deemed more injurious than burglary? Substantive criminal-law doctrine and theory provides few clues here, because it does not distinguish degrees of harm in systematic fashion. Measures of subjective victim suffering also do not seem helpful, because these can vary so much among individual victims. How, then, may criminal harm be gauged? My Swedish colleague Nils Jareborg and I developed an analysis, based on Amartya Sen's conception of the *standard of living*. Sen's approach is concerned, not with particular individuals' happiness or well-being, but with the 'means and capabilities' for achieving a certain quality of life. Notwithstanding significant differences in how a given offence affects individual victims, this approach permits an assessment of criminal harm by reference to standardized interests; and an assessment of the importance of those interests on the basis of generalized conceptions of the means and capabilities for a good life.

2. Rationale for State Punishment's Existence. My work on sentencing theory led me, in turn, to the more fundamental question, of the warrant for existence of a system of state-imposed criminal prohibitions and punishments. Why have such a state punishment system—rather having no coercive response at all, or leaving the response to neighbors or community organizations? After various unsatisfactory attempts, I came up with the following account.

Efforts to explain the criminal law's existence have been impeded by the assumption that the explanation must either be wholly instrumental and preventative, or else wholly deontological in character. Neither of these 'pure' conceptions seems plausible, however. Exclusively instrumentalist explanations, viewing the criminal sanction as just a disincentive to crime, fail to treat the actor respectfully, as an agent capable of moral deliberation; and fail to give adequate support to the fault-based limits of substantive criminal law and the proportionality requirements of sentencing. Exclusively censure-oriented accounts have difficulty explaining why a purely symbolic censuring response would not suffice.

The institution of criminal punishment, I came to think, needs to be supported by both deontological and consequentialist reasons. Its censuring element, of visiting the offender with formal disapprobation for his conduct, involves a moral appeal that cannot be reduced to the preventative effects of threatened unpleasant consequences. Its hard-treatment element, however, seems clearly to be concerned (at least in part) with inducing people to desist from certain kinds of injurious conduct. Hence the most plausible direction of analysis is toward a principled account that both includes deontological features and is concerned with consequences.

The censuring element in punishment, on this perspective, should be viewed as primarily deontological in character: as an appeal to actors and potential actors, treated as agents capable of moral deliberation. It is this censuring feature which supports requirements of wrongdoing in criminalization theory, of fault in substantive criminal-law doctrines, and of proportionality in sentencing. Hard treatment (i.e. the deprivation-element in punishment) is also an integral aspect of the criminal sanction: it is both the means through which penal censure is expressed, and serves as a prudential disincentive against offending that operates within a censuring framework. Having such a prudential disincentive – rather than solely symbolic censuring response – helps enable human beings (as moral agents but fallible ones) to resist the temptations to offend. Because punishment still must centrally involve the element of censure, however, that censuring feature serves as an essential constraint on whether and how much to punish. The *raison d'etre* of the criminal sanction should thus reflect the interaction of moral and instrumental concerns. The institution of punishment calls for justification on moral grounds; but this justification must also address punishment as a social institution, involving the exercise of state power, with pragmatic goals involving the welfare of citizens.

3. **Criminalisation issues.** My interest in the foregoing question (of 'why punish at all?') led me to explore issues of criminalization. This subject, concerning the proper scope and limits of the state's criminal prohibitions, had been given much impetus by the writings of Joel Feinberg in the 1980's. He identifies two differing kinds of reasons for prohibiting conduct, in virtue of its adverse effects on other persons: the Harm Principle (concerning the conduct's injuriousness), and the Offence Principle (concerning its character as an affront to sensibility). His view emphasizes the conduct's consequences: he analyses harm in terms of its intrusion into people's interests, and offence in terms of its effects on the attractiveness of public environments. Such a perspective, however, needs to be supplemented by a conception that addresses why the behavior is *wrongful*.

With harmful behavior, the problem becomes clearly apparent with 'indirect' harms—for example, harms (or risks) that are mediated by other intervening actors' choices. Suppose a given type of conduct, harmless in itself, is proscribed because it purportedly leads other persons to commit injurious acts—as when, for example, peaceable begging is prohibited on account of its supposed tendency to foster neighborhood deterioration and higher crime rates. Should the conduct of the initial actor, A, thus be criminalized on account of its leading others, B and C, to do harm? Feinberg maintained that it could be, provided A's conduct was done with the requisite criminal intent or negligence, and there was sufficient likelihood that it would induce others to do harm. Such intervening-choice liability, however, seems morally problematic: it involves criminalizing conduct in virtue of subsequent harmful choices by *other* persons, whom the initial actor does not control. To impose criminal liability—solely in virtue of the supposed causal link to subsequent actors' injurious behavior – would ignore the separability of persons as choosing agents. To make liability justifiable, I thus argued in a 1996 essay, the original actor needs to have some 'normative involvement' in subsequent actors' choices: that is, his own acts need to be of a character that provides normative support for those subsequent harmful choices. (I also tried to sketch what some of the criteria of normative involvement might be.) In the just-cited instance, however, it would be difficult to see how the beggar, by peaceably asking for alms, affirms in any fashion the commission of a higher rate of crimes by third persons.

With offensive behavior, there likewise exists a problem of establishing why the conduct is wrongful. Feinberg's criterion for criminalization – that a sufficient number of persons be sufficiently affronted – does not establish the conduct's wrongfulness; thus peaceable begging does not become wrongfully offensive merely because the behavior irritates numerous others using the public space. In two recent essays, Andrew Simester and I have thus put forward a wrongdoing requirement: namely, that the offensive conduct must also involve treating others with *gross lack of respect or consideration.* This calls upon the proponent of criminalization to put forward reasons why the ostensibly offensive behavior is wrongful, in this sense of being grossly disrespectful; and Simester and I evaluate the legitimacy of various offence prohibitions on this basis. (On our view, aggressive begging is wrongful, because it infringes others' entitlement to anonymity in public space; but peaceable begging would involve no such infringement.) We also suggest certain further mediating principles that should narrow further the scope of criminalization – for example, a principle of tolerance for varying styles of self-presentation in a plural society.

III. Salient issues in the philosophy of criminal law; bearing on legal policy

What are the salient issues in penal theory today? Consider the quartet of major issues mentioned previously: the rationale of the criminal sanction's existence; criminalization theory; the rationale for the substantive criminal law's central doctrines; and sentencing theory. A literature now exists on each of these issues, but there remain numerous questions calling for further exploration.

In criminalization theory, for example, some of these questions – concerning the limits of the Harm Principle, and the rationale for the Offence Principle – have been mentioned already (§II-3 above). An additional interesting criminalization issue is that of *indirect paternalism*. It is widely assumed that attempted suicide and other directly self-harmful conduct should be free from criminal penalties. However, self-harm by indirection (for example, killing another at the latter's request) remains subject to substantial sanctions. The legitimacy of such prohibitions needs examination: given the principal's consent and his entitlement to self determination, why should such conduct criminalised at all? In substantive criminal law, there has been extensive philosophical discussion of certain issues – such as the concept of culpability and the criteria for excuses; yet other questions have been relatively neglected – for instance, legal justifications and their rationale.

However, I doubt that it would be desirable, or possible, to try to make a definitive catalogue of the principal issues of penal theory. The normative issues arising from the criminal law policies will be defined, in significant part, by those policies themselves as they develop. Contemporary criminal policy, for example, has recently become increasingly concerned with risk, and novel forms of risk-related liability have been emerging. These new legal norms raise a variety of important moral issues with which legal philosophers need to be concerned.

Should penal theorists try to influence legal policymaking and if so, in what manner? A useful mode of analysis has been put forward by Douglas Husak in his 1992 volume, *Drugs and Rights*. Professor Husak addresses drug-prohibition laws, and asks whether these are supportable on paternalistic grounds. While mainly relying on philosophical argumentation, he also examines carefully the empirical evidence concerning ostensible harmful effects of drugs, and the structure of drug prohibitions. By doing so, he shows how his philosophical claims may be made germane to practical decisions about drug policies, and he thereby enhances the persuasiveness of his case against prohibition.

In my work on sentencing theory, I have tried to bring philosophical claims to bear in a policy-making context (see §II-1(c) above). Such influence as my views have had on sentencing policy may stem from my having addressed specific questions of penal desert—such as scaling penalties, gauging of crimes' seriousness, and deciding upon what weight should be given previous convictions. Policymakers may become more willing to heed arguments from penal theory, when these can offer guidance on the particular issues they must confront. .

The willingness of policymakers to listen, however, depends on the overall political environment in which they operate. With the recently changed political mood in English government circles, for example, liberal reform perspectives have diminishing influence. Yet even in such unpropitious political environments, theoretical perspectives may be utilized for the purpose of criticizing government policies. I thus recently was able to make use of my conceptions about the limits of criminalizing offensive behavior, in order to argue against the Labour Government's drastic measures against 'antisocial' behavior. Thus as a last resort, one can at least try to make a bit of trouble.

Selected Bibliography

Proportionate Sentencing: Exploring the Principles [with A. Ashworth]. Oxford: Oxford University Press, 2005.

Censure and Sanctions. Oxford: Oxford University Press, 1993.

Past or Future Crimes: Deservedness and Dangerousness in the Sentencing of Criminals. New Brunswick, N.J.: Rutgers University Press, 1985.

Doing Justice: The Choice of Punishments. New York: Hill & Wang, 1976.

"Gauging Criminal Harm: A Living-Standard Analysis", *Oxford Journal of Legal Studies* 11 (1991), 1–38.

"Proportionate Sentences for Juveniles: How Different than for Adults?" *Punishment & Society* 3 (2001), 221–236.

"Specifying Aims and Limits for Restorative Justice: A 'Making Amends' Model?" in A. von Hirsch, J. Roberts, A.E. Bottoms, et al. (eds.), *Restorative Justice and Criminal Justice: Competing or Reconcilable Paradigms?* 21–42. Oxford: Hart Publishing, 2003.

"Extending the Harm Principle: 'Remote' Harms and Fair Imputation", in A.P. Simester & A.T.H. Smith (eds.), *Harm and Culpability* 259–276. Oxford: Oxford University Press, 1996.

"Der Rechtsgutsbegriff und das 'Harm Principle'", in R. Hevendehl, A. von Hirsch & W.Wohlers (eds.) *Die Rechtsgutstheorie: Legitimationsbasis des Strafrechts oder dogmatisches Glasperlenspiel?* 13–25. Baden-Baden: Nomos Verlagsgesellschaft, 2003.

"Toleranz als Mediating Principle", in A. von Hirsch, K. Seelmann & W. Wohlers (eds.), *Mediating Principles: Begrenzungsprinzipien bei der Strafbegründung* 97–108. Baden-Baden: Nomos Verlagsgesellschaft, 2006.

"Penalising Offensive Behaviour: Constitutive and Mediating Principles" [with A.P. Simester], in A. von Hirsch & A.P. Simester (eds.), *Incivilities: Regulating Offensive Behaviour* 115–131. Oxford: Hart Publishing, 2006.

"Rethinking the Offense Principle" [with A.P. Simester] *Legal Theory* 8 (2002), 269–295.

Indirekter" Paternalismus im Strafrecht – am Beispiel der Tötung auf Verlangen" [with Ulfrid Neumann] *Goltdammer's Archiv für Strafrecht,* Dec. 2007 (forthcoming).

8
Tony Honoré

Regius Professor of Civil Law Emeritus, Oxford University
All Souls College, Oxford University, UK

Why were you initially drawn to the philosophy of law?

At school in South Africa I came into contact with philosophy through reading some of Plato's dialogues as a part of a mainly classical education. At the same time I became interested in law through a controversy in the 1930s about the status of the Episcopal Church of the Province of South Africa in relation to the Church of England. In that schism the lawyer representing the Church of the Province, Frank Reid Q.C., was a family friend who liked to discuss, even with a youngster such as myself, the cases in which he was involved and the issues they raised. The controversy in question (reported in *Mills v. Registrar of Deeds* 1936 Cape Provincial Division 417) involved constitutional issues, the registration of title to land, the law relating to the frustration of a trust object, and the criteria governing the identity of an ecclesiastical association. This last issue, debated against the background of court rulings that held that church identity was bound up with belief and so changed if beliefs changed, might be said to have had a philosophical aspect

At the time I did not match these theoretical and legal interests or see them as closely linked. But after five years in the army during the Second World War I was lucky enough to be able to come to Oxford to resume academic studies. I read law and was soon (1948) appointed to teach the subject at The Queen's College, Oxford. The college tutor in philosophy was Tony Woozley. He was influenced by the contemporary interests of philosophers such as Gilbert Ryle and J.L.Austin in the analysis of ordinary language; but his interests, like most of theirs, stretched more widely and included a concern with problems of responsibility and identity. Applied disciplines such as law often raise general problems which coincide to some extent with philosophical areas of interest. In moral and political philosophy many of the same concepts were employed as were prominent in law and many of the same problems about the conditions for and limits of responsibility emerged. Woozley and I therefore thought it would be of value to students of both law and philosophy to know something of the methods, style of thinking and examples current in the other discipline; there had been something of a divorce between the two subjects after the nineteenth century contributions of Jeremy Bentham, John Austin and John Stuart Mill.

So we arranged to take university seminars together in 1951 and 1952 in which the participants were invited to read materials from both law and philosophy. This would enable them, we hoped, to form a view about the extent to which each could contribute to an understanding of the other. The topics we studied were among those on which articles, chapters or cases were available in both disciplines: topics such as acts, cause, negligence, promises, meaning and interpretation, identity and attribute, personality, and implication. Fifty years later, when I was teaching legal philosophy in retirement along with a younger colleague, we noticed that the earlier books, articles, and cases were nearly all outdated, but that the topics discussed remained as lively as before.

This series of seminars did not continue after 1952 because H.L.A. (Herbert) Hart, who had come to some of them and had given a paper in one, was appointed professor of jurisprudence (meaning the theory and philosophy of law) in the university in 1952. He had been a successful practising lawyer at the Chancery Bar before the war. After it he switched from law to philosophy, which he was then teaching as a philosophy tutor at New College, Oxford. He quickly emerged as a leading figure in legal philosophy. Indeed he was the key scholar in establishing or re-establishing the subject as a serious academic discipline in the English-speaking world, and more widely. This it has remained ever since.

Though he was fourteen years my senior, we became friends and discussed issues that straddled philosophy and law. To him I was a 'natural philosopher'. We took one of the topics of the 1951–2 seminars, causation, and gave university classes on it in 1953–4. In the end this led to an ambitious joint book on the subject, *Causation in the Law* (1959).This was meant as a statement of our views about the relation between the philosophical and legal notions and applications of cause, not as a textbook. As it happened, however, it went into a second edition, with a substantial introduction developing certain themes and answering criticisms, in 1985. Though we drafted different chapters the text was agreed in detail by both. It was directed equally to lawyers and philosophers. It sought to bring to the attention of lawyers and laymen the philosophical foundations of the theories they implicitly adopted, of the decisions of courts and juries, and of the informal causal judgements of ordinary people. For philosophers it tried to demonstrate the benefit to be gained from studying a wide range of examples, such as were to be found in different branches of the law and different legal systems, European as well as English-speaking. It sought to bring an interdisciplinary element into questions such as What is it to cause harm? and When are we responsible for causing harm to others?

An account of this joint enterprise is to be found in chapter 9 of Nicola Lacey's *A life of H.L.A.Hart. The Nightmare and the Noble Dream* (2004). No more need be said about it here since my interest in the relation between law and philosophy existed before we embarked on it. In the same decade, the fifties, when we were working together and usually meeting weekly, Herbert was refining his more general views about the relation of law to philosophy. These culminated in the *Concept of Law* (1961). In that way, without endorsing all his opinions, in particular his rather idiosyncratic view of the separation between law and morals, I learned a great deal from him.

My interest in the philosophy of law was therefore nurtured through the study of law, particularly real or reported instances of occurrences that had given rise to litigation. It was reinforced by my collaboration with Hart. We were both lawyers, though of a rather different sort. I doubt if it is possible in modern conditions for a serious contribution to legal philosophy to be made except by a scholar who has undergone a legal training or has experience of the law in practice. A lively philosophical interest is necessary, but not sufficient.

For which of your contributions to legal philosophy so far would you most like to be remembered and why?

It is presumptuous to suppose that any of one's contributions deserve to be remembered. But there are topics to which I hope to have made some contribution. The first is to help explain how action, causation, and responsibility are related. Their mutual relationship is important in moral and social philosophy on the one hand and law on the other. The differences between their relationship outside and in the law throws light on the relationship between moral, political, and legal obligation and, indeed, on how law relates to morality and politics.

In the first place the contribution that Hart and I made to our understanding of causal language and causal judgements was an advance on the previous theories which thought of causal judgements as in principal uniform across disciplines or, alternatively, so diverse as to preclude helpful comparison. We drew a distinction between explanatory and attributive uses of causal notions. There is certainly a connection between these functions because what is attributed to people's conduct or non-human events as a consequence of those actions or events is very often something that human conduct or those events serve to explain. Nevertheless, the use of cause for purposes of attribution presupposes agreement on what the initial act or event is the outcome of which is to be traced out. This initial act or event may not be what would most plausibly explain the outcome. Indeed, in legal contexts the law always lays down the conduct or event that is a potential source of legal liability, so that it fixes the starting point of the attributive inquiry. It was important for us to demonstrate in this context the connection between causal judgements and the function they are intended to serve.

We also gave an account of the common sense principles that underlie the assertions of judges and writers that in many legal and moral contexts a causal connection relating to a particular sequence of events raises a question of fact. It is a question to be decided by criteria such as the abnormal character of the supposed cause in the context or its voluntary and deliberate character. These features are available for ordinary people to judge and are used by them in everyday life even when they are not conscious of the criteria they are employing. At the same time we made clear, in a somewhat Wittgensteinian spirit, that around the central notion of cause were clustered a number of analogous relations: providing or failing to provide reasons and opportunities for, or help in bringing about, desirable or harmful outcomes. These 'para-causal' relations often reflected forms of responsibility, moral and sometimes also legal, for the voluntary actions of others. They bore some resemblance to but were distinguishable from the responsibility of a person who directly causes harm to another, a form of responsibility that is usually cut short when the voluntary conduct of the person harmed or another intervenes between the agent's conduct and the harm. There were both a variety of possible causal relations between action and consequence and a variety of possible grounds of responsibility. These could lead to a wide range of obligations, moral and legal.

Our work was largely descriptive and needed to be supplemented, as I have recently sought to show, by relating causal judgements more closely to the different functions they serve. The core function seems to be that of bringing about a desired aim, and assembling the conditions that will ensure this. But this function has been supplemented by that of explaining or predicting classes of events or particular events and that of attributing legal, moral and historical responsibility to people or events for their conduct or for particular occurrences. On this analysis the central form of human responsibility is responsibility for one's own conduct and its outcome but this is extended to responsibilities imposed by society for one's failure to act for the conduct of others such as employees with whom the employer stands in a special relationship.

I hope to have succeeded in giving a plausible account of the reasons why people who are on the whole capable of doing what they choose to do should be treated as responsible, though not always legally responsible, for the outcome, even when unintended, of their conduct. I have argued that it is in the interest both of the agent who is held responsible and of society to accept and endorse this basic form of responsibility for one's conduct. This responsibility makes a contribution to the agent's own well-being in that it secures to the agent credit for successes as well as discredit for failures and botches, and so gives the person held responsible an identity that rests in part on the history of their actions and failures to act and the outcomes of their actions and failures. This approach to identify and responsibility rests on a view of human conduct according to which action inevitably involves taking some risks, since we can never entirely foresee or control the outcome of what we do.

At the same time the allocation to us by other people and by society as a whole of responsibility for the outcome of our conduct can be defended on moral and practical grounds. Not only is the system in the social interest in that it tends to promote good standards of conduct but it is fair to the agent, provided that it is confined to people who are broadly speaking capable and who are therefore on the whole likely to benefit from the system by which responsibility is allocated. The contribution that this system makes, both positively and negatively, to the agent's sense of his own identity and that of others, and to his identity in the eyes of others, is of very great value. In a legal context it explains and serves to justify the imposition of strict liability in law in cases when there are special reasons for imposing it, such as the potentially dangerous character of the conduct in question.

The second topic to which I hope to have made some contribution concerns certain aspects of the relation between law and morality. This is not a topic on which anyone can contribute a fundamentally original idea. My thoughts derive from and carry forward the theme that, when the law imposes duties or obligations or allocates rights or, in general, requires or endorses conduct, it implicitly claims to be morally justified in doing so. It impliedly asserts that the conduct required or authorized is not inconsistent with sound moral principles. This is an idea, proposed by others, that I find convincing, though the claim often turns out to be hypocritical or mistaken. From it I have drawn two consequences, but these apply only when the claim of the law not to be inconsistent with morality is justified. One is that a great deal of morality is encapsulated solely in law, either because the type of obligation in issue is one that only the law can impose, like paying taxes, or because the expertise necessary to determine the proper content of the obligation is not available to the ordinary person. Moreover the value to philosophers, spoken of earlier, of access to a wide range of practical examples rests to a considerable extent on the careful analysis of moral issues to be found in legal decisions. The detailed analysis of facts and issues that courts and administrative authorities are required to undertake in order to reach defensible decisions provides a pool of resource on which moral and political philosophers can draw.

The other consequence I have drawn from the claim of the law to be morally in order is that, in determining what the law is, it is always relevant, though not always decisive, to inquire whether what the law requires or endorses is consonant with sound morality. By that is meant not necessarily popular morality, which may be open to criticism, but those moral principles that are rationally defensible – a matter on which there is a rather more agreement among philosophers than is sometimes thought. In other words, interpretation of the law should, if possible, be such as to make it morally proper to conform to it. Admittedly this is not always possible, for example because the wording of a statute does not admit of the desired interpretation. But it often does, and many legal doctrines, such as those relating to fairness, equity and good faith, expressly give effect to the possibility of adopting a morally coherent interpretation of the legal authorities. This openness to moral argument rules out, I believe, a certain form of positivism, which would restrict law to what is socially recognized, though it does not rule out the view that the greater part of the law derives its validity from social recognition.

Lastly, my contribution to the analysis of property rights has been to suggest a standard model of ownership and to advocate that the decision whether to describe a holder of more limited property rights as an 'owner' is a contingent matter to be decided by each legal system and in each branch of the law in accordance with the internal requirements of that system or branch of the law.

What are the most important issues in legal philosophy and why are they distinctively issues of legal philosophy rather than some other discipline?

The most important issues in legal philosophy concern the distinctive character of a society that attaches value to law. In a sense all societies do this, since one function of law, that of officially authorizing the use of force in certain circumstances, is common to virtually all societies. The question of when the use of force is justified either officially or informally is therefore a central one in legal philosophy.

Another function of law, at least as conceived in western society, is that of allocating the power to decide issues between government and citizens and, within government, between different arms of government such as the executive, legislative and judicial. The function of legal philosophy in this context is to consider the optimum distribution of powers both between the state and the individual or associations of individuals and between the various branches or organs of the state. Assuming that a society is better if it recognizes a private sphere in which people are free to choose what to do as well as a public sphere in which they are subject to constraint, many issues of legal philosophy, including those relating to human rights and obligations, are concerned with how best to draw the line between the private and the public.

It is also a task of legal philosophy to consider the optimum distribution of governmental powers, since one function of law is to settle the system of government. The same applies in the modern world to the optimum distribution of powers between individual states and the international community and its institutions, and to the distribution of powers between these and international organizations and businesses. These are fundamentally issues of political philosophy, but their formal aspect is specifically legal. This aspect of legal philosophy is further concerned with considering the relation between formal rules of the distribution of power and informal conventions relating to its exercise.

This formal-informal divide is also central to the relations between law and morality. What aspects of conduct should be left to social pressure to regulate and what aspects require to be formalized and enforced by a state apparatus which ultimately rests on force? A great deal of customary behavior either becomes law in the course of time or is formalized by the recognition of custom as a type of law, but it remains of value from the point of view of human freedom not to resort to the formal mechanism where informal methods are adequate or the enforcement of formal requirements is likely to be ineffective. There is also an important issue about the extent to which individuals, organizations and states should be permitted to choose between adopting formal or informal methods of conducting their affairs. Since formal as opposed to informal rules for conducting affairs are very often those that are legally enforceable these issues clearly form important elements in legal philosophy.

A topic in legal philosophy that is specially the concern of law is justice. There are those who equiparate justice with the overall conditions for the existence of a good society. But there is a narrower sense in which justice is specially the concern of law and legal procedures. In this narrower sense of justice there is a special emphasis on impartiality, on hearing both or all parties to a dispute, and on the giving of defensible reasons for a decision, whether or not the outcome contributes to the overall good of the society in question. One of the tasks of legal philosophy in this connection is to demonstrate, if possible, the connection between the rational resolution of disputes by acceptable procedures and the conditions for the existence of a good society in which most people will find it comfortable to live.

In general the study of the relationship between law and other elements that make for a good society such as wealth, economic welfare, provision for the needy and the acquisition of knowledge through education and freedom of expression are important elements in legal philosophy.

What is the relationship between legal philosophy and legal practice? Should legal philosophers be more concerned about the effect of their scholarship on legal practice?

It is often tempting for a legal philosopher to press a view that he hopes will influence the outcome of litigation. There is nothing improper in doing this, provided the professional impartiality that philosophy demands is observed. But there is no reason to require legal philosophers continually to direct their views towards the solution of problems rising in practice.

But to answer the question proposed adequately one needs to attend to a more fundamental issue. As in most theoretical disciplines, there are two basic techniques for pursuing issues in legal philosophy. One is to proceed from the general to the particular, the other from the particular to the general. A role of legal practice in relation to a form legal philosophy that proceeds from the particular to the general is to provide examples of instances that have occurred or that might occur in practice and that demand a legal solution but relate to morality, economics, politics, sociology or some other non-legal discipline. Knowledge of such examples invites the legal philosopher to consider whether they throw light on the relationship between law and these other disciplines.

Although in principle the examples selected can be and sometimes are pure inventions, quite divorced from practice, it is likely that events which have in fact occurred and have been assessed by lawyers from different points of view will be helpful in unravelling the relationship of law to those disciplines that bear on the solution to legal problems. This is often because they suggest alternative solutions to the problem. My own preference has been for the down-up method in legal philosophy rather than the up-down one, but no special merit attaches to this personal preference. The reason for adopting it has been that as an aspiring lawyer I had to study many cases and examples, and it was natural to ask questions such as: is the solution adopted by the law in this instance morally justified? For example, does the distinction between acts and omissions, which plays an important part in some branches of the law, correspond to a significant moral distinction? Is there a significant moral distinction between liability for fault and strict liability?

While it is natural and often profitable for a legal philosopher to be stimulated by examples drawn from legal practice, it is not essential. In particular legal philosophy need not in the Dworkinian mode be oriented towards guiding judges on how to decide cases. That is a valuable strategy, but is not the only way of fulfilling the main function of legal philosophy, which is to throw light on the recurring structural or functional problems that confront legal systems and those that bear on the optimum conditions for a society that respects co-operation and co-existence.

To which problem, broad issue or broad area of legal philosophy would you most like to see more attention paid in the future?

There are two. One concerns the relation between law and political and private morality. It is to elucidate further the concept of necessity (emergency, preventive action) both as a ground of legal/moral obligation and as justifying departures from what law/morality ordinary requires, in particular in relation to the use of force. The theory underlying resort to this ambiguous notion has not yet been sufficiently explored.

The second area to which I would like more attention to be paid is an aspect of law and economics. Law imposes formal requirements and conditions for the acquisition of rights and facilities but often without a clear assessment of the costs of doing so, whether directly assessable in monetary terms or in terms not easily monetarized such as consuming time and foregoing other, arguably more important concerns. We live in an age of increased regulation without the regulators (whether politicians, legislators, administrators or judges) having clear theoretical guidance about the appropriate balance between likely cost and benefit that will justify formal intervention. Within the ambit of a society governed by the rule of law, there are theoretical as well and practical issues about the extent of regulation and so of the intervention of the law. These deserve more philosophical attention than they have so far received.

Partial Bibliography.

(with H.L.A.Hart), *Causation in the Law* (1959, 2nd ed. 1985)

'Ownership' in *Oxford Essays in Jurisprudence* (ed. A.G. Guest 1961) 107–147.

'Can and Can't' in *Mind* 73 (1964) 463–479.

'Reference to the Non-Existent' in *Philosophy* 46 (1971) 302–308.

'Groups, Laws and Obedience' in *Oxford Essays in Jurisprudence* (2nd series ed. A.W.B.Simpson 1973) 1–21.

'Property, Title and Redistribution' in *Archiv für Rechts- und Sozialphilosophie Neue Folge* 10 (1977) 107–116.

'Real laws', in *Law, Morality and Society. Essays in Honour of H.L.A.Hart* (ed. P.M.S.Hacker & J.Raz 1977) 99–118.

'The Right to Rebel' in *Oxford Journal of Legal Studies* 8 (1988) 34–54.

'Responsibility and Luck. The Moral Basis of Strict Liability' in 104 *Law Quarterly Review* (1988) 530–553.

'A Theory of Coercion' in *Oxford Journal of Legal Studies* 10 (1990) 94–105.

'Are Omissions less Culpable?' in *Essays for Patrick Atiyah* (ed. P.Cane and J.Stapleton 1991) 31–53.

'The Dependence of Morality on Law', in *Oxford Journal of Legal Studies* 13 (1993) 1–17.

'The Morality of Tort Law. Questions and Answers' in *Philosophical Foundations of Tort Law* (ed. D.G.Owen 1996) 67–93.

'Necessary and Sufficient Conditions in Tort Law' in *Philosophical Foundations of Tort Law* (ed. D.G.Owen 1996) 363–385.

'Being Responsible and Being a Victim of Circumstance in *Proceedings of the British Academy* 97 (1998) 169–187.

'Causation in the Law' in *Stanford Encyclopaedia of Philosophy* (2005)

'The Necessary Connection between Law and Morality' in *Oxford Journal of Legal Studies* 22 (2002) 489–495.

'Property and Ownership' in *Properties of Law. Essays in Honour of Jim Harris* (ed. T.Endicott, J.Getzler and E.Peel 2006) 129–137.

Several of the above essays are revised and reprinted, with others, in two collections:

Making Law Bind. Essays Legal and Philosophical (1987).

Responsibility and Fault (2002).

9
Douglas Husak

Professor of Philosophy

Rutgers University, USA

I was drawn to the philosophy of law entirely by accident. My story will not be helpful or relevant to someone deciding to embark on a career in legal philosophy, but I think it is sufficiently interesting to be worth retelling. This narrative has a happy ending, and illustrates how wonderful consequences can follow from events that seem awful at the time.

As an undergraduate, I aspired to be a lawyer. I'm not sure why. But I expected to attend the University of Michigan Law School – the only school to which I had applied – immediately after graduation, in the Fall of 1970. Unfortunately, I was drafted for military service by lottery in May of my senior year, and had to interrupt my plans to attend law school. I was devastated by the news from my local draft board. Fortunately, lots of advisors were available in universities in those days to assist students who opposed the Vietnam War. I discussed my situation with many such persons. Some of these well-intentioned advisors suggested that I would be deferred from military service if I became a Teaching Assistant in a graduate program. The difficulty, or so I thought, was that I had not planned to be a graduate student, applied to any graduate program, or taken the Graduate Record Exam – and the deadlines had long since expired. These apparent obstacles posed no problem in those remarkable days of political turmoil. I was assured that good universities – like The Ohio State University, where my advisor had friends – routinely set aside teaching assistantships for promising late applicants like me. I did not need much time to decide what to do; happily, self-interest and morality coincided in this case. I suddenly found myself a graduate student in the Ohio State Department of Philosophy – something I had not imagined even as a remote possibility as late as May of my senior year.

I began to enjoy my graduate studies, but still expected my future would be in law. I tended to concentrate on those areas in philosophy – ethics, political theory, and philosophy of law itself – that I believed would help my eventual transition to law school. But why not also earn a degree in philosophy? When I planned to leave after obtaining an M.A., the Chairman, Robert Turnbull, made an excellent suggestion. If I stayed at Ohio State, he said, I could finish my Ph.D. and earn a law degree virtually free, since I would be able to use my tuition remission to attend law school while remaining full-time as a teaching assistant working on my dissertation. I followed this sage advice and within six years I received both my Ph.D. and J.D. from Ohio State, and paid virtually nothing for the privilege. I did not set foot in the University of Michigan Law School until I came as a Visiting Professor in 2006, thirty-six years later than my original plan. .

Along the way, I became hooked on philosophy. It was simply too fascinating to abandon for a career in law. I was able to enjoy law school more than most of my peers because I took interesting courses that would not have been especially helpful in legal practice. While other students struggled through Bankruptcy, I elected such options as Soviet Criminal Law and Procedure. I decided to write my dissertation on legal paternalism, a topic that had just begun to receive scholarly attention in the wake of Gerald Dworkin's pioneering article[1]. The information I learned in law school became grist for a philosophical mill. Every time I came across a doctrine in tort, contract, constitutional law, or criminal law that seemed relevant to my project, I wrote about it in a special notebook. Law and philosophy fit together beautifully.

I must mention one interesting footnote to my story. My beliefs about earning a deferment from the draft by teaching in graduate school turned out to be false – not entirely unreasonable, but false nonetheless. I was called for duty anyway, and had to undergo the stressful and tedious process of resisting induction into military service. My situation would have been dire but for all of the courageous draftees who came before me. Massive resistance made prosecution virtually impossible. When all was said and done, I wound up in a discipline I hadn't expected to enter, in a place I hadn't expected to be, for a reason that turned out to be wrong. If my career had proceeded according to plan, I would almost certainly be a lawyer today. Now, however, I am happy to

---

[1] Dworkin, G., 1972 , "Paternalism" *The Monist*, 56: 64-84.

say that I don't know anyone who loves his job more than I.

After graduating with both a Ph.D. and a J.D., I spent a very enjoyable year as a Visiting Assistant Professor at Indiana University. I probably could have stayed for another year, but received a tenure-track offer from Rutgers. I was not eager to leave; Indiana was a terrific job for an Ohio State graduate, and (at the time) was clearly a better department than Rutgers. What to do? I benefited from more good advice, and set off for New Jersey. I began by concentrating on many of the usual topics in legal philosophy: the nature of law, the justification of punishment, the obligation to obey the law, the nature of rights, and the relation of law to morality. My contributions to these issues were unremarkable, but good enough to earn me tenure at Rutgers—a department that became world-class over the years. Since I played almost no role in its vast improvement, I realized that my good luck charm was still working. If Indiana had been able to offer me a permanent appointment, I am sure that I would not have applied to Rutgers. Most academics need to change jobs to move up in the profession, but my department became great while I was able to remain at home in my first tenure-track position..

In 1979, I stumbled across George Fletcher's *Rethinking Criminal Law*[2] – the single most important book in my intellectual development.I discovered original insights on every page. It is only a slight exaggeration to say that much of my career has been devoted to a critical examination of ideas I first encountered in *Rethinking*. The topics Fletcher raised were not only important, but also largely undeveloped. That is, few legal philosophers seemed to be working on them, despite their obvious significance. Part of the attraction in specializing in criminal theory was that the area was not crowded, which increased my chance of making a genuine contribution. I continue to try to identify and write about issues that other theorists neglect, rather than to add to a discussion that already has attracted a great deal of commentary. With a little imagination, one can find dozens of important topics that philosophers barely have touched.

Fletcher's book stimulated me to think seriously about specific philosophical issues in the substantive criminal law. At the time, many philosophers of law resembled the philosophers of science of that era: they were fine philosophers, but were not very proficient in the discipline about which they purported to philosophize. In

---

[2] George Fletcher, *Rethinking Criminal Law (Brown, Little 1978)*.

other words, they didn't really know – or think they needed to know – much about the law. I became persuaded that I had to learn more criminal law in order to say anything important about it. During my sabbatical in 1980, I spent a great deal of time reading textbooks in criminal law – an exercise regarded by some of my peers as boring and unproductive. For some reason, most of the best treatises in criminal law happen to be British, so I learned something of how a different legal system responds to the same set of problems faced in the United States (which is one of the strengths of Fletcher's *Rethinking*). Criminal theory remains one of the few philosophical specialties that may be more highly developed in Great Britain than in the United States. I remain fascinated by criminal law textbooks, and spend as much time reading law reviews as philosophy journals.

Legal philosophers who specialize in criminal theory are roughly divisible into two camps. The first is composed of academic philosophers who are extraordinarily knowledgeable about moral responsibility and attempt to apply their insights to issues of criminal liability. Some write whole books (allegedly) about the criminal law while barely mentioning a single case or statute. The second camp is composed of law professors who know a great deal about statutes and cases but are not especially conversant with philosophy. Often their philosophical sophistication does not extend beyond their discussion of how their views would be received within the deterrence and retributive traditions. Of course, given legal philosophers fall on a continuum between these two extremes. In any event, I believe that my scholarship lies squarely in the middle of these two poles. I try to be firmly anchored in existing criminal law while drawing heavily from contemporary moral, political and legal philosophy. Along the way, I also borrow from the empirical research of criminologists. I hope that my efforts capture the best these disciplines have to offer. I aspire to write books and papers that are neither too philosophical for legal theorists nor too legalistic for philosophers. The corresponding risk, of course, is that my scholarship will fall between the cracks, attracting the attention of neither discipline. Nonetheless, the scholars from whom I learn the most tend to share a similar orientation.

In the course of thinking about the many philosophical issues in the substantive criminal law, I came to wonder about my country's drug policy – a topic Fletcher had not addressed. Surprisingly, almost no other criminal theorists addressed it either. 1979 was the year of peak illicit drug use in the United States; well over 60%

of high-school seniors and college undergraduates experimented with illicit substances. Many users were excessive, but few seemed to suffer any significant harm from their experience – unless they were arrested. Some of my students got into quite a bit of legal trouble from using and selling small amounts of drugs. I noted an astounding disconnect between the issues covered in casebooks and treatises, and those that arise in the real world of criminal law. Drug offenses are the meat and potatoes of our criminal justice system, yet no theorists were talking or writing about them. Many of the normative principles defended in scholarly textbooks were qualified or simply ignored when drugs were involved. Even philosophers strongly opposed to paternalism tended to make an exception for drug prohibitions, although the grounds for this exception were rarely explained. The questions that arise about drug policy are the most basic issues one might pose: What are drugs? How harmful are they, and how might their harmful effects be ameliorated? Should we have a special policy that differentiates between drugs and non-drugs? Do principles of justice allow us to continue to rely on our punitive approach, which makes the use and possession of given kinds of drugs a criminal offense? What are the alternatives to prohibition, and would they promote the legitimate objectives of drug policy more effectively?

I did not begin my inquiry into drug policy with an unshakable conviction that no rationale could be found for imposing penal liability on persons who use illicit substances. I remain willing to allow the arguments to take me wherever they happen to lead. Nonetheless, I have yet to find a defense of prohibition that strikes me as remotely persuasive. To assess given rationales effectively, I believe it important to actually learn something about drugs – how they affect the persons who use them, and how they affect the communities in which these persons live. It is not enough to proclaim – as some libertarians do – that drug prohibitions are unjust because drugs are put into one's body, in which everyone has a property right. Everything depends, I contend, on what happens to one's body when drugs are ingested. Expertise on this topic requires a willingness to stray far outside the boundaries of philosophy – to pharmacology, history, economics, criminology, psychology, biology, sociology, and elsewhere. Most of the arguments in favor of drug proscriptions fail for empirical reasons. Empirical investigation convinced me that drug proscriptions are not justified for any of the reasons typically offered on their behalf: to prevent crime, to protect juveniles, to preserve health, or to send a moral message. Still, new drugs – or new findings about existing drugs – might make the case for prohibition more plausible. Here is where philosophical imagination is essential. One needs to think about what *would* count as a good rationale for drug prohibitions if given empirical assumptions were true. In other words, one needs to identify the properties a drug must have before the state would be justified in punishing persons who use it.

To this day, I am equally proud of my work in the philosophy of criminal law and my work on (what I take to be) the injustice of contemporary drug policy. The latter is a topic of immense practical and theoretical importance. If I am correct to conclude that no good reason to punish drug users exists, our drug policy has produced massive injustice – the greatest injustice perpetrated by law, I believe, since the institution of slavery. In my lifetime, tens of millions of Americans have been arrested, and many millions have been incarcerated, for nonviolent drug offenses. The scale of this injustice dwarfs that of other domestic injustices our government has perpetrated. I have tried to persuade other philosophers of law to become more interested in this important topic, but with very limited success. I am amazed that many of the legal and political philosophers who are most outspoken about other repressive practices are not more vocal about the injustice of our contemporary drug policy..

Of course, no one can decide whether the state has good reasons to punish persons for using drugs unless he has a reasonable grasp on what would count as a good reason to punish anyone for anything. Thoughts about drug offenses in particular lead inexorably to thoughts about criminalization more generally. Yet no theorist – with the possible exception of Jeremy Bentham – has produced a sophisticated theory of criminalization: that is, a theory of what the criminal law should and should not proscribe. This lacuna must be filled. One would think that the question of what conduct the state may require its citizens to perform (or not to perform) on pain of punishment would be among the most central topics in legal and political philosophy. For whatever reason, however, the issue has not received the treatment it deserves. Moreover, many of the issues that have been discussed more thoroughly – political obligation, the justification of punishment, and the like – cannot be resolved in the absence of a respectable theory of criminalization. No one could hope to show that the state may punish persons, or that citizens are obligated to obey the law, without making assumptions about what people are punished for, or about the content of the laws they might be obligated to obey. The last few years of my career have been devoted to attempts to fill this enormous gap in legal philosophy. I hope to produce a set of principles to retard the phenomenon of overcriminalization from which we currently suffer. At present, some 7 million Americans are under the control and supervision of the criminal justice system; 2.2 million are incarcerated. It is time to give the plight of these persons the attention it deserves. I hope to have more success persuading my colleagues to address this issue than I have had in convincing them to think seriously about our drug policy.

When someone is absorbed by a given subject matter, it is hard to understand why others do not share this passion. I admit that I have this attitude about legal philosophy generally and about criminal theory in particular. The state imposes power through law, and the coercive power of the government is exercised most directly through the criminal sanction. Ultimately, the criminal law backs up everything else done by a political system. Anyone interested in political authority and the coercive power of the state should be interested in the criminal law. Or so it seems to me. Yet criminal theory attracts fewer specialists in the academy than many other subject matters that seem, to my mind, far less important.

The philosophy of criminal law includes many outstanding issues. Even a partial list of these issues is lengthy. What *is* the domain of criminal law? Should criminal laws be defined as those that subject offenders to punishment? What *is* punishment? Does it differ in degree or in kind from civil sanctions? What criteria must be satisfied before criminal statutes are justified, and how are these criteria to be defended? How does the principle of legality apply to criminal offenses? Does it pertain to defenses in the same way it pertains to offenses? How should the contrast between offenses and defenses be drawn? How do utilitarian and deterrence considerations interplay in our thinking about criminal liability? Should punishment be imposed only for acts that are voluntary? Or may punishment be imposed when conduct *includes* a voluntary act—whatever "includes" means in this context? When may persons be punished for their omissions? What mental states make agents culpable for their criminal conduct, and should the criminal law countenance greater or lesser numbers of culpable states? What is harm, and should all penal offenses be required to proscribe it? Under what circumstances, if any, is it worse to cause a harm on purpose rather than unknowingly? Should persons ever be punished for their negligence? Can liability for negligence be reconciled with the intuition that punishment requires choice? Is the latter intuition defensible? To what extent should tests of recklessness and negligence be sensitive to the peculiar characteristics of given defendants? How should intoxication bear on criminal liability? Under what conditions should ignorance of law excuse criminal behavior? What conditions must be satisfied before an agent can be said to have caused a result, and should results ever be relevant for criminal liability? How should justifications be differentiated from excuses, and is the contrast between these two types of defense important? Might defendants have a justification defense even though they were unaware of the circumstances that create the justification? Why should the state recognize any excuses, and which excuses should it allow? Is justification somehow prior to excuse? How should a test of insanity be formulated? Is the character of the defendant ever material to criminal liability? Should persons be punished in order for law to serve an expressive function? Under what circumstances should the criminal sanction protect persons from offense? Which problems are best addressed through the criminal law, and which are more appropriately resolved by non-criminal means? How do answers to any of these questions bear on how others should be resolved? Is there a grand, unifying theory of criminal law? Needless to say, positions on each of these matters invite further questions that have spawned a massive literature. Contributing to these debates is an ongoing challenge.

Despite the plethora of important issues that require consideration, criminal theory is only a tiny subfield of philosophy of law. Legal philosophy today consists of two fairly clearly demarcated specialties. The first area is jurisprudence, sometimes called analytical jurisprudence. This field examines the nature of law and the many complex issues that are related to that investigation. Theorists attempt to determine the conditions that need to be satisfied before a system of rules, or individual rules, qualify as law. This topic leads naturally into questions about the connection between law and morality, the nature of legal reasoning, the authority of law, and a host of others. The second area involves philosophical work in particular domains of law, such as contract, tort, and my own field of criminal law. Most of the issues that arise here are peculiar to the particular area of law under examination, but a few questions reoccur in virtually all domains. Questions about causation and responsibility, for example, are common to just about every area of law. The same could be said about principles of interpretation. To my mind, the most important question in each domain involves the purposes for which that kind of law may be used. Might the law of tort be used to require people to pay compensation for harms they have caused without negligence? Under what circumstances, if any, should contract law refuse to enforce an agreement because it is unconscionable? I trust, however, that other contributors to this volume will have substantially more to say about such matters – as well as about the familiar division between the two fairly clearly demarcated specialties in legal philosophy.

Which topics should legal philosophers examine in the immediate future? In keeping with what I described as my own research agenda, I believe that they should try to discover important issues that have not been thoroughly discussed already. There are many such issues. Data about the leading causes of preventable death and serious injury in the United States, for instance, bear surprisingly little correlation to the specific issues that legal philosophers have scrutinized. Let me mention two examples. First, persons in the United States between the ages of 4 and 40 are most likely to die or suffer serious injury from an automobile accident. If Americans drove less frequently, or simply drove different kinds of vehicles, thousands of these deaths and injuries would be prevented. Yet legal philosophers have precious little to say about how the law might accomplish this important objective without violating other principles we value. Second, thousands of Americans – perhaps as many as 400,000 each year – die prematurely from diseases exacerbated by obesity. Many respond to these facts by claiming that diet and exercise are strictly matters of personal responsibility. This facile response does not begin to tap the imagination to find strategies to alleviate this epidemic without trampling on personal autonomy. Here is yet another important topic waiting for legal philosophers to make a valuable contribution.

I have never been too inclined to define the borders of a discipline or sub-discipline too sharply. I rarely complain that a given topic "isn't really philosophy" or "isn't really legal philosophy." I am aware that some legal philosophers regard many questions within criminal theory as not within the domain of legal philosophy at all. Instead, they conceptualize these debates as belonging within political philosophy. They are even less inclined to believe that an investigation qualifies as philosophical when it includes a substantial empirical component. To my mind, these debates are fruitless and unimportant. Unless I can be persuaded that something significant depends on how they are resolved, I refuse to become too engaged in them. The borders of philosophical inquiry are themselves a topic of philosophical inquiry – but a topic I am largely content to leave to others.

Should legal philosophy connect more directly to legal practice? Probably. Sometimes our debates are conducted at too high a level of abstraction to be easily applied to existing problems. But I hasten to point out that much of the blame for the lack of intersection between legal philosophy and the real world lies with individuals in the latter rather than with the former. Philosophers of law have contributed much from which the world of legal practice might draw. Consider my own specialty of drug policy. It is remarkably hard to provide a balance in a conference on drug law by finding knowledgeable and articulate commentators who are willing to defend the status quo. Almost no thoughtful person within the academy believes that our present strategy is just and effective, yet the present policy remains. For deep reasons about which I can only speculate, the political processes in the United States tend not to draw on academic scholarship. At the same time, I admit that legal philosophers do not always have practical advice to give. When we do, however, few officials with policy-making authority seem particularly interested in what we have to say. This same pessimistic observation can be made about criminal justice generally, which proceeds along merrily despite enjoying almost no support from the academic community. One can only wonder how much our criminal justice system would benefit if it were influenced more directly by legal scholarship.. A closer connection would probably improve the quality of work in legal philosophy as well.

Although I would prefer to see legal philosophy move in a more practical direction, however, I am happy to know that the profession includes many whose opinions differ. The philosophy of law in particular, like philosophy generally, is a very broad tent, with lots of room for persons with diverse and varied interests. The fact that many of the most important figures under this tent disagree about the most important topics in legal philosophy is a healthy state of affairs. Philosophy is and ought to be a discipline in which persons pursue a range of issues with no straightforward practical application. I would not regard a greater amount of consensus on these matters as necessarily a sign of progress.

Selected Bibliography

Overcriminalization (Oxford University Press, forthcoming, 2007).

Drugs and Rights (Cambridge University Press, 1992).

Legalize This (London: Verso, 2002).

The Philosophy of Criminal Law (Rowman & Littlefield, 1987).

"On the Supposed Priority of Justification to Excuse," 24 *Law and Philosophy* (2005) 557.

"Vehicles and Crashes: Why Is This Moral Issue Overlooked?" 30 *Social Theory and Practice* (2004) 351.

"Is the Criminal Law Important?" 1 *Ohio State Journal of Criminal Law* (2003) 261.

"Addiction and Criminal Liability," 18 *Law and Philosophy* (1999) 655.

"Partial Defenses," XI *Canadian Journal of Law and Jurisprudence* (1998) 167.

"The Nature and Justifiability of Nonconsummate Offenses," 37 *Arizona Law Review* (1995) 151.

"Date Rape, Social Convention, and Reasonable Mistakes," (George Thomas, co-author) 11 *Law and Philosophy* (1992) 95.

"Why Punish the Deserving?" 26 *Nous* (1992) 447.

"Motive and Criminal Liability," 8 *Criminal Justice Ethics* (1989) 3.

"Malum Prohibitum and Retributivism," in R.A. Duff and Stuart Green, eds: *Defining Crimes: Essays on the Special Part of Criminal Law* (Oxford University Press, 2005) 65.

"Strict Liability, Justice, and Proportionality," in A.P. Simester, ed: *Appraising Strict Liability* (Oxford University Press, 2005) 81.

"Limitations on Criminalization and the General Part of Criminal Law," in Stephen Shute and Andrew Simester, eds: *Criminal Law: Doctrines of the General Part* (Cambridge: Cambridge University Press, 2002) 13.

"Does Criminal Responsibility Require an Act?" in R.A. Duff. ed: *Philosophy and the Criminal Law* (Cambridge University Press, 1998) 60.

"Legal Paternalism," in Hugh LaFollette, ed.: *Oxford Handbook of Practical Ethics* (Oxford University Press, 2003), 387–412.

10

Nicola Lacey

Professor of Criminal Law and Legal Theory
London School of Economics, UK

Why were you initially drawn to the philosophy of law?
The answer to this question needs to be set within the specific context of British legal education, where law is typically a three year undergraduate programme. When I arrived at University College London as an undergraduate in 1976 I was, like most of my fellow students, primarily motivated by my intention to qualify as a lawyer. But I quickly realized that the subjects which commanded my real interest were those which considered law from what one might call an external perspective. In the first year, the relevant courses were legal history and the sociology of law; but it was really in my second year, when I studied criminal law, that I started to feel excited about legal philosophy. For the first time, I encountered a doctrinal area in which my teachers, and the scholars whose work I was reading – even, sometimes, the judges! – seemed interested in how the subject fitted together. Instead of merely mugging up the substantive rules for the purposes of an exam, I was being asked to think about whether they made sense; about what their underlying assumptions were; about the justification for criminal law and punishment; about the relationship between criminal law and morality on the one hand and political force on the other. I wouldn't have put it this way at the time, but I think that I had already realized that I was more interested in law as a social phenomenon than as a doctrinal system – though, of course, law's doctrinal form is one of its interesting and significant features from a social and theoretical point of view.
My experience of studying criminal law – H.L.A. Hart's *Punishment and Responsibility*[1] and *Law, Liberty and Morality*[2], Bar-

---
[1] Oxford: Clarendon Press 1968.
[2] Oxford: Oxford University Press 1963.

bara Wootton's *Crime and the Criminal Law*[3], and Glanville Williams' *Criminal Law: The General Part*[4] stand out in my memory – gave me tremendous excitement about studying jurisprudence the following year. I was not disappointed. The course which I followed was quite a standard one. It focused on analytical jurisprudence – Austin, Bentham, Kelsen, Hart, Dworkin, natural law theory. Though legal realism and sociological jurisprudence received some attention, one did not have to be an astute reader between the lines to know that these were not generally regarded as of the same intellectual stature as the positivist or natural law traditions. It was some time before I re-evaluated this position: at the time, I was an enthusiastic and relatively uncritical consumer of analytical jurisprudence, particularly of a positivist temper. I was fortunate in having a tutor – Stephen Guest, an avid Dworkinian – who enjoyed debate and responded generously to what he regretfully regarded as relatively rare instances of genuine student enthusiasm for legal philosophy.

With Guest's support and encouragement, I began to think in terms of pursuing postgraduate studies, and went on to Oxford to read for the BCL. I remember my tutor, John Finnis, asking me on my arrival what I wanted to study. I replied that I had not decided on all six courses, but that I was sure about two things: first, that I wanted to study and write my dissertation in Jurisprudence: second, that I didn't want to study Restitution. (Quite why private law held so little attraction for me I now find it difficult to explain.) Finnis assured me that restitution was 'good for the soul', and to my retrospective amazement, I duly studied it, though without much enjoyment. I leave it to others to judge what, if any, impact it had on my soul.

The BCL jurisprudence syllabus combined a focus on the analytical jurisprudence to which I had already been introduced with a strong element of political theory, and I now immersed myself in Rawls, Nozick et al. It was a marvellous time to be studying jurisprudence in Oxford. The main BCL seminar was run by Ronald Dworkin, John Finnis and Joseph Raz, all of whom were publishing around that time some of their most important works, many of which were piloted in draft at the seminar. Hugh Collins and Denis Galligan held a seminar on Marxist jurisprudence, which debated among other things the main ideas published in Collins'

---

[3] London: Stevens & Sons 1963.
[4] London: Stevens & Sons 1961.

monograph in 1982.[5] Dworkin regularly teamed up with philosopher and economist colleagues like Jerry Cohen, Derek Parfit and Amartya Sen to put on joint seminars – known among the students as 'circuses', which gives a sense of both their entertainment value and their occasionally alarming quality—which drew large numbers of mesmerized colleagues and students. Equally important from my point of view was the fact that this constellation of scholars attracted a very strong group of graduate students to Oxford. During my time they included Jeremy Waldron, Leslie Green and Denise Rëaume, all of whom became friends and regular co-members of reading and discussion groups. In addition, George Cawkwell, classics fellow at University College, organized a termly dinner for the graduate students in law, philosophy, economics and politics, at which we were able to meet and talk informally (if occasionally somewhat nervously!) with philosophical luminaries such as John McDowell, John Mackie, Peter Strawson and – best of all from my point of view – Herbert Hart.

Seminars in legal and political philosophy, and debates with my fellow students in those fields, were undoubtedly a highlight of my two years as a graduate student: they confirmed both my appetite for jurisprudence and my feeling that an academic career would be more satisfying to me than a career in legal practice. But my intellectual development and theoretical views were shaped equally decisively by my experience of two other courses: Criminal Justice and Penology – the only genuinely socio-legal course on the BCL syllabus – and Comparative Human Rights. Like my criminal law course, these courses excited my interest in the potential for applying ideas from analytical and normative theory to substantive fields: though I still had what I now regard as a surprisingly keen appetite for very abstract theory, even at that stage I felt a yet stronger motivation when confronted with issues arising out of practices or institutional arrangements on which theoretical ideas could be brought to bear. I was also – particularly as a result of studying criminal justice – beginning to see the relevance to legal theory of the context in which legal rules and arrangements exist and are enforced, as well as interpretive and enforcement practices themselves, and to feel some dissatisfaction with the relatively narrow way in which many legal philosophers delineated the conceptions of law on which they focused. I was, in short, feeling the pull towards what might be called 'applied jurisprudence'

---

[5] *Marxism and Law* Clarendon Press 1982.

and 'socio-legal studies', as well as a resistance to the idea that jurisprudence and socio-legal studies occupy two entirely difference universes. These impulses have shaped much of my later work.

In the light of this, it might seem surprising that I opted to write my dissertation on a highly abstract question of analytical jurisprudence: the place of the distinction between momentary and non-momentary legal systems in legal theory. This distinction had first been formulated by Joseph Raz in what many scholars regard as his most difficult book: *The Concept of a Legal System*[6]. It had then been taken up in John Finnis's fascinating (and no less complex) 'Revolutions and the Continuity of Law'.[7] I was fortunate enough to be able to persuade Raz to supervise my dissertation. His meticulous commentary on successive drafts, as well as his warm encouragement, were a model of thesis supervision, and made a large contribution to my development of skills in putting together an integrated theoretical argument. My interest in the notion of non-momentary legal systems prefigured my later fascination with the relationship between sociological and philosophical jurisprudence; indeed I have returned to it in several papers written over the last decade. But I can now see that my decision to write my dissertation on Jurisprudence had to do not only with intrinsic intellectual interest but also with the hierarchy which characterized Oxford's intellectual culture. This hierarchy became startlingly apparent when one of the most eminent legal philosophers in Oxford described the BCL to me as 'a degree of no intellectual substance'. Notwithstanding the stature of legal scholars like John Morris, Rupert Cross, Peter Birks and many others whose ideas and teaching shaped the BCL syllabus, jurisprudence enjoyed a special allure lent it by its association with, as Herbert Hart put it,[8] 'the queen' of the Oxford disciplines: philosophy. As for social science approaches to law, they were firmly at the bottom of the heap. Much later, I came across a wealth of evidence about this hierarchy while researching my biography of Hart. But it was not difficult to trace even at the time: think for example of Tony Honoré's comment in an essay for the 1973 Oxford Essays in Jurisprudence: 'Decade after decade, Positivists

---

[6] Oxford: Clarendon Press 1970

[7] 'Groups, Laws and Obedience', in A.W.B. Simpson (ed.) *Oxford Essays in Jurisprudence: Second Series* (Oxford: Clarendon Press 1973) p.1

[8] In a letter to his wife, Jenifer, from Harvard in 1956: see Lacey, *A Life of HLA Hart: The Nightmare and the Noble Dream* (Oxford University Press 2004) Chapters 7 and 8.

and Natural Lawyers face one another in the final of the World Cup (the Sociologists have never learned the rules).'[9]

Of the senior legal philosophers teaching in Oxford at the time, only Honoré had any serious reputation as a scholar in a substantive law field. With the next generation – Jim Harris, Colin Tapper, Hugh Collins, Peter Cane, John Bell, John Eekelaar – this was changing. The change was reflected in the development, just after my departure from Oxford in 1981, of a BCL course on 'Philosophical Foundations of the Common Law'. The course was probably conceived as a contribution to increasing the 'intellectual substance' of the BCL. For the younger generation, it opened however the possibility not only of a more theoretical approach to legal scholarship but also of a legal theory more grounded in the specificities of particular areas of law.[10] As such, it was in my view a more radical development than its originators perhaps realized. While the traditional parameters of legal scholarship would be challenged by a confrontation with legal philosophy, in other words, legal philosophy would not remain untouched by the encounter. When I returned to Oxford as a member of the Faculty in 1984, my three years teaching Jurisprudence at UCL during William Twining's tenure of the Quain Chair had further shaped my views about the importance of integrating theoretical with contextual and historical scholarship, and teaching on the Philosophical Foundations course afforded me a regular dialogue with Andrew Ashworth, Hugh Collins and Anne de Moor which was of decisive importance in the development of my ideas.

What are the most important issues in legal philosophy, and why are they distinctively issues of legal philosophy rather than some other discipline?

It makes sense to me to take this question next, and to take its two parts in reverse order.

It will be apparent from what I have already said, as well as to anyone who has read my work, that I entertain very serious doubts about the extent to which legal philosophy ought to be regarded as an autonomous discipline. Though we must be careful to avoid an arid definitional debate, the question's reference to

---

[9] Simpson (ed.) op cit

[10] The impact of this development was reflected in the Third Series of the *Oxford Essays in Jurisprudence*, edited by John Bell and John Eekelaar and published by the Clarendon Press in 1986.

issues which are 'distinctively issues of legal philosophy' perhaps needs some unpicking here. I am perfectly comfortable with the idea that philosophy, as a discipline, develops relatively distinctive procedures and methods: certain kinds of linguistic analysis would be one example. Further, it is obviously true that philosophy, like other disciplines, sets up or poses issues in distinctive ways. But two further things are also true. The first is that philosophy itself – or perhaps I should say 'philosophers themselves' – use a number of methods: these are both an object of debate and contestation within the discipline and imply different relationships between philosophy and other disciplines. The second is that the issues which are of interest to legal philosophers are also – even if they may be posed in slightly different ways – of interest to legal scholars generally and to social scientists and historians, and that what each of these disciplines has to say about the issues is of potential relevance to the others.

I will take each of these points in turn. First, the differences among philosophical approaches. Several examples are of clear relevance to legal philosophy – perhaps most notably the long-running debate about the relationship between description and prescription, reflected both in the natural law/positivism debate and in the debate about Dworkin's conception of law as an interpretive practice. But I would like to take another example: that between different versions of the linguistic analysis which has been so central to post-war analytical jurisprudence. As I argued at greater length in my biography of H.L.A. Hart,[11] one could argue that Austin's famous notion of analyzing language to generate 'a sharpened awareness of the phenomena' would have generated a rather different kind of jurisprudence had it been interpreted along Wittgensteinian lines. While the Austinian approach, reflected for example in Hart's and Honoré's famous treatise on causation,[12] reduces linguistic usage to a body of doctrine, a Wittgensteinian approach would see that usage as a social practice which takes place within a context the specific nature of which requires investigation because it inflects the relevant concepts. For Wittgenstein, language games are embedded within social practices and forms of life. This implies that conceptual and socio-institutional

---

[11] Op. cit. chapter 9; see also Lacey, 'Analytical Jurisprudence versus Descriptive Sociology Revisited' (2006) 84 *Texas Law Review* 945–86.

[12] *Causation in the Law* (Oxford: Clarendon Press 1959: second edition, 1985).

analysis cannot be neatly separated. This is not, of course, to recast Wittgenstein as a social scientist manqué. Despite his injunctions about the limits of philosophy, Wittgenstein was, after all, a philosopher, and his method was analytic rather than empirical: his own reaction to the insights which I am emphasizing here was to adopt a famously defeatist view of the power of philosophy rather than to launch a case for the social sciences. Rather, my point is that a more socially contextualized, less philosophically autonomous approach is implied by, and could be constructed through a supplementation of, Wittgenstein's work, as could a more equal and intimate relationship between philosophy and other disciplines.

It is legitimate to ask what kind of analytical jurisprudence Hart would have developed had he been inspired more by Wittgenstein's than by Austin's linguistic philosophy. I would argue that we could expect him to have explored questions such as the institutional factors which restrict the extent to which judges will appeal to pragmatic or policy arguments – their sensitivity to the need to legitimate their decisions, their (system-specific) understanding of their constitutional role and so on. As an empirical matter, these institutional factors shape not only the appeal to policy in legal cases but also the development of legal concepts themselves. This is, it must be admitted, an unpalatable argument to legal philosophers: for, if fully pursued, the Wittgensteinian message undermines the pretensions of philosophy as the 'masterdiscipline' which illuminates our access to knowledge about the world. For once the notion of 'context' is broadened out, the inexorable conclusion is that illumination of legal practices lies not merely in an analysis of doctrinal language but equally in an attempt to locate the analysis within some general account of the history and social role of the institutions and power relations within which that usage takes place. A full acceptance of the implications of Wittgenstein's thought, in other words, threatens the philosophical boundaries of jurisprudence.

Let me now move to the second point: the fact that many of the phenomena which interest legal philosophers – 'law', 'legal systems', 'legal rules' and so on – are also of interest to scholars in other disciplines. Here we begin to touch on an issue at the core of 'philosophical foundations' scholarship: when we claim that our account is an account *of* a concept or phenomenon which has a 'real' social existence, what, precisely, are the criteria of accountability involved? How many aspects of the phenomenon are we allowed to jettison as mistaken or confused? How, in other words, do we square the normative/conceptual clarification aspect of the philosophical enterprise with its positive aspect? The project of analyzing philosophical foundations of legal doctrines and arrangements is rooted firmly in the tradition of analytical jurisprudence revived by Herbert Hart. Yet the commitment to analyzing 'the common law' – indeed, in many of its manifestations,[13] to analyzing specific aspects of the common law – implies a vision of law as the sort of spatially and historically specific phenomenon which is susceptible of social-scientific inquiry. The values and ideals of a political society change over time; conceptions of conduct, agency and responsibility shift; geo-political and economic circumstances change; the implications of these and many other factors for not only the substance but also the conceptual framework and even the idea of law are evidently an important object of research.

The idea of legal systems as developing over time and within complex social, economic, cultural and political environments is well captured by Joseph Raz's idea of the 'non-momentary legal system'.[14] Raz's argument is that the identity of the non-momentary system is determined primarily by its content rather than by its criteria for the identification of valid legal standards. It is the latter – the normative conditions under which a momentary legal system exists – which is the proper object of analytical jurisprudence. This object can be theorized independently of any consideration of the non-momentary system to which it belongs. Hence Raz may be taken to imply that the social-theoretic analysis of law can be neatly bracketed off from the analytic; that in tracing the philosophical foundations of, say, English criminal law, we have no need of any broad understanding of the social functions or meaning of criminalization understood as a connected sequence of practices, of the historical development of the values informing those practices or of the conceptual frameworks in terms of which they have been carried forward. This resolute distancing of social and historical context is reproduced in analyses of philosophical foundations which are concerned with the moral coherence of particular common law doctrines. The result is that law is implicitly (mis)represented as founded – actually or ideally

---

[13] Notably in the Third Series of the *Oxford Essays in Jurisprudence*, J. Eekelaar and J. Bell (eds.) op cit..

[14] *The Concept of a Legal System op cit* Chapter VIII.

– on a metaphysics: a moral or conceptual structure whose validity transcends space and time. My argument, by contrast, is that if we are interested in the philosophical foundations of law and of other social institutions, we must be concerned with accounts of how these social institutions operate. It is a mistake to think that law can afford to ignore insights into the operation of the institutions whose practices it seeks to shape, or that the structure of those practices places no constraints on the development of adequate legal policy. Both policy and theory are, in short, answerable to context. Hence a radical separation between the analytic and the contextual will in fact occlude our understanding of law.

From my point of view, therefore, the most interesting and important questions – though they would not be identified by many legal philosophers as jurisprudential questions – can only be tackled by bridging the philosophy/history/social science divide. Such work, though still regarded as outside the jurisprudential canon by many legal philosophers is, happily from my point of view, flourishing. For example, Brian Tamanaha[15] has sought to push Hart's approach further in the direction of its constructionist or conventionalist aspects and away from its functionalism and essentialism, providing a broader, 'socio-legal positivist' conception of law which purports to fulfill many of the aims which Hart saw as central to his own jurisprudence. Sociological jurists such as Niklas Luhmann and Gunther Teubner have developed sociologies of law[16] which have a strong philosophical component. William Twining's recent work on legal theory[17] shows a similarly eclectic embrace of different methods and disciplinary resources, while

---

[15] *A General Jurisprudence of Law and Society* (Oxford: Clarendon Press 2001); in relation to the themes of this paper.

[16] *A Sociological Theory of Law* (London: Routledge and Kegan Paul 1985); *Law as an Autopoietic System* (Oxford: Blackwell 1993)

[17] *Globalisation and Legal Theory* (London: Butterworths 2000); see also Twining's review essay on Tamanaha, 'A Post-Westphalian Conception of Law' *op cit.*; and 'General Jurisprudence', in M. Escamilla and M. Saavedra (eds.) *Law and Justice in Global Society, Anales de la Catedra Francisco Suarez* (2005) pp. 563-608.

Hamish Ross[18] has traced the echoes of classical social theory in the work of legal philosophers including Kelsen and Hart. In a recent paper, Simon Roberts[19] has even gone so far as to question the broadening out of conceptions of law beyond the state in the work of scholars like Tamanaha and Twining in response to the long-running debate about legal pluralism, arguing on empirical grounds in favour of the giving just the kind of priority or distinctiveness to state law for which legal pluralists have so long criticized Hart. And most consistently of all, Roger Cotterrell[20] has argued for a mutually respectful and informed division of labour between sociological and analytical jurisprudence. For me, however, the most compelling questions remain those of applied or, as Bentham would have had it, 'special' jurisprudence, as is reflected in my current work on criminal responsibility described below.

For which of your contribution(s) to legal philosophy so far would you most like to be remembered, and why?

For the reasons explored in the previous section, I am not inclined to make a hard distinction between philosophical and non-philosophical contributions. All of my work has been influenced by legal philosophy. I regard even my most 'legal' works – my jointly authored criminal law textbook for example – as making a contribution to legal theory. I mean by this that it expresses and advocates a particular, contextual way of understanding and studying law, even though it does not explicitly confront many issues of legal philosophy as conventionally understood.

---

[18] *Law as a Social Institution* (Hart Publishing 2001); '*The Pure Theory of Law* and Interpretive Sociology – A Basis for Interdisciplinarity?', forthcoming in Michael Freeman (ed.), *Law and Sociology* (*Current Legal Issues* Vol. 8: Oxford University Press); see also, for a philosophical approach defending the relevance of empirical knowledge to Hart's conceptual project, Veronica Rodriguez-Blanco, 'A Defense of Hart's Semantics as Nonambitious Conceptual Analysis' *op cit.*

[19] 'After Government? On Representing Law Without the State' 68 *Modern Law Review* (2005) 1–24. Roberts argues that pluralist conceptions of law beyond the state risk diluting the analytic purchase of the concept of law, depriving comparative social science of tools to make important distinctions between centralized, hierarchical and governing-oriented normative systems and genuinely negotiated normative orders. Hence in his view Hart's concept of law indeed has an empirical and ethnographic basis, albeit one which Hart himself failed to elaborate.

[20] See in particular *Law's Community* (Clarendon Press 1995).

In terms of what I would like to be recognized for among legal theorists, I would select three contributions, which I will discuss in chronological order.

Feminist Theory

While working in Oxford in the late 1980s, partly as a result of the experience of working in a heavily male-dominated environment, and partly as a result of some marvellous seminars run by Jennifer Hornsby, Sabina Lovibond and Elizabeth Frazer among others, I became interested in feminist philosophy. At the same time, I was a member of a reading group exploring some of the contributions to North American 'critical legal studies'. What I found interesting about the literature I was reading (and continue to find interesting, notwithstanding the virtual demise of 'CLS') was the thought that apparently neutral conceptual frameworks might be marked by the vectors of power which characterized the social order in which they developed and operated. This was, of course, an idea central to Marxist thought, but feminists, critical race theorists and others were now exploring a wider range of intersecting vectors in an attempt to uncover what we might crudely call the 'gender' or 'color' as well as the 'class' of law and other social institutions (and indeed disciplines). In the UK, the early examples of feminist legal scholarship had been marked also by a strong socio-legal commitment which I found intellectually congenial: there was little point in having an acute critique of 'law in the books' if the law as enforced was the main, or an equal, problem from the point of view of gender justice. Over the years, I published a number of essays exploring the nature of feminist and critical method in legal scholarship, and deploying that method in the analysis of particular issues such as the construction of sexuality in sex offences or the proper shape and likely impact of anti-discrimination law. In 1998 I brought these together in a published collection.[21] Though I am ultimately doubtful – not least for socio-legal reasons – about any sweeping generalizations about 'the sex of law', I remain convinced of the importance of the sort of critical analysis which unearths both the assumptions on which conceptual arrangements are based and their connection with broader socio-structural dynamics. To the extent that my essays express and defend these insights, I hope that they will have some impact on the field.

---

[21] *Unspeakable Subjects* (Oxford: Hart Publishing 1998).

A Life of H.L.A. Hart: The Nightmare and the Noble Dream

Some readers may quibble with the idea that the biography of H.L.A. Hart, which I was fortunate to have the opportunity to write in the early 2000's, counts as a contribution to legal philosophy. I would argue that it does, for two reasons. First, it sheds light on the development of, and influences upon, the ideas of one of the two most important legal philosophers of the Twentieth Century. Second, it advances a critical interpretation of Hart's work (further developed in an article in the *Texas Law Review*[22]) which articulates my own view of the field. The book also shows that there is a human, emotional side to the production of ideas, as well as a set of psychological, historical and institutional conditions for their realization. These are, perhaps, no bad things for philosophers to be reminded of from time to time ...

The Nightmare and the Noble Dream is very much my interpretation of Hart's life, personality and work: it is genuinely 'A Life', and someone else would – indeed may – write a very different account. It is, however, the piece of work which I have found most emotionally and intellectually engaging, and I regard it as my most fully realized project to date. I am not sure that I want to be 'remembered', but I do hope that the book will be read for many years to come, and in particular that it will be read by students.

In Search of the Responsible Subject: criminal law history and theory

For the last seven years I have been working, in the interstices of other projects, on a long term research programme which explores the historical development of ideas of responsibility for crime since the mid-Eighteenth Century. At the start of the Twenty-First Century, it is little exaggeration to say that responsibility stands as the central question of normative criminal law theory. The state's obligation to prove not only that a defendant has committed criminal conduct but that he or she is responsible in the sense of being fairly held accountable for doing so is seen as the key to justifying the imposition of liability and punishment. It may be that appellate cases in most legal systems of the common law world are as often concerned with the interpretation of the conduct element

---

[22] Nicola Lacey, 'Analytical Jurisprudence versus Descriptive Sociology Revisited' 84 *Texas Law Review* 945.

of criminal offences as with the responsibility condition or the defences. However, a brief survey of not only legal texts and theoretical monographs but also draft codes such as the American Model Penal Code testifies to the contemporary preoccupation with questions about the 'fault element', i.e. the conditions under which it is appropriate to hold an individual responsible for his or her actions. These responsibility conditions are widely seen as being grounded in broader conditions of human capacity: people are responsible for what they do intentionally, knowingly, recklessly or negligently because such action – unlike inadvertent conduct – engages their powers of understanding and self-control. This vision of responsibility as grounded in capacity is in turn embedded in notions of human agency which underpin the great Enlightenment philosophies so widely diffused in European culture during the Eighteenth Century. Yet there has been little research on how and when these ideas found their way into the doctrines of the common law.

This project raises both substantive and methodological questions about the treatment of responsibility in criminal law theory, and has two substantive purposes. First, it examines the way in which English criminal law's conception of responsibility has changed since the mid-Eighteenth Century. Second, it examines the relationship between these changes in legal framework and broader social, political and economic changes.[23] This aspect of its argument is premised on the assumption that criminal law may usefully be examined not only as an institution in its own right but also as an index of broad social changes. The project therefore seeks to contribute as much to social theory as to legal analysis and history.

Methodologically, the project contributes to the general question in legal theory which I regard as of the greatest interest and importance: how do the disciplinary resources of philosophy, history and the social sciences contribute to our understanding of law? Most research in criminal law works within one of three disciplinary frameworks: doctrinal legal scholarship, analytic philosophy, or the social sciences. My aim, by contrast, is to produce a multi-disciplinary study which explores the relationship between

---

[23] My papers 'In Search of the Responsible Subject: History, Philosophy and Criminal Law Theory' 64 *Modern Law Review* (2001) 350-371 and 'Responsibility and Modernity in Criminal Law' 9 *Journal of Political Philosophy* (2001) 249-277 give a more detailed picture of this project.

the legal basis of criminal liability and the broader ideas of responsibility influenced by socio-economic and political changes and by the rapid expansion of the social sciences over the relevant period. The project therefore moves away from a conception of criminal law theory as founded primarily in analytic philosophy and the systematic analysis of legal doctrine, towards what might be called a 'genealogical' approach. Its aim is to historicize the structure as well as the content of criminal law within a broad socio-theoretic framework, drawing links between the conceptual structure of criminal law doctrine and the substantive social functions which criminal law and punishment have been expected to perform at different points in history. The project thus attempts to construct a dialogue between criminal law theory of a doctrinal and philosophical temper and socio-historical studies of criminal justice.

What is the relationship between legal philosophy and legal practice? Should legal philosophers be more concerned about the effect of their scholarship on legal practice?

I would prefer to explore the relationship between legal philosophy and *law as a set of social practices* – a broader idea than legal practice, though one which incorporates the practice of law as one important aspect of the phenomena under consideration.

As I have already argued, all legal philosophy – with the possible exception of some wildly utopian, purely prescriptive project setting up a blueprint for some entirely new kind of law or legal arrangement – is engaged in theorizing social phenomena which have a 'real' existence, and to the contours of which the philosophical account is hence in some sense answerable. I have also argued that legal philosophers have to be concerned not just with 'law' in a conceptual or doctrinal sense, but in the sense of a dynamic social practice which is interpreted and enforced, with decisive effects on individuals, groups and the social order. Some concerns of legal philosophy are of particular relevance to legal practice. Perhaps the most obvious examples would be theories of legal reasoning, accounts of legal professional ethics and constitutional theories exploring the responsibilities of judges. It would hardly be human for a legal philosopher to be uninterested in whether his or her work has an impact, as for example when an appellate judge picks up on an argument about the best interpretation of a legal concept such as causation. And it surely goes without saying that legal philosophers have a general responsibility – like all scholars – to think about the effect of their work, on practices generally and not merely on legal practice. But the primary concern of scholars, legal philosophers among them, should be the intellectual quality of their ideas and arguments rather than their impact or reception.

To which problem, issue or broad area of legal philosophy would you most like to see more attention paid in the future?

My answer to this is sufficiently indicated by my answers to the second and third questions. I look forward to reading, and contributing to, further debates both about the second-order question of the relative contributions of philosophy and the social sciences to our systematic and theoretical understanding of law, and 'applied jurisprudence' drawing on the disciplinary resources of history and the social sciences alongside philosophy. As I have argued elsewhere, I regard these genres of work as making good on H.L.A. Hart's aspiration to contribute to both 'analytical jurisprudence' and 'descriptive sociology'. Unlike many legal philosophers, I regard this aspiration as a key insight rather than an unfortunate mistake on Hart's part.

It is perhaps appropriate also to say something about the style of the work which I should like to see in the field. As a teacher of jurisprudence, it distresses me that much of the contemporary scholarship is both so complex and abstract and so strongly concerned with debates internal to particular sectors of the discipline. I aspire to teach jurisprudence as a living subject: as a continuing debate, rather than a history of ideas. But I do not feel that I can recommend to students books and articles which I can scarcely make sense of myself. I do not mean this as merely a snide swipe at unidentified scholars: I would include some of my own work within the criticism. Given the 'interview' framework of this essay, it is perhaps appropriate to conclude with an autobiographical anecdote. Soon after the publication of my feminist theory essays, a distinguished judge and scholar told me, regretfully, that he had felt unable to review the book because he found it too difficult to read. I was deeply affected by this, and much influenced by it in my approach to the Hart biography. On (painful!) reflection, I felt that my feminist theory book could have been written more simply without loss of substance; and I questioned the justification for

writing something which was intelligible only to a relatively small
côterie of fellow professionals.[24] For these reasons, I would very
much welcome a return to the readable and relatively economical
style exemplified by Hart's work, and which his work shows us to
be entirely compatible with real intellectual sophistication.

Principal Publications

Books

A Life of H.L.A. Hart: The Nightmare and the Noble Dream (Oxford University Press 2004): winner of the Swiney Prize and shortlisted for the James Tait Black Prize for biography and for the British Academy Book Prize.

Regulating Law (edited by Christine Parker, Colin Scott, Nicola Lacey and John Braithwaite: collection including introduction co-authored with the other editors and a single-authored article) (Oxford University Press 2004).

with Celia Wells and Oliver Quick, *Reconstructing Criminal Law: Critical Perspectives on Crime and the Criminal Process* (third edition, Cambridge University Press 2003) (Law in Context Series: first edition 1990: second edition 1998).

Unspeakable Subjects: Feminist Essays in Legal and Social Theory (Hart Publishing 1998).

with Elizabeth Frazer, *The Politics of Community: A Feminist Analysis of the Liberal-Communitarian Debate* (Harvester Wheatsheaf/University of Toronto Press 1993).

State Punishment: Political Principles and Community Values, (Routledge 1988).

Criminal Justice: A Reader, (Oxford University Press 1994) (edited collection: original introduction, pp. 1–36).

Articles

'Analytical Jurisprudence versus Descriptive Sociology Revisited' 84 *Texas Law Review* (March 2006) 945–982.

---

[24] This is not to say, of course, that technical (and hence inaccessible) vocabularies are never justified. Sometimes – as in the case of formal logic – they are indispensable. Their currency in contemporary legal philosophy in my view however oversteps any reasonable conception of their necessity.

'Feminist Legal Theories and the Rights of Women', in Karen Knop (ed.), *Gender and Human Rights* (Oxford University Press 2004) pp. 13–56.

'Partial Defences to Homicide' in Andrew Ashworth and Barry Mitchell (eds.) *Rethinking English Homicide Law* (Oxford University Press 2000) pp. 107–131.

'In Search of the Responsible Subject: History, Philosophy and Criminal Law Theory' 64 *Modern Law Review* (2001) 350–371.

'Responsibility and Modernity in Criminal Law' 9 *Journal of Political Philosophy* (2001) 249–277.

'Philosophical Foundations of the Common Law: Social Not Metaphysical' in Jeremy Horder (ed.) *Oxford Essays in Jurisprudence* (4th series) (Oxford University Press 2000) pp. 17–39.

'Bentham as proto-feminist?' (1998) *Current Legal Problems* 441–466.

with Lucia Zedner, 'Community in German Criminal Justice: A Significant Absence', 7 *Social and Legal Studies*, 1998 7–28.

with Lucia Zedner, 'Discourses of Community in Criminal Justice' (1995) *Journal of Law and Society* 93–113.

'Government as Manager, Citizen as Consumer', (1994) 57 *Modern Law Review* 534–54.

'A Clear Concept of Intention: Elusive or Illusory?', (1993) 56 *Modern Law Review* 621–642.

11
Brian Leiter

Hines H. Baker & Thelma Kelley Baker Chair and Director of the Law & Philosophy Program
The University of Texas at Austin, USA

Why were you initially drawn to the philosophy of law?

The explanation for my *initial* interest in philosophy of law is rather mundane and somewhat accidental. I had gone to college in 1980 with an interest in being a lawyer, motivated in large part by my political sympathies. These were formed, it is important to recall, in the late 1970s in America, before the election of the reactionary Ronald Reagan and the extraordinary rightward turn in U.S. political life: so one might have thought at that time that human progress could be achieved through law. In high school, I was particularly taken with the story of the remarkable American labor and civil rights leader A. Philip Randolph, and so lawyering (though Randolph himself was not a lawyer) seemed like a way in which to advocate effectively for important social, political, and economic causes. At the same time, I went to university at Princeton with an interest in philosophy, an interest that had grown out of high school study of Sartre. The only philosopher I knew of at Princeton at that time was Walter Kaufmann, who, sadly, died before my first year! But the study of philosophy gripped me nonetheless. In April of 1982, I discovered Nietzsche, in a course with Richard Rorty (it was his last term at Princeton). This made a deep impression on me (though I later came to think Rorty's particular view of Nietzsche totally wrong-headed). By the time I was ready to graduate, the choice between pursuing a law degree (law being a post-graduate degree in America) or a doctorate in philosophy now seemed stark. Being a person of a risk-averse temperament, I decided to apply for both—after all, a law degree guaranteed a job, while a philosophy degree did not—and was accepted to both programs at the University of Michigan at Ann Arbor.

The first year of law school I found quite uninspiring. I had a couple of intellectually serious and engaging teachers—James Krier (in property law) and James J. White (in contracts) stand out—but the others were quite feeble as pedagogues and sometimes as intellects. But having committed to law study, I naturally thought to engage points of intersection between law and philosophy. A course by Frederick Schauer on "Legal Realism and Critical Legal Studies" was quite important in shaping my interests. In the Realists, I found the jurisprudential analogues, as it were, of Nietzsche: thinkers who were sceptical, irreverent about the "received wisdom," who had no patience for moralistic nonsense, and who were ready to report unpleasant truths. In the final years of law school, I wrote a series of papers – for seminars and independent studies – on various aspects of Legal Realism and the jurisprudential issues about the indeterminacy of legal reasoning it raised. These papers constituted, as I like to say, my "second dissertation" (the *actual* one being on Nietzsche's moral philosophy, written under the primary supervision of the moral philosopher Peter Railton). Through the American Legal Realists, but mediated by a general philosophical education, I first found my way into problems in the philosophy of law.

For which of your contribution(s) to legal philosophy so far would you most like to be remembered, and why?

First, I hope I have redeemed "Realist jurisprudence" as a serious topic for philosophically-informed thinking about law. The Realists were lawyers, not philosophers, but unlike many of the philosophers, they understood how judges and courts actually work. I have tried to supply some recognizable philosophical motivations for their perspective on law and courts, and, at the same time, offer a rigorous reconstruction of their distinctive theses. We ought to think sympathetically about what the Realists were doing and what they have to teach us, and we ought to notice that Hart and other "mainstream" jurisprudents who critiqued them did not really understand their opponents.

Second, I hope I have made legal philosophy more self-conscious about its methodology. Because I came to philosophy of law partly by (happy) accident, as well as from the standpoint of broadly "naturalistic" sympathies in philosophy, I have tried to force philosophers of law to be self-conscious about their armchair method and, in particular, about the costs of solving problems about the nature of X – whether it be law or anything else – by reference to the intuitive judgments of a wildly non-selective group of respondents. In most areas of philosophy, this worry has come to the fore in recent decades, though not legal philosophy, perhaps because of the unusually insular network of jurisprudents who have been thought to count. I may not be right about the upshot of the skepticism about the methodology of legal philosophy, but I hope its methodological innocence will now be a thing of the past.

What are the most important issues in legal philosophy, and why are they distinctively issues of legal philosophy rather than some other discipline?

What *had* been the most important issue in general jurisprudence for fifty years or more – namely, what demarcates legal norms from other norms common in human societies – was dealt with powerfully by H.L.A. Hart (who drew on, but correctly amended, Hans Kelsen's account) and then his student Joseph Raz. Positivism is now fairly clearly the *default* position with respect to the "demarcation problem," even for most serious natural law theorists, like John Finnis. Why this is distinctively a problem of legal philosophy is clear enough.

There are problems of what is often denominated "specific jurisprudence" – namely, investigations into the philosophical foundations of the various substantive law fields (for example, criminal law, torts, and contracts) – that also seem to be distinctively problems of legal philosophy. I must confess that these distinctive topics have always struck me as rather odd, involving, as they do, attempts to provide conceptual rationalizations for bodies of doctrine arising over long periods of time and in response to diffuse economic and political interests. It would be extraordinary if these doctrines had much conceptual coherence, and, of course, it turns out they do not. To the extent special jurisprudence connects up, though, with law reform efforts it no doubt has a point.

Beyond these two broad rubrics of general and special jurisprudence, I do not think there are "distinctive" problems of legal philosophy, nor do I think that the distinctive ones are necessarily the most interesting ones any longer. Law has so many similarities with other systems of normative guidance, both in its theoretical character (e.g., in purporting to provide reasons for action and impose obligations; in its reliance on familiar patterns of practical reasoning; in its dependence on normative concepts like responsibility, guilt and blame; and in its concern with questions about proof and truth) and its institutional context (e.g., in utilizing organized coercion and hierarchies of official decision-making) that it would be astonishing if philosophical reflection on law did not intersect at multiple levels with questions of moral and political philosophy, semantics, metaphysics, epistemology, and decision theory. Beyond that, of course, the naturalistic turn in philosophy – the recognition of the extent to which philosophical problems turn on empirical facts in the sciences – means that we should also expect the theoretical and institutional features apparently distinctive of legal systems of normative guidance and control will fall within the scope of psychological and sociological inquiry as well. Intellectual specialization, a consequence of the rise and proliferation of research universities, especially in the advanced capitalist societies, means that there will likely be institutional incentives for students and theorists of the demaracation problem, and its progeny, for many years to come. But this same economically driven development may also create conditions under which the idea of "distinctive" problems of legal philosophy will seem antiquated.

What is the relationship between legal philosophy and legal practice? Should legal philosophers be more concerned about the effect of their scholarship on legal practice?

Most philosophical inquiry aims at truth and understanding, not effect on practice, and it is not obvious why legal philosophy should be any different. Even if one embraces a Marxian dictum about philosophy to the effect that all questions that do not affect practice are merely "scholastic"—that would consign, e.g., most of armchair metaphysics, blessedly, to the trash bin—I still don't see any reason why *legal* philosophy bears a special burden on this score. Moral philosophy is almost wholly irrelevant to how people conduct their lives and philosophy of science has no effect on scientific practice (indeed, most scientists are notorious for their indifference to and contempt for philosophical reflection on their endeavors). If legal philosophy, alone among the branches of philosophy, is supposed to affect the practice about which it philosophizes, then a special reason will need to be supplied.

Now it might be said that, at least in the United States, professional postgraduate schools of law often support the study of legal philosophy, and, given their mission, they are entitled to expect legal philosophy to affect practice. The comparison with medical schools is instructive, since the one branch of philosophy they often support, namely bioethics, is offered precisely because of its purported relevance to clinical practice. So here, it might seem, is an institutional reason that legal philosophy, at least insofar as professional faculties support its study, ought to affect practice.

But this observation simply forces us to get clear about what is meant by "affecting practice." Most legal scholarship in the United States—from jurisprudence to the economic analysis of law to constitutional theory–does not, in fact, affect practice, in the sense of influencing directly how lawyers advise clients or courts decide cases or legislatures draft statutes. But another way of affecting practice is, of course, by affecting the mindset or outlook or intellectual repertoire of the practitioners, and here legal philosophy offers as much, if not more, than most other branches of modern legal scholarship. Indeed, given its traditional emphasis on clarity, analytical rigor, and making explicit conceptual and normative presuppositions, legal philosophy is – at least in my experience – among the more "practical" offerings in the curriculum. (A student of contemporary constitutional theory in the United States, for example, would not come away thinking that it teaches analytical or argumentative rigor.) Certainly when the field of jurisprudence is construed naturalistically–so that, e.g., Realist claims about what courts *really* do are a central topic of inquiry–then the practical benefit for lawyers-in-training is clear.

To which problem, issue or broad area of legal philosophy would you most like to see more attention paid in the future?

General jurisprudence strikes me as being, at present, a slightly moribund field. This is partly because Hart and Raz offered plausible answers, given their methodological tools, to some of the main problems (as discussed earlier), and partly because Ronald Dworkin has so disfigured honest intellectual inquiry in the field through his repeated misrepresentations of the views of legal positivists and his endless promulgation of confusing and often pointless new distinctions and categories with little regard for how they map on to existing debates or positions in those debates. (There is still work to be done clearing the debris from Dworkin's interventions, though I imagine within the next ten or twenty years we will be done—but clearing debris is not the same as advancing understanding). Still, general jurisprudence, within the powerful framework bequeathed us by Hart and Raz, presents some topics that demand further scrutiny, for example, about the nature of rules and the normative force and status of conventional rules. Hart taught us that you can not explain the social phenomenon of law without recourse to the idea of a "rule," and perhaps we shall have to treat "rules" as explanatorily primitive, but it is still too soon to draw that conclusion. Natural law theorists have always put pressure on the idea of "legal obligation" as distinct from moral obligation, and Hart, himself, as we learned from Nicola Lacey's biography, was uneasy about how to understand the former. Yet we do have the notion of conventional obligations – those playing chess have an obligation to move bishops only diagonally – but we do not have a satisfying account of conventional obligations and whether they are explanatorily adequate to the notion of obligation in law.

Outside general jurisprudence within the tradition set by Hart and Raz – or perhaps supplementing that tradition – there are a variety of topics and problems that warrant attention. In no particular order, here are a few that I think worthy of more scholarly attention:

(1) Scandinavian Realism deserves a sympathetic reconsideration, along the lines of what I have tried to do for its (distant!) American cousin. It is true that the Scandinavians suffer from the vice of being motivated almost exclusively by logical positivist doctrines in semantics, epistemology, and ontology, doctrines which are largely moribund (for good reasons) in philosophy. Yet the general naturalistic conception of the world that animated their theoretical writings is *not* moribund, and the question of how to accommodate norms within such a world view is very much a live one. Perhaps the Scandinavians still have something to teach us? Certainly they have not yet received sympathetic scrutiny within Anglophone jurisprudence.

(2) The rise of "experimental philosophy" – which integrates the methods of empirical psychology into philosophical inquiry – ought to change the practice of legal philosophy. Oxonian claims about ordinary intuitions about the concepts of law, authority, and obligation should be made to answer to empirical evidence about these intuitions. And to the extent these intuitions vary along demographic dimensions – e.g., ethnicity, class, nationality, perhaps even gender – general jurisprudence will have to undertake a kind of meta-philosophical reflection to which it has been

unaccustomed. It may turn out, to be sure, that Hart's intuitions about what the ordinary person knew about the modern municipal legal system were spot on. But if intuitions about the concepts pertaining to law turn out – like the concepts pertaining to epistemic justification or moral wrongness – to be hostage to economic and social variables, then legal philosophy will have to explain why its results *matter*. These issues are intimately connected with the general question of whether or not the concept of law is a hermeneutic concept, that is, one whose extension is fixed by how people use it to make sense of themselves and their practices. If the concept of law is, as both Hart and Raz appear to think, a hermeneutic concept, and if it turns out to be sensitive to economic and social variables, then general jurisprudence will turn out to be a kind of *particular* jurisprudence–though in a way quite different from the way in which Hart, correctly, diagnosed Dworkin's theory as an instance of particular jurisprudence. But this specter only looms over general jurisprudence as currently practiced because of its allegiance to a method – analyses of the extension of concepts by reference to intuitions about possible cases – that may be inapt for its subject. Social scientific theories of law are, as things stand, not epistemically robust or impressive in their results, but perhaps the metaphysical and epistemological principle that only the causally efficiacious is real and knowable should still trump the hermeneutic understanding of the concept of law? This will demand that general jurisprudence engage with broader issues in the philosophy of the natural and social sciences to a greater extent than heretofore.

(3) "Ought implies can" is a plausible constraint on theorizing in both ethics and epistemology, but it deserves more consideration than it has received to date in general jurisprudence, especially the theory of adjudication. Jerome Frank, the most extreme and often least sensible of the American Legal Realists, claimed that we can only understand how judges think by understanding what he took to be a brute psychological fact about human decision-making, namely, that it starts with hunches about outcomes and then works backwards to reasons. Our understanding of the psychology of decisions and reasoning has increased substantially since the time of Frank, yet none of it plays any role in the best-known theories of adjudication and judicial reasoning. That would be fine if we are willing to renounce "ought implies can," but not otherwise. To be sure, there will be political motivations for resisting this incursion of psychology into the theory of

adjudication, given the popular myth about the autonomy of legal reasoning and the "rule of law, not men." But cynical political considerations provide no excuse for scholars, so jurisprudence will have to answer to psychology if it deserves to be taken seriously in the decades ahead.

(4) Legal philosophy in the last hundred years has always been the beneficiary (or victim!) of general philosophical developments. Scandinavian Realism was the jurisprudential handmaiden of logical positivism, Kelsen's theory of law has the imprint of German NeoKantianism all over it, and Hart brought J.L. Austin's ordinary language philosophy (and some soft Wittgensteinianism) to philosophy of law in the 1950s and 1960s. The naturalistic revolution in late 20th-century Anglophone philosophy is making some inroads into legal philosophy, but the most significant problems of the future will no doubt be forged in the smithy of more general philosophical developments. When I think about the creative intellectual giants who have contributed the most to theorizing about systems of normative power over the last two hundred years, three stand out for their profundity: Marx, Nietzsche, and Freud. I have argued for their continuing importance as part of a general naturalistic turn in normative theory, one that ought to encompass legal theory as well. That means legal philosophers ought to be thinking about the psychology of morality and agency; the role of economic interests in both substantive law and its theoretical articulation; the constraints that human nature imposes upon law and legal regulation; and perhaps, most importantly, what the fundamental pretense of human beings to *rational* behavior conjoined with their equally fundamental irrationality means for all systems of normative governance, legal or otherwise.

Selected Bibliography

Books

Naturalizing Jurisprudence: Essays on American Legal Realism and Naturalism in Legal Philosophy (Oxford: Oxford University Press, 2007).

Nietzsche on Morality (London: Routledge, 2002). (Ed.).

Objectivity in Law and Morals (Cambridge: Cambridge University Press, 2001).

Articles (not reprinted in any of the above books)

"The Case for Nietzschean Moral Psychology," in *Nietzsche and Morality*, ed. B. Leiter & N. Sinhababu (Oxford: Oxford University Press, 2007) (with Joshua Knobe).

"Determinacy, Objectivity, and Authority," *University of Pennsylvania Law Review* 142 (1993): 549–637; also in *Law and Interpretation*, ed. A. Marmor (Oxford: Oxford University Press, 1995) (with Jules Coleman).

"The End of Empire: Dworkin and Jurisprudence in the 21st Century," *Rutgers Law Journal* 35 (2005): 165–181.

"The Hermeneutics of Suspicion: Recovering Marx, Nietzsche, and Freud," in *The Future for Philosophy*, ed. B. Leiter (Oxford: Clarendon Press, 2004).

"Naturalism and Naturalized Jurisprudence," in *Analyzing Law: New Essays in Legal Theory*, ed. B. Bix (Oxford: Oxford University Press, 1998).

"Naturalized Epistemology and the Law of Evidence," *Virginia Law Review* 86 (2001): 1491–1550 (with Ronald J. Allen).

A number of articles are also available on-line for free download at:

> http://papers.ssrn.com/sol3/cf_dev/
> AbsByAuth.cfm?per_id=119223

12
David Lyons

Professor of Philosophy and Professor of Law, Boston University, USA

Susan Linn Sage Professor of Philosophy Emeritus and Professor of Law Emeritus, Cornell University, USA[1]

From Politics to Philosophy

Politics led me to philosophy. Not the conventional politics of the two big American political parties but street-level agitation for peace and civil rights during the decade following World War II. The government actively discouraged our activities. Unlike the measures it employed against dissidents like us, our actions were non-coercive, lawful, and public. As my political orientation and experiences have greatly influenced the choice and content of my philosophical projects, I shall interweave the personal narrative with the philosophical account and will include more detail than might be expected for purely academic purposes. Besides, the political background is not likely to be familiar to my readers and may be more interesting than the philosophical story.

My earliest political memory is of an experience in the early 1940s, when I was about seven. A friend came to school with traces of knife strokes on his face. That they bore the shape of a swastika was no coincidence, for anti-Semitism infected our divided Brooklyn neighborhood. The hatreds were mutual. Contempt for "gentiles" was commonplace on our side of the line.

Our public elementary school, situated on the neighborhood's fault line, reflected the social division, but its policies were not even-handed. In school assemblies, for example, we celebrated only Christian holidays. I declined to participate in singing Christmas

---

[1]I am grateful to Aaron Garrett, Matthew Lyons, and Sandra Lyons for comments on earlier drafts.

carols – though that minor bit of passive resistance was probably not noticed.

My critical faculties were sharpened in an experimental class that occupied the last four years of elementary school. Our teachers led us into research projects and engaged us in critical analysis. We took apart advertising and political propaganda. Newspapers provided ample material, as a Red Scare was under way – the one that was later called McCarthyism.

By the time we entered high school, a close friend and I had become active in a left-wing youth organization – the Young Progressives of America, which was the youth branch of the Progressive Party of the late 1940s and early 1950s. Given the government's repressive measures, we assumed that our telephone conversations were not private. There was too much of a risk (later amply confirmed) that our conversations would be overheard by illicit, though official, eavesdroppers. So we omitted identifying references to persons and places.

In high school, I became one of the "usual suspects." On one occasion my friend and I were suspended following the distribution of political leaflets near the school. We were summoned from class to see the Assistant Principal, who held us in his office for hours while he grilled us about our politics and our parents' choice of publications. It was assumed that we had helped distribute the leaflets, although in fact we had nothing to do with that particular action.

In that political climate, I chose to study engineering in college, partly because of its political neutrality. By then I had become active in the Labor Youth League, which was the functional equivalent of a Young Communist League. Preoccupied with politics, after two years I dropped out of college. A friend suggested a machine shop where I might find suitable work. He advised me not to give his name as a reference, as he had earlier tried to unionize the workers.

It was a small shop, in which a handful of machinists produced specialized equipment that required careful, close-tolerance work. The crew was cheerful and friendly. Seeing my aptitude, they taught me not only how to operate the various machine tools but how to "set them up" to meet the product specifications and how to grind tool bits for differing materials and applications. I quickly became a capable machinist.

A few months later, another friend told me of an apprenticeship that was open next to his workbench in a tool-and-die shop within a large factory. I was soon working with another group of friendly, skilled workers, who were responsible for creating and adapting the machines that were used in the manufacturing process. They too were happy to train a newcomer. I refurbished machine tools in our shop and made emergency repairs on the production lines in the larger factory.

The work was good, but the wages were low. This became significant another few months later, when my wife-to-be and I decided to get married. I sought a job that would support us both. A third political friend helped me find one in a factory that employed him as a pipe fitter.

The work was mainly on thick-walled high pressure pipes that had to be bent to precise angles, often in three dimensions, for installation in power plants abroad. Although it involved working with lengths of pipe that weighed three thousand pounds, the bending process was an art. At crucial stages, the pipe fabricating process required skilled machine tool work, and the company's increasing production orders could no longer be met by the shop's one machinist. So my friend told the foreman of my background, and before long I was once again working as a machinist, sometimes directing a crew.

I worked in that shop for more than a year, along with experienced welders and boilermakers who introduced me to their crafts. The shop was integrated, the workers comprising an ethnic rainbow, which was most unusual at the time, especially in the plumbers' union, to which we were affiliated. Although the work we did was exceptionally technical and difficult for the industry, the shop was subject to discrimination by the union.

During this time, the Old Left was in crisis, the result of governmental harassment as well as disillusioning revelations about the American Left and the Soviet Union. Without regretting the path we had taken and without abandoning our political ideals, my wife and I dropped out of organized political activity. Reading more widely – especially in contemporary Marxist theory, philosophy of education and philosophy of science – I came to think that in the long run I would prefer work that used more of my mental skills. I valued and enjoyed the work that I was doing – the camaraderie no less than the machine tool work – but I decided to change directions.

Lack of financial resources and ignorance of the possibilities limited what seemed feasible. I was aware, however, that fine, tuition-free colleges were accessible – the engineering school I had left and New York City's public municipal colleges.[2] Thinking that a workable plan was to complete my engineering degree and seek a teaching career in that field, I returned to those studies. This time, however, I took evening classes, so that I could continue working full-time while my wife completed her studies. My job was physically demanding and involved much overtime, which were incompatible with studying at night. With a reference from my older brother, I was able to secure work as a draftsman in the engineering department of a large sugar refinery.

It was a marvelous arrangement. Armed with measuring tape, pad, and pencil, I would go into the refinery when changes were needed. After studying the situation, I'd return to my drafting desk to draw up a proposal. My engineering supervisor had me design as well as draw. It was sobering to realize that a real structure, filled with heavy machinery, based on my calculations, built from my plans, would arise nearby: this was not merely a problem set for a class. I held that job for two years, until I returned to college full-time during my wife's last year of graduate school.

After my thermodynamics class one evening, the instructor took me aside to urge me to move into a field that was more theoretical than mechanical engineering. His advice fitted my evolving interests. I thought at first of physics, which seemed a reasonable move from engineering. When I finally recognized what issues in my recent reading sparked my interest, however, I moved all the way to philosophy.

During all of this time, the FBI made sure that political activists knew that they were continuing to monitor us. Even after I had dropped out of regular political activity, FBI agents would come to my workplace, seeking information from me about others, issuing threats when I declined to cooperate. Agents would visit my employers, presumably to make good on their threats.

One personal confrontation was, for a change, more amusing than intimidating – at least in retrospect. When I declined once again to cooperate with their inquiries, one of the agents said angrily that I would never be able to get work as an engineer. They knew that I was back in engineering school. But they did not yet know that I had decided to switch from engineering to philosophy.

---

[2] The Cooper Union School of Engineering, while private, provided free tuition to its students, as did the municipal colleges New York City at the time.

At a later point I thought they might make good on their threats. This part of the story begins in 1957, when the U.S. was still drafting men into its standing army. After a lengthy and intimidating process, the U.S. Army formally determined that, for political reasons, I was unfit to serve in the military. I had mixed reactions to that outcome. I did not wish to participate in American military interventions abroad. I also knew that I took more seriously than my government did the ideals of American democracy that had been so strongly emphasized as I was growing up during the war against fascism.

This story continues: After I entered graduate school three years later, the FBI continued in various ways to let me know that I remained a target of their attention. When I had all but completed my doctoral studies, my mentors offered to nominate me for a traveling fellowship. I hesitated to accept the nomination, partly because I was unsure the U.S. government would issue me a passport.[3] I had been a prominent activist and had been disparaged officially by the Army. When I explained the predicament, my dissertation supervisor (John Rawls) assured me of university support. My wife and I decided that I should accept the nomination. In due course I was awarded the fellowship, and the government issued the passport – perhaps because by then (1963) it had turned most of its attention away from the Old Left in order to concentrate on harassing activists in the civil rights movement.

In graduate school I was drawn to moral philosophy,[4] for I discerned a tendency in the utilitarian literature to favor socially conventional rules. (I'll explain that in a moment.) That perception was enough to engage my dissident inclinations: I determined to counter any academic bias towards social conformism. But utilitarian theories varied along several dimensions. One day, while trying to think about them systematically, I sketched a dialogue between two differing theories, which I personified for the purpose. When pressed to explain how they evaluated conduct, their judgments seemed unavoidably to converge. This led to the conclusion that competing versions of utilitarianism are "extensionally

---

[3] As we were expecting our first child, I was also hesitant to turn down the attractive job offers I had received, which would be necessary if I allowed myself to be nominated.

[4] My account will include work in moral and political as well as legal philosophy because they are central to my story and, in any case, legal philosophy is often understood broadly enough to encompass the issues on which I have worked.

equivalent": when applied rigorously, they come to the same exact evaluations of individual actions. The argument fully supporting that thesis was complex and had to be developed carefully. The result, drafted in two weeks of intensive work, was my doctoral dissertation. My attempt simply to understand the theories led unexpectedly to my project becoming relatively abstract, far removed from my counter-conformist concerns.

Now to explain. Utilitarian theories evaluate conduct relative to the promotion of welfare[5] but differ in the way they do so. "Act utilitarianism," for example, holds that an act is morally permissible if, and only if, it promotes welfare at least as much as any alternative course of action. That theory had generally been regarded by theorists as the standard version of utilitarianism. Critics cited examples to show that the theory conflicted with our most reflective moral judgments by failing to take adequate account of our moral obligations, such as those that flow from promises and special relations. Some utilitarian theorists, sensitive to these examples, constructed utilitarian theories to withstand such criticism, e.g., by providing a utilitarian account of moral obligations. "Rule utilitarian" theories judge conduct by social rules that are believed to promote welfare and impose obligations. (The rule utilitarian theories that originally attracted my critical attention hold that rules of conventional morality promote welfare better than alternatives.) Other theories judge conduct by asking questions like "What if everyone did that?" The extensional equivalence argument holds that seemingly different utilitarian theories come to the same practical conclusions in their evaluations of conduct. More generally, such variations on utilitarianism could not solve its assumed problems, and some made them worse.

The following year, supported by the traveling fellowship, my wife, our infant son, and I lived in Oxford. My examining committee had urged me to turn the dissertation into a book. With further encouragement from my Oxford supervisor (Herbert Hart), I

---

[5] The extensional equivalence argument is actually broader, applying not just to utilitarian theories but to "consequentialist" theories generally – theories which may embrace basic values in addition to or other than welfare. The extensional equivalence argument compares analogous theories, with identical theories of the good.. It concerns only the ways in which those values are applied, that is, whether it makes any difference to evaluate acts individually, as members of sets of similar acts, or as required by useful rules. I refer to utilitarian theories in the text because that terminology is more widely familiar..

pursued the project, which lasted the entire year. I developed the argument in much greater detail, until I felt that I could do no more. At Hart's invitation, I left the manuscript with the Clarendon Press.

My concerns about the extensional equivalence argument did not match those of its subsequent critics. I was unsure, for example, that it was legitimate to employ, as the argument demanded, descriptions of actions that were based entirely on the distinct concerns of the respective theories rather than descriptions that we would ordinarily use. That was an issue no critic mentioned.

The comment I found most worrisome was that I should have ascribed consequences to actions on a "marginal" rather than a "contributory" basis. In my argument I asked, in effect, how much of the difference an action helps make to the promotion of welfare is attributable to the act itself rather than to other contributing factors, such as the actions of other persons. My critic suggested that I should simply have asked what difference the act itself makes to welfare promotion, *given* the surrounding conditions. On reflection, I came to recognize that I often reasoned as the critic urged. Many years later I persuaded myself that the extensional equivalence argument works equally well when acts are judged on either basis – but I never confirmed that comforting thought with a fully-developed written argument.

The extensional equivalence argument may have influenced the development of utilitarian theory. I had the impression that it diverted interest from rule utilitarianism back to act utilitarianism. As the latter theory seemed to me at odds with sensitive moral judgment, I did not welcome that result. At any rate, the argument did not discourage the further development of utilitarianism in various configurations. Utilitarians are not easily discouraged.[6]

The most important contribution of the extensional equivalence argument may have been the example it sometimes seems to have set in attempting to reason rigorously about normative ethical theory. Theorizing about utilitarianism, for and against, often involves unsupported claims about the consequences of actions. The extensional equivalence argument does not rely on any such estimates. It aspired to, and suggested the possibility of, tight reasoning, even about a theory whose implications depend on contingent

---

[6] The same seems true of many philosophers who embrace general theories about right and wrong. They seem much more confident than I could imagine being about such matters.

facts.

When we returned to the U.S. from our year in Oxford, the immigration agent took some time consulting his books while processing my passport. I assumed then, and in similar situations later, that my name had triggered a search. The result, however, was only a brief delay, with an impatient toddler.

Upon our return we moved to Ithaca, New York, the home of Cornell University. Early on it appeared that I had been identified within the university administration as one of the "usual suspects." (Had the FBI already come to call?) In the spring of 1965, during my first year at Cornell, I was one of a small group of faculty members asked by a high university official for advice concerning a student protest which was expected that evening when Averill Harriman (then U.S. ambassador without portfolio) was to give a speech on campus. It was assumed that Harriman would defend widening American military interventions abroad – in Southeast Asia, where it was supporting a corrupt and unpopular government, and in the Caribbean, where it had just sent Marines into the Dominican Republic to insure that its government would be acceptable to ours.

It was agreed that Harriman should give a brief talk instead of his prepared speech and then respond to questions from the audience. In the event, the audience was well behaved but Harriman wasn't. He responded to students who questioned U.S. military interventions by suggesting that they were "communists." His stupid and intemperate response outraged the audience, and he hastily departed. The students thereupon decided to occupy the university meeting hall in symbolic protest. A clever faculty colleague prevented potential problems by securing permission from the university administration for the students to stay there overnight – provided that we two served as faculty chaperones! And so began my political career at Cornell.

Over the years, I would be drawn from time to time into campus developments that reflected the more troubled world outside. In the spring of 1969, for example, I helped pull together a tiny group of faculty members who urged the university faculty to change its mind and listen to African American students whose grievances had led them briefly to occupy a university building. When we feared that faculty intransigence would result in the occupation of another building by black students, outside police brought to campus, and the shedding of blood, we offered to put ourselves in the potential line of fire: if they occupied a building, we would go along to reduce the likelihood of an armed police attack. Fortunately for all, the vast majority of Cornell students agreed that the faculty should listen to the black students' grievances, the faculty reconsidered its position, and violence was averted.

Another crisis developed in 1985, when students remained in the university's central administration building after it closed for the day, as part of the international campaign to seek divestment from companies doing business with South Africa, so as to put pressure on the South African apartheid government to accept major reforms. The small initial contingent of students committing this most decorous form of civil disobedience was thereafter joined each day by hundreds of other Cornellians. Within a week the campus police had made twelve hundred arrests. As I was on sabbatic leave for the academic year and thus had more free time than most other faculty members, I assumed a good deal of responsibility for working with student and staff organizers. The campaign was long and frustrating. The university president and the board of trustees were anxious to defend a benefactor to the university whose company was heavily invested in South Africa.

For a variety of reasons, my philosophical work expanded into legal and political theory. My last graduate school seminar had devoted half the semester to Hart's recently published *The Concept of Law*. In Oxford the following year I attended Hart's lectures and seminars, among others. Shortly after joining the Cornell philosophy department, a senior colleague suggested that I look into the topic of rights. I sought advice about readings on the subject and Hart's suggestions led me into the jurisprudential literature. When the department reformed its undergraduate offerings, I created a course on the philosophy of law. I taught seminars on topics such as punishment. In 1969 a new member of the law faculty asked me to help him introduce analytical jurisprudence to the law school, and I co-taught his seminar on legal theory. I was soon invited to teach my own courses in that school and in 1979 to join its faculty. And so I came to divide my teaching and research between the two academic units, philosophy and law.

An early research project that bridged the two fields was on Bentham. Agreeing to contribute a volume on Bentham to a new series, I taught a seminar on some of his principal works, and found myself puzzling over his explanation of utilitarianism. Conventionally regarded as a creator of utilitarian theory, Bentham differed in his focus from most theorists who supposedly followed his lead. Save for John Stuart Mill, most utilitarian philosophers have seemed preoccupied with particular acts performed by individuals, whereas Bentham was chiefly concerned with law and other institutions. In his *Introduction to the Principles of Morals and Legislation*, however, Bentham distinguishes the two realms and offers distinct criteria for them: the community's interest for public policy and the agent's interest for private action. Only such a "dual" interpretation seems to take Bentham at his word. The publications in which I presented that reading may have encouraged others to look more closely at what Bentham actually wrote – which was a message that Hart was more forcefully conveying in his revelatory work in the new collection of Bentham's writings.

Around the time my Bentham project ended, John Rawls's *A Theory of Justice* appeared, which some appreciative reviewers declared meant the demise of utilitarianism. I was no champion of the condemned theory, but the history of ethics suggests that its obituary was premature. Rawls himself treats utilitarianism as the chief alternative to his conception of social justice.

Although Rawls compares his theory of justice with a version of utilitarianism, he does not consider the only significant theory of justice that had been developed by a utilitarian, namely, John Stuart Mill's. That theory has two stages. Mill first analyzes morality in terms of rules that determine moral obligations and, in the case of justice, moral rights as well. Then he argues that the rules are to be identified by means of a utilitarian test. The theory is presented sketchily, but my work on Bentham offered some clarifying clues. Mill criticized much in Bentham, but not Bentham's conception of rules. That suggests how to explicate Mill's theories of justice and morality, in terms of useful rules with sanctions attached.

My Mill project asked, in effect, whether utilitarianism could ground a plausible theory of moral rights. Mill's theory might do so if his conceptual analysis of rights in terms of moral rules reasonably excludes the possibility of approving the violation of useful rules when welfare would be maximized by doing so. I argued that Mill does not justify such a theory of rights and, in any case, that such a view would be incompatible with a utilitarian's overriding commitment to promoting welfare. Generalizing from Mill's case, it looks as if any utilitarian approach to moral rights would be undermined by the compromises it must make with direct utilitarian reasoning. Of course, some utilitarians disagree; some do not care; and others have reconstructed Mill's theories differently.

Beyond Bentham, my work in legal theory has had two main parts: the "separation" of law and morals and the problem of legal interpretation.

In *The Concept of Law,* Hart seems to endorse the view "that there is no necessary connection between law and morals, or law as it is and law as it ought to be." As he would probably have agreed, that formulation of the separation thesis needs refinement. Some "necessary connections" are irrelevant to the thesis. On the one hand, Hart acknowledged that prevailing moral values interact with law, which means that there may be *causally* necessary connections between the two. On the other hand, it is sometimes suggested that those who presume to speak on behalf of the law characteristically claim that it does justice. Even if such a claim were a conceptually necessary feature of law, it would seem irrelevant to the separation thesis.

The central idea of the thesis seems to be expressed by the platitude that laws (in the ordinary, everyday sense) can be just or unjust, morally defensible or indefensible. Hart did not frame the separation thesis in this way, perhaps because he believed that a book like *The Concept of Law* should be neutral between skeptical and objectivist views of moral judgment. Hart suggested that laws lack conceptually necessary connections with any moral standards by which they *may* be judged. As a critic of skeptical conceptions of morality, I prefer to say that laws lack conceptually necessary connections with the standards by which they are *properly* judged.

One commonplace qualification of the separation thesis is implied by the idea that adherence to law constitutes a species of justice – "formal" justice. The idea seems to over-generalize a valid point: that injustice can be done not only by applying unjust law but also by officials failing to follow the law. While Hart seems to embrace the idea of formal justice, he also suggests how the valid point requires qualification; for he says that injustice occurs *when* official deviation from the law embodies "prejudice, interest, or caprice." So qualified, the valid point does not imply that an official acts unjustly when he refuses to follow an unjust law precisely in order to *prevent* an injustice. No injustice of any kind would have been done, for example, if a Nazi official deliberately refused to accept conclusive evidence that a particular person qualified for transport to an extermination camp.

A point related to the separation of law and morals is that the burden of proof falls on one who claims there is a moral obligation to obey the law. That is because a law's injustice generates a moral presumption *against* compliance with it. Theorists who embrace the idea that we have a moral obligation to obey the law generally recognize that the obligation does not exist in all circumstances and that, when it does exist, it might be overridden. So the idea is best understood as the claim that there *may* be good moral reason for all persons in a given community to comply with each and every one of its laws, the unjust as well as the just.

I argue that this idea requires further qualification. I see no reason to suppose, for example, that one could be morally required to participate in genocide or some other violation of a fundamental right. It is not that the moral obligation would be overridden in such a case but rather that a moral obligation could not normally extend so far.

These points apply to officials as well as to private persons. It seems possible for those who assume a public trust to acquire a special, more stringent moral obligation of fidelity to law. Such an obligation depends, however, on the circumstances of the case and the character of the law. If an individual is coerced into official service by a repressive regime, she may have no moral obligation to enforce the law. And some of the laws she is called upon to implement may involve systematic violations of fundamental rights. For such reasons, it is implausible to suppose that officials *always* have a moral obligation of fidelity to *all* of the laws that they are legally required to implement or enforce.

Now to legal interpretation: Soon after joining the Cornell law faculty I was urged by colleagues to venture into constitutional law because of its philosophical assumptions. That was an intriguing prospect for someone interested and experienced in political action that was dedicated to the realization of democratic principles. Embarking on the project, I quickly came to appreciate how atypical it had been for the U.S. courts, in the third quarter of twentieth century, to enforce our most prized constitutional rights. I learned how the Supreme Court's desegregation decision in *Brown v. Board of Education* had not been welcomed by a number of legal academics and had engendered a politically charged but theoretically confused field of constitutional theory.

Consider the theory that asks courts to follow "original intent" – a view I'll call intentionalism. When legislation and written constitutions must be applied, lawyers and theorists often seek guidance from the "intentions" of the lawmakers. I have argued that this theory, taken literally, is implausible. An individual lawmaker may support a statute intending it to have certain *applications* so that it might serve some intended *purpose*. But the lawmaker may be mistaken about what applications of the law would serve the desired end. If the law were applied as intended, it might undermine rather than serve the intended purpose, in which case intentionalism generates conflicting imperatives – to apply and not to apply the same law to the same fact-situation – which, of course, is guidance it is impossible to follow – and arguably self-contradictory. Also, when a legal change results from the actions of several persons, such as the members of a legislative assembly, sometimes no intention is shared widely enough within the group to justify ascribing an intention to the law makers or their enactment, in which case intentionalism implies, implausibly, that a perfectly intelligible law has *no* meaning or proper application!

In any other field, such consequences would discredit a theory. It is unclear, however, that my arguments have had any impact on theorists who work on the issue of legal interpretation.

One reason may be that those who employ intentionalist legal reasoning appeal indiscriminately to intended applications and intended purposes, without considering whether those intentions are in fact compatible or, indeed, whether any relevant intention was widely enough shared within the enacting body.

Another reason is that frequently the attribution of an intention to a set of law makers (or to the law they have enacted) seems tacitly to reflect a value judgment about the law: that it can readily be seen to serve a *reasonable* (and thus reasonably justifying) purpose. On the one hand, because the value judgment is uncontroversial, it is not identified as such. On the other hand, the (justifying) purpose is ascribed to the law without any evidence that there was an intentional consensus among its enactors. This practice is significant because some who embrace intentionalism insist that laws can be interpreted without exercising value judgment and should always be interpreted in a value-neutral manner. That claim and the accompanying aim are defeated when a purpose is ascribed to a law not on historical grounds but rather because the alleged "purpose" provides a justifying rationale for the law.

A related theory holds that the meaning of a law is determined not by the lawmakers' intentions but by the "original understanding" of what the law meant when it was enacted or ratified. As an original understanding can concern the law's purpose as well as its applications, this theory faces the difficulties that seem fatal to intentionalism. If the theory refers instead to an original understanding of the text, it will be incapable of helping if there had been no original consensus about the text's meaning or if the consensus does not determine how the law should apply to the unanticipated fact situation that must now be addressed.

Intentionalist and comparable theories focus entirely on written law, such as legislative enactments and written constitutions. They ignore some of the law in a "common law" system like ours – the part that is generated when courts provide authoritative interpretations of the law. Because judicial precedents contribute to our law, our system requires a more complex interpretive theory.

This gap was addressed in the 1980s when interpretive legal theory was revived by Ronald Dworkin.[7] Dworkin argues that interpreting law involves the exercise of moral judgment as well as the attribution of moral principles to the law. He grounds this view on a more general theory about the interpretation of social practices.

Dworkin's theory holds that past authoritative decisions – constitutional, legislative and judicial – should be understood in terms of those moral principles that show past practice in the best light, which involves *justifying* past decisions (as far as that is possible). This approach is by no means foreign to legal practice; examples are readily found in judicial opinions and scholarly writings. Dworkin does not claim, however, that judges or lawyers always reason in this way but rather that the approach is more defensible than the alternatives.

I have argued that Dworkin's theory cannot apply generally. The problem is that legal practice (like other social practices) is not always justifiable. Dworkin is aware, of course, that it may not be possible to justify all past authoritative decisions, and that some judicial precedents may reasonably be regarded as "mistakes." That is familiar judicial practice. But it does not solve the problem. Trouble arises not only when an entire legal system is morally corrupt, as some systems have seemed to be, but also when individual statutes or constitutional provisions are morally indefensible.[8] Dworkin's theory, which requires that statutes and constitutional provisions be interpreted so that they serve some truly justifying rationale, encounters the following predicament: first, we have no reason to assume that every statute or constitu-

---

[7] Dworkin's earlier work, in my view, was neither clear nor general enough to ground a theory of legal interpretation.

[8] It is arguable, for example, that the fugitive slave clause of the U.S. Constitution was morally unjustifiable.

tional provision enjoys even a minimal measure of moral justification, and some reason to suppose the contrary; second, courts are not free to discount totally unjustifiable statutes or constitutional provisions as "mistakes" that need not be enforced; third, such a statute or constitutional provision can be meaningful enough to have determinate applications in some range of cases. Because Dworkin's theory holds that the legal meaning and proper application of statutes and constitutional provisions are determined by the principles that provide them with some measure of genuine moral justification, it implies that a morally indefensible statute or constitutional provision cannot be interpreted and lacks legally appropriate application. It would seem to follow that the theory is false or, at best, crucially incomplete.

We are left with a conundrum – whether we can identify a plausible, generally applicable approach to the interpretation of law.

My recent work has concentrated on the experiences of peoples of color in the United States and the antecedent British colonies over the past four centuries. This is political history, but it raises continuing questions of political morality. Governmental policies in this area have involved systematic discrimination, enslavement, and genocide. Two of the most obvious issues are what forms of resistance can morally be justified and what kinds of corrective justice are now morally required.

Prior to my recent work in this area I had addressed the issue of civil disobedience. I was moved to do so upon finding that some of the recent literature misrepresented the judgments I associate with principled criticism of social injustice. Test cases were available in three of the leading theorists and practitioners of civil disobedience: Henry David Thoreau, Mohandas Gandhi, and Martin Luther King, Jr.

A significant portion of the recent philosophical literature assumes that those who engage in civil disobedience regard the systems within which they act as sufficiently just to generate a moral presumption favoring obedience to law and thus that such activists faced a moral dilemma framed by a duty of justice and an obligation of fidelity to law. This view of the matter represents a striking gap between political theory and political practice. As the political concerns of Thoreau, Gandhi, and King centered, respectively, on chattel slavery, British colonial rule, and Jim Crow, it would have been unreasonable for any one of them to have regarded the prevailing system as generating a moral presumption favoring obedience to all of the law, including the laws supporting slavery, enforcing British colonial rule, or giving us Jim Crow. And they were reasonable men.

The writings of Thoreau, Gandhi, and King confirm their radically negative judgments of the systems under which they lived. King, for example, emphasized the awful gap that existed between America's democratic ideals and its outrageous political practice under Jim Crow. Following a suggestion made by Rawls, I argued that a moral obligation to obey the law is impossible in any community with deeply entrenched, systematic injustice. In such circumstances, there is *no* moral presumption favoring obedience to *some* of the community's laws. This does not tell us what kind of disobedience can be justified, or precisely when, but it clears the way for a more realistic and defensible conception of political deliberation.

The second issue, of corrective justice, has often been framed in terms of reparations for slavery. As slavery was abolished a century and a half ago, this way of thinking about the issue suggests that individuals' claims for compensation today must be based on estimates of the disadvantages they currently suffer that can be traced to wrongs that were done long ago by slaveholders to slaves. As many generations have intervened, estimates of compensation that is morally required today would be, at best, practically impossible. The same applies to the identification of valid claimants and of those who today can justly be called upon to pay.

But that way of framing the corrective justice issue is misleading. It obscures the fact that Reconstruction was aborted after the Civil War and that government policies at all levels led to the creation of Jim Crow, another violent system of racial subordination, which continued well into the second half of the twentieth century. Current conditions flow from practices of racial subordination that persisted until the relatively recent past.

Slavery and Jim Crow were abolished, but without compensation for their victims. And their legacy is measurable, e.g., in the enormous wealth gap between white and black Americans. It is exemplified in the deeply rooted disadvantages of African American children, whose conditions challenge the American ideal of equal opportunity. In their case, corrective justice calls for massive, sustained programs in medical services, housing, education, and other necessities of contemporary life.

That returns us to politics, as seems appropriate.

Bibliography

Forms and Limits of Utilitarianism (Oxford: Clarendon Press, 1965).

In the Interest of the Governed: A Study in Bentham's Philosophy of Utility and Law (Oxford: Clarendon Press, 1973; Revised Edition, 1991).

Ethics and the Rule of Law (Cambridge: Cambridge University Press, 1984).

Moral Aspects of Legal Theory: Essays on Law, Justice, and Political Responsibility (New York: Cambridge University Press, 1993).

Rights, Welfare, and Mill's Moral Theory (New York: Oxford University Press, 1994).

"Ethical Relativism and the Problem of Incoherence," *Ethics* 86 (1976) 107–21.

"Normal Law, Nearly Just Societies, and Other Myths of Legal Theory," in *Archiv für Rechts- und Sozialphilosophie* 55 (1993) 13–26.

"The Balance of Injustice and the War for Independence," *Monthly Review* 45 (1994) 17-26, 38–40.

"Political Responsibility and Resistance to Civil Government," *Philosophic Exchange* (1995–96) 5–25.

"Moral Judgment, Historical Reality, and Civil Disobedience," *Philosophy & Public Affairs* 27 (1998) 31–49.

"Original Intent and Legal Interpretation," *Australian Journal of Legal Philosophy* 24 (1999) 1–26.

"Open Texture and the Possibility of Legal Interpretation," *Law and Philosophy* 18 (1999) 297–309.

"The Moral Opacity of Utilitarianism," in *Morality, Rules, and Consequences: A Critical Reader*, ed. B. Hooker, E. Mason, and D.E. Miller (Edinburgh: Edinburgh University Press, 2000), pp. 105–120.

"Unfinished Business: Racial Junctures in US History and Their Legacy," *Justice in Time: Responding to Historical Injustice*, ed. L.H. Meyer (Baden-Baden: Nomos, 2004), pp. 271–298.

"Corrective Justice, Equal Opportunity, and the Legacy of Slavery and Jim Crow," *Boston University Law Review* 84 (2004) 1375–1404.

13
Sir Neil MacCormick

Regius Professor of Public Law and the Law of Nature and Nations in the University of Edinburgh, Scotland, 1972–2008
Leverhulme Research Professor 1997–9, 2004–8

How I became involved in philosophy of law

My first University degree was in Philosophy and Literature (although I had initially embarked on a degree in classics, philosophy took a grip of me in my second year). My second degree was in law, because at that time various respected seniors advised me that I seemed to them better cut out for an active life at the bar than for the contemplative life of a philosopher. I initially took up an academic position with the aim of paying my way through qualification as a Scottish advocate, since after six years of study I wanted to get married and to have an income sufficient for that. Already, however, in my first job, I was growing [getting?] much involved in jurisprudence and the philosophy of law. When my second job took me to Oxford and to working within the orbit of H L A Hart along side of a fascinating group of colleagues, the die was almost cast. The conclusive moment was when, five years after arrival in Oxford, I was appointed to the Regius Chair of Public Law and the Law of Nature and Nations in the University of Edinburgh. There, I had a specific mandate to take charge of teaching and research in jurisprudence, interpreted widely enough to embrace the philosophy and sociology of law, and socio-legal studies more generally.

To put all this in proper context, it may be of interest if I give some more detail about my education and what followed thereafter. After schooling at the High School of Glasgow, I attended Glasgow University 1959–63 and graduated M.A. with honours in Philosophy and Literature. I then won a scholarship (a 'Snell Exhibition') to continue my studies at Balliol College in the University of Oxford, where I took a degree in law ('B.A. in Jurisprudence') 1963–65.

In my time as a student, philosophy in the Scottish universities, particularly in Glasgow, had not yet come greatly under the influence of 'ordinary language philosophy'. My interests in practical philosophy were particularly focussed on the neo-Kantian ideas of W.D. Lamont, on Deontology as advocated by W.G. Maclagan and W.D. Ross, and on eighteenth century British moralists such as Hume, Butler, Adam Smith and Thomas Reid, an interest which some years later led to a long-term involvement with the legal philosophy of the Scottish Enlightenment. I also started reading the moral philosophy of R.M. Hare, which connected well to my Kantian interests, and I found J.L .Austin's writings on *Sense and Sensibilia* and other subjects extremely challenging. We were exposed also to a certain amount of Wittgenstein, but I was never attracted by his way of writing and thinking. John Stuart Mill and the English Utilitarians were also of considerable interest, and Mill's essay *On Liberty* exercised great influence on my thinking both philosophically and in politics.

In Oxford, I learned quite a lot of English and Roman Law, but in particular I came under the influence of H.L.A. Hart, then Professor of Jurisprudence. I attended his lectures (On Rights and Duties, and on Kelsen) and read *The Concept of Law*. At that time my intention was to return to Scotland and enter into legal practice in Edinburgh, so when I was offered a teaching job in St Andrews University (at Queen's College, Dundee) I accepted this as a means to an end. My interest in legal philosophy became focused because I had already become fascinated by philosophy, yet intended to make a career in legal practice. When the opportunity to move from Dundee to Balliol College arose, and all the more when I had the good fortune to be appointed to the Regius Chair at Edinburgh, I decided that philosophy of law was, after all, my calling in life. I have not regretted it, though it would have been a good thing had I had the opportunity to undertake a period in professional legal practice.

Teachers whose example and enthusiasm made a real impact on me as a philosophy student in Glasgow were: William Maclagan, Professor of Moral Philosophy; William Lamont, Reader in Moral Philosophy; Robin Downie, lecturer, and subsequently Professor of Moral Philosophy; J.J. Russell, lecturer in logic and subsequently Professor of Philosophy in the University of Kansas; Howard Horsburgh, lecturer in Moral Philosophy, subsequently Professor in the University of Victoria, British Columbia.

Then, in Oxford: D.R. Harris (Fellow of Balliol College, and subsequently Director of the Centre for Socio-Legal Studies, University of Oxford; W. A. J. [Alan] Watson, Fellow of Oriel College, and subsequently Professor in successively Glasgow, Edinburgh, Pennsylvania and Georgia Universities. And H. L. A. Hart as well. Since he was incomparably the outstanding academic figure among those intellectual influences, it is right to say a little more about Hart's influence on me.

When I took up a position as Fellow of Balliol College in 1967, I regarded him with some awe as a giant of my subject, whose work I found very persuasive. I had attended his lectures, but had never met him as a person. He gave me a very friendly welcome as a younger colleague also involved in philosophy of law, and in due course I worked with him in certain matters concerning the Oxford Union Society, of which he was a Trustee and I was for a period Acting Senior Treasurer. Along with John Finnis and Richard Buxton, I took on responsibility for a postgraduate seminar (aimed at candidates for the BCL (Bachelor of Civil Law – a postgraduate degree – and also for doctoral candidates) on some selected texts in jurisprudence. Hart regularly attended these, as in due course did Joseph Raz and Ronald Dworkin. Hart gave up the Jurisprudence Chair quite early in my time at Oxford, and the rather surprising appointment of Ronald Dworkin took place at the end of my first year.

A discussion group including all those named and Gareth Evans, Brian Simpson, David Bentley, Philip Lewis, Jean Floud and occasional visitors such as Adam Podgorecki, Philippe Nonet, Philip Selznick and Harry Frankfurt met in Hart's room in University College, and subsequently in that of John Finnis, then that of Ronald Dworkin. I remained in touch after departing to Edinburgh in 1972, but inevitably contacts weakened over time.

I wrote a book about Hart in Edinburgh in 1979–80, and it was published in 1981 as the first in the 'Jurists' series edited by William Twining. This was an attempt at a short statement about and appraisal of his contribution as a scholar, taken in the light of such basic biographical information as seemed necessary to put the juristic work in context. Up till then most of my own writing and teaching had been very much done within the Hartian paradigm, and my conclusion in the book was one of broad agreement with Hart's work as I interpreted it. Subsequently, it became clear that my interpretation took Hart much closer to the 'natural law' tradition than he wished to go. His own final years and the posthumous postscript to *Concept of Law* (2nd edition) were marked by a yet more determined adherence to inclusive positivism than previously.

The *Hart* book had been preceded by my *Legal Reasoning and Legal Theory* of 1978, in which I effectively attempted to advance a comprehensive theory of legal reasoning that was in part based on and in every respect compatible with the general theory of law in the *Concept of Law*. This was published in the Clarendon Series under Hart's editorship – and he gave me very helpful editorial comments.

In the early eighties, I was therefore rightly characterised as a member of the same school of thought as Hart, indeed of his circle, though with a certain deviation towards acknowledging a greater mutual inter-penetration of law and morality than Hart considered correct. Over the period of all this work, I became personally friendly both with Herbert Hart and (to a lesser extent) with his wife Jenifer, but we never became intimate friends, and (for example) I was never one of those who joined the Harts in their country home in Cornwall.

As an intellectual he was quite austere and very critical in judgement of what he considered slipshod or badly thought-through. He sometimes seemed to me too hasty in judgement, and not inclined to see the strength of views he disagreed with. He was a wonderful and kindly, though stringent, critic of colleagues' work in preparation. He thought well enough of me to support my appointment to the Edinburgh Chair in 1972, though I was still only 31 years of age. He was quite a shy person, but genial and kindly in demeanor with those who were members of his – wide – circle of friendly colleagues in Oxford and elsewhere. He had a dry wit, and could be funny in an acerbic way.

I admire Nicola Lacey's book *A Life of H L A Hart: The Nightmare and the Noble Dream* (Oxford, 2004). While it disclosed many aspects of his private life and thoughts of which I had no knowledge, it confirmed rather than displaced my overall picture of him, and it did not diminish my admiration for either Herbert or Jenifer Hart, but, if anything, enhanced it. To my relief, I found that the biographical sketch in my own book turned out to have been broadly accurate, even in the light of the much more searching biography produced by Lacey.

I have just (in early 2007) finished a major book called *Institutions of Law* that states my own (probably) final conclusions in the way of general jurisprudence undertaken in an interpretative-analytical way, and with due regard to recent advances in socio-legal studies. This is, in short, my version of the Institutional Theory of Law that Ota Weinberger and I commenced to propose in the 1980s.

In that light, my view of Hart is now as follows. Hart's greatest and most enduring insight concerns the need to understand rule-governed conduct from the 'internal point of view'. This is essential to developing a clear and convincing theory of norms – but rules are only one kind of norm. The analysis of law as a union of primary and secondary rules, though full of valuable insight, is in the end incomplete and unsatisfactory. A fresh start is needed. A version of a 'basic norm theory' is more satisfactory than a 'rule of recognition' theory in explaining how a legal system comes together in the framework of a constitutionalist state (*Rechtsstaat*, *Estado de derecho*). Legal institutions interface with politics and economics and are foundational for the state and also for civil society. Criminal law is one essential part of the foundations of social peace and thus of civil society. All this takes one quite far from the Hartian conception of law, though the development out of a Hartian position is easily traced. Law and morality are indeed conceptually distinct, but it remains also true that minimal elements of respect for justice are essential to the recognition of a normative order as 'legal' in character.

For Which of My Contributions to Legal Philosophy do I wish to be Remembered?

What a difficult question this is – the truth is I would be delighted if it were vouchsafed to me now to know that I shall be remembered for anything at all! So far as I can discover from relative frequency of citation, *Legal Reasoning and Legal Theory* is the work which has in my lifetime so far been the most noticed. Now, however, it has to be read in the light of the later *Rhetoric and the Rule of Law* (Oxford, 2005). From my own point of view, I am clear that my *magnum opus* is *Institutions of Law* (Oxford, 2007). That itself is by no means the whole story, for the full significance of *Institutions* depends on the way it underpins and casts light on most of the rest of my work. It is not possible to give a sensible answer to the question posed here without putting my latest work in the context of what went before it. So here is an account of what I have been doing from 1965 up till the present (March 2007.).

Among the interests that stayed with me from my philosophical education at Glasgow was an interest in issues of logic and informal reasoning. During my first teaching appointment, 1965–7, at Queen's College Dundee (St Andrews University), my mentor there, Professor Ian Willock, asked me to prepare a course of lectures on logic and legal reasoning. Connected with this was a very early paper, 'Can *Stare Decisis* be Abolished?' (1966 *Juridical Review* 197). I continued with this interest when in 1967 I moved to Oxford, and during the years 1967–72 became engaged in controversy with Ronald Dworkin, taking the side of H.L.A. Hart in then current disputes about the place of principles in law and legal reasoning. The eventual outcome of this was my *Legal Reasoning and Legal Theory* (Oxford, Oxford University Press, 1978; 2nd edn 1994).

While in Oxford, though again with reference back to interests initially stimulated in Glasgow, I did some work on the theory of speech acts in ways that seemed to me of considerable importance for law and legal concepts, still closely connected to my interest in Hart"s' work. Two papers which exhibit this interest are 'Voluntary Obligations and Normative Powers'(1972 XLVI *Aristotelian Society Supplementary Volume*, pp.59–78) and 'Legal Obligation and the Imperative Fallacy' in *Oxford Essays in Jurisprudence, 2nd Series*, (ed. A. W. B. Simpson; Oxford: Clarendon Press, 1973; pp.100–130) This connects directly to the theory of institutional facts and hence to the theme of my 1973 inaugural lecture as Professor at Edinburgh University, 'Law as Institutional (1973: Edinburgh, Edinburgh University Inaugural Lecture No.52; also published in *Law Quarterly Rev* 70 (1974) 102–129).

My early years in Edinburgh were much engaged with developing a full account of legal reasoning. The above-mentioned main work was published in 1978, but not before I had met Chaim Perelman at a conference in Stirling in 1976, which had a considerable influence on my thinking, and led later to some papers published at his invitation.[1]

In 1979, at the IVR World Congress in Basel, I took part in the same plenary session as Ota Weinberger of Graz, presenting a paper 'On Analytical Jurisprudence'. In this, I picked up a theme

---

[1] 'Formal Justice and the Form of Legal Arguments' 1976 VI *Études de Logique Juridique* 103-118;

'The Motivation of Judgement in the Common Law', *La Motivation des Décisions de Justice*, ed. Ch. Perelman and P. Foriers 1978 Brussels, Bruylant, pp 167 – 94;

'On Reasonableness', in *Les Notions à Contenu Variable en Droit* ed. Ch. Perelman et al.,1984, Brussels: Bruylant pp.233-48

from Peter Hacker concerning the 'hermeneutic' aspect of Hart's thought on the nature of rule-governed behavior and its 'internal aspect'. The encounter with Weinberger led to mutual recognition that there was considerable similarity in our approaches to the 'institutional' aspect of law. This interaction continued later the same year at a conference organized by Aulis Aarnio in Finland, then again in Edinburgh at an ALSP Conference on Kelsen, in 1981 and at the IVR World Congress in Helsinki in 1983. All this led eventually to our collaborating in a jointly edited set essays, translated both into German (my essays) and English (Weinberger's), published both as *Grundlagen des institutionalistischen Rechtspositivismu* (1986), and as *An Institutional Theory of Law* (1987)

Other significant encounters in 1979 at the World Congress were with Robert Alexy and Aleksander Peczenik, along with Aulis Aarnio. During a visit to the University of the Saarland in the Spring of 1979, undertaken with the purpose of remedying my ignorance of German, I had discovered Alexy's *Theorie der juristischen Argumentation*, and Aulis Aarnio's *Reasoning on Legal Reasoning*. Peczenik's work on *Causes and Damages* I discovered only during the Basel Congress. It was clear to me, and to my colleagues, that all four of us were converging in our interests about legal reasoning, while exhibiting also certain characteristic differences attributable to the philosophical traditions from which we were moving forward. In due course I wrote what I think was the first English language paper drawing attention to Alexy's work[2] and its importance. Subsequently my former doctoral student (and dear friend) Ruth Adler and I prepared an English-language translation of *Theory of Legal Argumentation* (1988), having first established our ability to collaborate in translation by the work we had done on the Weinberger/MacCormick translations.

In 1980, John Finnis's *Natural Law and Natural Rights* came out. As a friend of John Finnis, I had read the typescript and made some very minor suggestions prior to publication. This work made a huge impression on me, and led me completely to reassess my understanding of 'natural law', as a number of subsequent papers confirmed.[3] Around that time, too, at the instigation of William

---

[2] 'Legal Reasoning and Practical Reason', *Midwest Studies in Philosophy* VII (ed. P. A. French et al., Ninneapolis, 1982) 271-286

[3] See in particular "Natural Law and the Separation of Law and Morals, in R. P. George (ed) *Natural Law Theory* (Clarendon Press, Oxford, 1992) pp. 105 - 33

Twining, I had undertaken to write the first volume of a series of short and partly biographical studies of significant legal thinkers – the 'Jurists' series. My *H.L.A. Hart* was published in the spring of 1981.

This has been a quite well-received account of the main elements in Hart's legal philosophy. Even after the recent publication of Nicola Lacey's full-scale biography *H. L. A. Hart: The Nightmare and the Noble Dream* (2004) it appears that my *Hart* book is a widely accepted account of Hartian legal theory. Perhaps under the influence of Finnis, however, but also in ways linking back to my Scottish philosophical training, it made Hart seem more of a natural lawyer than he (Hart) wanted to be, as he once told William Twining. In due course, the new Preface to the second edition of *Concept of Law* that was published posthumously showed how Hart had hardened the positivistic line in his own thought. This ran counter to the ideas I had suggested as the most attractive line of development of certain principal ideas in *The Concept of Law*. Thus the publication of *H.L.A. Hart* marked the high water mark of my strongly 'Hartian' period as a jurist. Without in any way belittling the enormous influence his thought and personality had on me, I came thereafter to develop lines of thought that diverged ever more widely from Hart's thought, certainly his later thought.

Also from the early 1980s is my *Legal Right and Social Democracy: Essays in Legal and Social Philosophy* (Oxford, 1982), a collection of essays and papers published over the preceding decade. These deal with issues about the legal establishment or disestablishment of moral principles, the possibility of a liberal society with a social democratic – not Marxist – approach to distributive justice and various other politico-legal questions. Looking back, it is almost impossible to remember how loud was the drumbeat of Marxist and *marxisant* thought in legal and social theory in the sixties, seventies and eighties of the twentieth century. I disagreed, considering that Rawls and others had given a more inspiring view, and that Adam Smith had left an insufficiently explored legacy in political and legal philosophy. It also seemed to me, then and subsequently, that the 'critical' epithet arrogated to itself by the Critical Legal Studies movement was one that other approaches ought to contest rather vigorously. I now believe that the ideas I put forward at that time have stood the test of time better than many of the rivals that were then more fashionable.

In the later eighties and into the nineties, my work on legal reasoning, in collaboration with my close Edinburgh colleague and friend Zenon Bankowski, concentrated increasingly closely on issues of interpretation considered comparatively. This developed through the work of the group of scholars initially brought together through an initiative of Bob Summers of Cornell University, and later jointly organized by Bob and myself, with considerable input from Zenon. The so-called *'Bielefelder Kreis'* (a name deriving from several workshops held in ZiF at Bielefeld on the initiative of Ralf Dreier) went on to produce two interesting sets of essays on *Interpreting Statutes: A Comparative Study* (1991) and *Interpreting Precedents: A Comparative Study* (1997) (edited by Summers and MacCormick).

Bankowski and I jointly organized the IVR World Congress in Edinburgh in 1989 on the theme 'Enlightenment, Rights and Revolutions' and we co-edited a book of the plenary lectures with the same title, and after the Congress acted as editors-in-chief of a series on connected themes. This was partly a matter of duty to colleagues in the IVR, but it also expressed a long-standing interest of my own, attested in many writings, in the legal, moral and political thought of the Scottish Enlightenment, read in the light of its broader international connections.

Partly because of a long-standing political involvement outside the academic world, I was in the early nineties greatly interested to develop ideas about how the emergence and development of the 'new legal order' of the European Communities (and now European Union) challenged many traditional categories of jurisprudential thought, notably 'sovereignty'. My Chorley lecture of 1992, 'Beyond the Sovereign State' 56 *Modern Law Review* 1–18 (1993) has proved a quite influential starting point. It was in due course followed up with the publication of *Questioning Sovereignty: Law State and Nation in the European Commonwealth* (1999), which included revised versions of several papers published in the intervening years on connected themes. It also includes the most mature of my writings on the ideas of nation and nationalism, and the possibility of civic nationalism.

From 1999–2003, I served as a Member of the European Parliament for Scotland representing the Scottish National Party within the Group of the Greens and European Free Alliance, fourth largest of the party political groups in the Parliament. This led on to participating over two years as an alternate member of the 'Convention on the Future of Europe' chaired by former French President Giscard D'Estaing, which produced the Draft Treaty Establishing a Constitution for Europe. This was for me a most exciting practical development relevant to earlier theoretical work, on which I wrote in my quite concise *Who's Afraid of a European Constitution?* (Exeter: Imprint Academic, 2005)

I am sometimes challenged on the compatibility of my political activities with the intellectual stance I have taken as a proponent of 'liberal social democracy'. There are colleagues who doubt whether my philosophical position is compatible with the political role I have taken for the last forty years as an activist in and occasional office-bearer of, the Scottish National Party. My answer to this question is given in full in chapter 11 of my book *Questioning Sovereignty: Law, State and Nation in the European Commonwealth*. The following quotations, from pp 170 and p183 respectively give the essence of my view.

> ... To [the idea of 'liberal nationalism'] the idea of civic nationalism is strongly material. 'Civic nationalism' identifies the nation in terms of its members' shared allegiance to certain civic institutions. These are understood in broad terms to include, for example, legal norms and institutions, political representative organs, branches of public and local administration, the organization of education, churches and religious communities in their secular aspect, and other like institutions having an understood territorial location to which they refer. Institutions of civil society as much as of the state are relevant here. Territorially located civic institutions can be objects of allegiance, understood as 'ours' by the people among whom they perform their functions. As civic institutions, they are necessarily of great political significance to the community which, to an extent, they define.
>
> Naturally, it is possible, and perhaps desirable, for such civic institutions to go the length of including a constitution and the full panoply of statehood. Perhaps without that the civic quality of civic institutions is too precarious. But it would be a mistake to require this by definition, for to do so is simply to endorse the in-principle challenged assumption that the states that currently exist comprise also the totality of nations, at any rate, the totality of nations that can be understood in the civic sense
>
> Whether or not the civic nation is or has a state,

or a fortiori an independent sovereign state, the point of the idea of a civic nation is that it is in principle open to voluntary membership. The community defined by allegiance to institutions is open to anyone who chooses to dwell in the territory and give allegiance to the institutions. Departure to a different place and different allegiances is also possible, and not traitorous. One is guilty of treachery only if one who remains in place and surreptitiously undermines the institutions of that place while ostensibly giving them respect and allegiance. (There is all the difference in the world between such surreptitious subversion and open criticism, however robust, of civic institutions considered stultifying, obsolete, or the like.) (p.170)

There is at least a prima facie case for some kind of right to respect or national identities as a part of respect for persons, for implicit in respecting human individuals is respect for whatever goes into their individuality. Morally justifiable political principles have to take account of a sense of nationality that is intrinsic to the fabric of individuality, to whatever extent such a sense is vital for many individuals to their sense of themselves, and to their self-respect in being acknowledged members of some recognized and respected community of people.' (p. 183)

Throughout, I stress that while some form of representative political institutions are justified by reference to significant claims of national self-determination, it cannot be the case that every single one could be or ought to become a sovereign state in international law. But then my other thesis is that sovereignty is part of the problem, not part of the solution, hence the title of my book.

In 1997, after a long period in which I had both borne heavy administrative duties in Edinburgh University and spent a huge part of my spare time in political activity, I was so fortunate as to be awarded a Research Professorship by the Leverhulme Trust. This enabled me to devote not less than 80% of my working time to research and writing, to bring together the various strands of legal-philosophical work I had been engaged in during the 1980s and 90s. My project was entitled 'Law, State, and Practical Reason', and envisaged the publication of four books. *Questioning Sovereignty* was the first of these. During my five years in the European Parliament, I made only a little progress with others, but the Leverhulme Trust very generously renewed my award when I stood down from Parliament in June 2004. Since then *Rhetoric and the Rule of Law: A Theory of Legal Reasoning* (Oxford: Oxford University Press, 2005) has brought my theory about legal reasoning fully up to date. This work exhibits an evolution toward ground shared with Ronald Dworkin on the issue of objective 'right answers' to contested legal points of argument. Next, in January 2007 *Institutions of Law: An Essay in Legal Theory* (Oxford: Oxford University Press, 2007) brings my version of the institutional theory of law fully up to date. It does so in an avowedly post-positivistic form, developing an interpretative approach to analytical jurisprudence that is fully in tune with certain major recent developments in the sociology of law and socio-legal studies more generally.

My final goal is a book about practical reason in morality and law, for publication by mid-2009. This will fully explore the possibility of discursive ethics as a basis to develop objectively testable moral principles, and will give a credible account of the centrality of autonomy or self-command to moral action and moral thinking. It will seek to explore the connection of these findings with well-known positions in classical natural law theory. In its conclusions, this book will finally link together and reconcile my approach to legal reasoning and my post-positivist institutional theory of law, as well as the theory of sovereignty and the state.

Reduced to stages, I would say that 1965–81 was for me a period in which I was most closely engaged with Hart's work, as a follower of his, though one with independent connections derived from other influences. 1981–1995 was a period of re-consideration of main themes and steady distancing from Hart, especially the later Hart. Since 1995 I have developed a rounded account of my own mature thought, having at its centre the post-positivist institutionalism developed in *Institutions of Law*, and ultimately to be underpinned by my book on practical reason in morality and law. Meantime, as I have said, *Institutions of Law* should be deemed the *magnum opus*.

What are the Most Important Issues in Legal Philosophy?

As I near the end of a long career, both of activism and of writing and lecturing, I feel myself entitled to say that the topics I have covered do seem to me to be those which it has been most important to address. That was why I put my mind to them. If I were to summarize, these questions are as follows:

13. Sir Neil MacCormick 183

What is the best way to convey and enhance an understanding of the concept of law, especially in the context of the law-state?

Since law does not only manifest itself in the framework of the Westphalian sovereign state, and since Westphalian sovereignty is steadily dwindling, how do we locate state law within a wider and more pluralistic conception of law?

How does all this square with a conception of the human being as a norm-user yet more fundamentally than a norm-giver or norm-creator?

When we reason about issues in dispute as a matter of law, what are the forms of argument a reasonable person can use to justify one position or another on a disputed point?

Given the 'positive' character of any authoritatively issued decision on a disputed point of law, how does this contrast with morality conceived as a domain in which the autonomy of the moral agent is in some way paramount?

What is justice, and how far is there a necessary pretension to justice in any act of making law or of authoritatively determining its proper interpretation in a given case or practical context?

Is there a minimum necessary element of justice in whatever can be reasonably recognized and implemented as law?

How should we understand states and nations and other kinds of significant human community? Are there any moral claims that belong to states or to nations as such?

What is good and right, and how do we construct reasonable and reliable arguments about this?

What is the Relationship between Legal Philosophy and Legal Practice?

All human activities that have a direct and strong bearing on the interests of human beings deserve to be subjected to philosophical scrutiny, and all practitioners of such activities have some responsibility to have a tolerably articulate view of the foundations in which their practical activity is grounded. On the other hand, those concerned with accounting for the foundations have a responsibility to ensure that whatever they put forward by way of accounting for these foundations is intelligible to concerned practitioners. I see many failings on both sides of this gap at present. Of my own writings, I think that *Legal Reasoning and Legal Theory* has been of use to practitioners, and that some of the more recent work will in due course prove its worth in a similar way.

As a former member of a Parliament, I believe also that legal philosophy is of relevance to law-makers, and that legal philosophers should be more alert to this. Law making is a kind of practical legal activity, if not 'legal practice' in the narrower sense.

It is too easy, and happens too frequently, for legal philosophers to become so absorbed in the dialogue and dispute internal to their specialism that they neglect to write in a manner that is capable of detaining the attention of any non-specialist. This is a fault I have tried to avoid in all my writing, though surely I also will have failed on many occasions.

What Should Legal Philosophy Concentrate On?

I frequently remind myself of the watchword adopted by Bill Clinton's team during his first Presidential Campaign: 'It's the Economy, Stupid!'. My jurisprudential parallel would be: 'It's the Law, Stupid!' We ought not to become obsessed with issues like the dispute between negative and positive positivism or inclusive or exclusive positivism, or among the various species of natural law theory as though resolving these were an end in itself. We should always remember that our proper study is the law and the conditions of good or just law, and the possibilities of good and bad arguments about law and legal claims. We should always seek to clarify these, and subordinate concepts and institutions internally to them, and we get into wrangles about different juristic approaches with a view to answering such questions, not for some more parochially intra-disciplinary reason.

Principal Publications

As author

Legal Reasoning and Legal Theory (Oxford: Clarendon Press1978, 2nd ed 1994).

H L A Hart (London: Edward Arnold,1981).

Legal Right and Social Democracy (Oxford, Clarendon Press1982).

An Institutional Theory of Law (co-authored with Ota Weinberger; Dordrecht: D Reidel, 1985).

Questioning Sovereignty: Law, State and Nation in the European Commonwealth (Oxford: Clarendon Press 1999).

Rhetoric and the Rule of Law (Oxford, Oxford University Press 2005).

Who's Afraid of a European Constitution? (2005).

Institutions of Law: An Essay in Legal Theory (Oxford, Oxford University Press 2005).

As editor

The Scottish Debate; Essays on Scottish Nationalism (1970).

The Legal Mind (1985, co-edited with Peter Birks).

Enlightenment, Rights and Revolutions (1989, co-edited with Zenon Bankowski).

Interpreting Statutes: A Comparative Study (1991, co-edited with Robert S.Summers).

*Interpreting Precedents: A Comparative Study (*1997, co-edited with Robert S.Summers).

Constructing Legal Systems: "European Union" in Legal Theory (Dordrecht: Kluwer Academic Publishers, 1997.

14
Stanley L. Paulson

William Gardiner Hammond Professor of Law, and Professor of Philosophy

Washington University in St. Louis, USA

Why were you initially drawn to the philosophy of law?

On the question of why or, as I would prefer to put it, *how* I was initially drawn to the philosophy of law, I take the liberty of answering in purely autobiographical terms, focusing largely on a contingency stemming from my graduate studies in philosophy. I completed the graduate programme, leading to the Ph.D., "on schedule" as we say, including a year spent on the dissertation. The upside, finishing the programme on time, was, however, paired with a downside, namely, that having settled relatively quickly on a dissertation theme, a series of problems about the nature of explanation in psychology, I did not, as it turned out, really have my heart in it. Still, I was fascinated by issues falling within the rubric of "the philosophy of x", where the variable "x" ranges over the object disciplines – thus, philosophy of mathematics, philosophy of history, philosophy of social science, and so on.

Realizing in the late stages of my graduate work in philosophy that I had not yet found my niche, I began reading texts in jurisprudence and legal philosophy. However superficial my impressions may have been, I found the material rich and suggestive, prompting me, after completing my graduate work in philosophy, to enroll in law school, where I completed the standard three-year professional programme.

I had the good fortune to attend Harvard Law School, but, coming directly out of a philosophy graduate programme that I had found enormously stimulating, I found the study of law disappointing in one respect. I had naïvely expected a panoply of concepts along with structure, system, and the like. Instead, standard fare in the American law schools, mine included, was a steady diet of cases, cases, and still more cases, and this was true not only in the common law fields but also in fields governed by statute, say, commercial law. In order to supplement the traditional law school fare, I began to explore European legal science, initially as a challenging hobby of sorts. I even tried at one point early on to read Georg Friedrich Puchta's two-volume treatise on customary law, *Das Gewohnheitsrecht* (Erlangen 1828/37).

While I had no illusions about having come to a clear understanding of these matters, I did think I was on to something. European legal science, with its decided emphasis on things conceptual, was a reflection, as I would learn only later, of a Central European development of the mid-nineteenth century, the movement to "render the law scientific" (*Verwissenschaftlichung des Rechts*). This transformation of the field – a transformation, at any rate, in terms of the conceptual framework it wrought – would set the stage for everything that followed in European legal science. What is more, certain parallels between European legal science and classical analytic philosophy struck me as unmistakable. For example, Rudolf von Jhering wrote, in the 1860s, that while everyone uses the concept of legal construction, virtually no one is in a position to explicate the concept. A strikingly similar observation turns up, a half century later, in a paper by the Cambridge philosopher G.E. Moore. In a line that would become famous in philosophy circles, Moore wrote that while we all know that certain general propositions are true, we are unable to provide correct analyses of these propositions.

For me, the trappings of European legal science were just what the doctor ordered. I had found a congenial field of study. What is more, the figures in the United Kingdom whose work attracted me – above all, H.L.A. Hart and Joseph Raz – had been notably influenced by European legal philosophy and social science. In Hart's case, one thinks of the influence of Hans Kelsen and Max Weber, whose impact on Hart is abundantly clear albeit scarcely addressed in the literature. Raz's case is still more obvious, for his early work explicitly attests to the influence of Kelsen. My interest in Hart's and Raz's work, bolstered by my reading in European legal science, led me, in turn, to Hans Kelsen and the Vienna School of Legal Theory.

Kelsen's legal theory came to me as a revelation – or, more accurately, as a whole series of revelations. On the one hand, the core of the theory proved to be genuinely philosophical, with a profound influence stemming from the *fin de siècle* neo-Kantians. On the other hand, I found the colossus of Kelsen's juridico-theoretical explorations to be well nigh staggering in its breadth. There was, *first*, legal philosophy and legal theory, that is, Kelsen's own Pure Theory of Law along with everything from studies of historical figures to highly original contributions to norm theory, *second*, the theory of public law (*Staatsrechtslehre*) with special attention to constitutional law, *third*, Kelsen's central role in drafting the Austrian Federal Constitution of October 1920, including provisions for centralized constitutional review, *fourth*, public international law, including, in legal theory, Kelsen's epistemologically based doctrine of legal monism and, closer to practice, a detailed examination of the United Nations Charter, *fifth*, ethno-sociological studies directed to issues in the law, including the treatise *Vergeltung und Kausalität* (The Hague 1940), and, *sixth*, political theory in the broadest possible sense, ranging from an early commentary on Austrian election law to studies of federalism, hard-hitting criticism of Austro-Marxism, and a classical defence of democracy.

My research on themes in Kelsen's Vienna School of Legal Theory has been greatly promoted over the years by lengthy stints abroad – in Berlin, Vienna, Münster, Heidelberg, Göttingen, and, most recently, in Kiel. I have invariably found the work both stimulating and rewarding, and I am grateful to all of the good people – at home in St. Louis and here in Germany – who have made these extraordinary opportunities possible. By the same token, I remain grateful to the Alexander von Humboldt Foundation, Bonn, to the Deutsche Forschungsgemeinschaft, Bonn, and to my home institution, Washington University in St. Louis, for generous funding of my work.

For which of your contribution(s) to legal philosophy so far would you like to be remembered, and why?

Bearing in mind that the subjunctive mood governs this second question, I would answer that if I were to be remembered for contributing to legal philosophy at all, I would like the focus to be on my effort to lend philosophical respectability to Hans Kelsen's work by insisting on the significance of its neo-Kantian dimension.

I shall return to Hans Kelsen in a moment, but it is well, first, to place the issue of historico-critical research on Kelsen's legal philosophy within a greater framework, that of historico-critical research on issues in the history of philosophy generally. Fifty years ago – just ten years ahead of my own graduate study in philosophy – research in the English-speaking countries on the history of European philosophy was, for the most part, a wasteland. The exception in those days, important historico-critical work in ancient philosophy, establishes the rule. In the 1960s, things began to change, and developments in Kant scholarship are illustrative of that change.

As their remarkable reception over the years would make clear, no fewer than three seminal works on Kant's *Critique of Pure Reason* appeared in English in the mid-1960s: Robert Paul Wolff's *Kant's Theory of Mental Activity* (Cambridge, Mass. 1963), Peter F. Strawson's *The Bounds of Sense* (London 1966), and Jonathan Bennett's *Kant's Analytic* (Cambridge 1966). Today, Kant scholarship in the English-speaking countries is flourishing as never before. It has, indeed, been paid the utmost compliment: Many Kant scholars in Germany, who understandably regard Kant as their bailiwick, are conducting research in cooperation with their English-language counterparts. Exciting explorations of the themes in Kant's three critiques are complemented by significant work on Kant's theory of natural science – for example, Michael Friedman's *Kant and the Exact Sciences* (Cambridge, Mass. 1992) and Jeffrey Edwards' *Substance, Force, and the Possibility of Knowledge* (Berkeley 2000) – and by important work on the early, "precritical" Kant – for example, Martin Schönfeld's *The Philosophy of the Young Kant* (New York 2000). Philosophico-intellectual histories of German philosophy in the later eighteenth century and on into the nineteenth century include remarkable studies by Frederick C. Beiser, *German Idealism. The Struggle against Subjectivism 1781–1801* (Cambridge, Mass. 2002), and Terry Pinkard, *German Philosophy 1760–1860. The Legacy of Idealism* (Cambridge 2002). A major project, the English-language edition of Kant's works, published by the Cambridge University Press, will soon reach sixteen volumes. Fifty years ago, developments such as these were scarcely imaginable.

The reader sees where I am heading. Would it not be a splendid thing if historico-critical research on major figures in the philosophy of law were to follow the example set by studies on Kant? We in legal philosophy have a ways to go. Put less charitably, historico-critical research on figures in the philosophy of law remains in the dark ages. An exception is the important work over the last thirty-five years on Jeremy Bentham's legal philosophy, including much that is of jurisprudential interest in the *Collected Works of Jeremy Bentham*. Another exception is John Finnis's monograph, *Aquinas. Moral, Political, and Legal Theory* (Oxford

1998), and, for that matter, Finnis's earlier *Natural Law and Natural Rights* (Oxford 1980), with its discerning sections on Aquinas.

Where Kelsen's legal theory is concerned, I have worked from a historico-critical standpoint on various fronts, always with an eye to enhancing the philosophical dimension of the theory. I might invite attention to two of these fronts here: first, Kelsen's arguments against naturalism and, second, his neo-Kantianism, in particular in this connection, his normativity thesis.

Toward the end of the nineteenth century, in a paper entitled "Norms and Laws of Nature", the Baden neo-Kantian philosopher Wilhelm Windelband gave expression to the concept of normativity as Kelsen came to understand it, adumbrating a basic distinction between the normative disciplines and the natural sciences. Drawing on Windelband's distinction, Kelsen, at the outset of his first major treatise, *Main Problems in the Theory of Public Law* (1911), lists the normative disciplines and includes not only ethics, aesthetics, logic, and philology, but also legal science. From the beginning, Kelsen had condemned as wrongheaded the very real inroads made by naturalism into the legal science of the day, and Windelband's distinction was grist for the young legal theorist's mill. Legal science was a normative science, that is, a non-naturalistic science, and the task Kelsen set for himself was to demonstrate that this was indeed so.

To be sure, Kelsen's constructive work on an alternative to naturalism came for the most part later, taking neo-Kantian doctrines as the point of departure. Kelsen's task in his very early writings – in *Main Problems* and, a decade later, in *The Sociological and Juridical Concept of the State* (1922) – was to adduce arguments showing that naturalism in legal science was mistaken. As an illustration, it is instructive to consider his criticism of Georg Jellinek's legal theory. Jellinek's "two-sides" theory of law seemed to reflect a normative or non-naturalistic dimension, namely, a "juridico-normative" side that appeared not to be reducible to anything factual, along with a "social" or "historico-social" side that was supposed to represent the factual dimension of the law. Kelsen, however, argued correctly that, on Jellinek's view, legal norms cannot be "anything other than '*is*'-rules, with the 'ought' reflected – psychologically – in one's subjective consciousness of rule-governed action". On the basis of "this thoroughly psychologistic orientation" toward legal norms, Jellinek's legal theory is revealed for what it is, a species of naturalism. (Ibid. § 20, at p. 119, emphasis in original.)

It is no accident that Kelsen spoke of Jellinek's *psychologistic* orientation. The anti-naturalism of Kelsen's legal theory is a reflection of other anti-naturalistic programmes developed in philosophy at the same time, including the campaign against psychologism in logic and in the theory of knowledge, that is to say, against attempts to reduce the material of these fields to psychological phenomena. Among the critics of psychologically inclined – or, the pejorative expression, "psychologistically inclined" – logicians of the later nineteenth century were, above all, the philosophically inclined mathematician Gottlob Frege and the mathematician-turned-philosopher Edmund Husserl. Kelsen was aware of Husserl's role here.

Frege and Husserl were only the most prominent of a number of *fin de siècle* philosophers who campaigned against naturalism. The naturalistic turn in psychology serves as an illustration. The young turks in experimental psychology – most prominently Oswald Külpe and Edward Bradford Titchener – broke at the end of the nineteenth century with the master, Wilhelm Wundt, in order to reconstitute psychology on a purely empirical basis. Among the anti-naturalistic critics were the neo-Kantian philosophers Heinrich Rickert and Hugo Münsterberg. While endorsing the young turks' naturalistic position in the case of psychology, both Rickert and Münsterberg sought to preserve the autonomy of the *Geisteswissenschaften* or humanistic fields. Reflecting Wundt's influence, these disciplines had earlier been thought to be based on psychology, and they were therefore seen as threatened by the reconstitution of psychology in naturalistic terms.

In short, Kelsen was engaged in a common enterprise with others in philosophy, doing battle against naturalism with an eye to preserving the autonomy (*Eigengesetzlichkeit*) of the discipline in question – be it logic, be it one or another of the *Geisteswissenschaften*, be it legal science. When, at a later point, Kelsen works up rudiments of an alternative to naturalism, he draws on the work of the neo-Kantians.

As for the neo-Kantian dimension of Kelsen's legal theory, some commentators have drawn on Kant and the work of the Marburg neo-Kantian Hermann Cohen, contending that Kelsen's tack was to adduce a "regressive" version of the Kantian or neo-Kantian transcendental argument in order to establish his case on behalf of a non-naturalistic or normative theory of legal science. The basic norm or, more precisely, the category of imputation serves, however, as the presupposed category of a sound transcendental argument only if no viable alternative to the presupposed category exists. Neither Kelsen nor anyone else is in a position to show this, even if Kelsen sometimes writes as though he could.

Although there is textual support for attributing a transcendental argument to Kelsen, another approach, for which there is also textual support, is more persuasive. This approach reflects the influence on Kelsen of the Baden neo-Kantians. Of special interest here is the doctrine of methodological form, which, in legal science, serves as Kelsen's "law of normativity".

In the last chapter of his treatise, *The Object of Knowledge*, Heinrich Rickert, erstwhile student of Windelband's and the leading figure in the Baden School of neo-Kantianism after Windelband's death in 1915, distinguished "constitutive categories" of objective reality – for example, the category of permanence – from the "methodological forms" that are part and parcel of the various standing disciplines. (See generally Rickert, *Der Gegenstand der Erkenntnis*, 6th edn., Tübingen 1928, at pp. 401–432.) Rickert's basic idea is that objective reality, constituted transcendentally, must be sharply distinguished from the processing (*Bearbeitung*) of the material that is given in objective reality. Objective reality is constituted by means of the categories of reality, while the processing of the material of objective reality is the work of the methodological forms found in the standing disciplines. Rickert offers lawfulness (*Gesetzlichkeit*) as an example of a methodological form in the natural sciences. In fact, the example has to be taken as the *genus* of methodological forms in the natural sciences, for it has application to all of them. The various species of this generic form are peculiar to the various standing disciplines. Thus, as Rickert argues, physics has its own methodological form, and so does psychology.

Legal science, too, has its own methodological form, namely, imputation (*Zurechnung*) or, as Kelsen sometimes puts it, the "law of normativity" (*Rechtsgesetz*). As he explains: "Just as the law of nature links a certain material fact as cause with another as effect, so the law of normativity links legal condition with legal consequence (the consequence of a so-called unlawful act). If the mode of linking material facts is causality in the one case, it is imputation in the other, and imputation is recognized in the Pure Theory of Law as the particular lawfulness, the autonomy, of the law." (Kelsen, *An Introduction to the Problems of Legal Theory*, a translation of the First Edition of the *Reine Rechtslehre*, published in 1934, § 11(b), at p. 23.)

When the legal condition set out in the reconstructed, hypothetically formulated legal norm obtains, the methodological form of legal science – the imputation relation – marks the legal position of the legal subject, that is, the legal subject's *liability* to the imposition of a sanction. By the same token, the satisfaction of the antecedent condition marks the legal position of *empowerment* on the part of the legal official, namely, power to impose the sanction in question. In this way, Kelsen explicates the peculiarly juridical methodological form, imputation, in terms of the modalities of liability and power.

Kelsen's methodological form, his "law of normativity", plays itself out in normative legal science, understood by Kelsen as the alternative to naturalism in legal science. Normative legal science is a genuine alternative to naturalism, he argues, for the modalities of the reconstructed legal norm are immune to the naturalist's effort to restate and account for them in factual terms. In particular, the underlying law-like character of imputation, Kelsen's methodological form, serves to explain *non-causal change*. If an individual A is subject to an exercise of legal power by B, and B exercises this power, the legal position of A is thereby changed, and the change, Kelsen insists, is not a causal change. It is, rather, a "normative" change. Thus, "normativity" is understood by means of the contrast with causality. To be sure, this is but one reading of "normativity" in legal theory. It is Kelsen's reading, and it reflects his Baden neo-Kantian heritage.

Kelsen's "law of normativity" speaks to the analytic and systematic dimension of his theory. In my own case, the discovery of Kelsen's "law of normativity" stemmed from historico-critical research, requiring, *inter alia*, a fair bit of attention to the neo-Kantian doctrines that Kelsen assimilated. There is no occasion sharply to distinguish analytic and systematic work from historico-critical research. In philosophy, they are inextricably interwoven.

What are the most important issues in legal philosophy, and why are they distinctively issues of legal philosophy rather than some other discipline?

In some juridico-philosophical circles it has become common practice in recent years to declare that the fundamental problems in the philosophy of law have been solved and that what calls for attention now are "applications". I take issue with this view. The question of the nature of law – in a word: what is law? – is the leading issue in legal philosophy and it will remain so for as long as people pose questions about the law that go beyond things prosaic.

Legal philosophy counts as a field of conceptual exploration alongside the other standing fields of philosophy, where the basic issues are addressed in such questions as: what is existence or being?, what is knowledge?, what is beauty? To dismiss the leading question in legal philosophy is tantamount to dismissing the field.

Conceptual exploration into the niceties of the nature of law may well have been led down a blind alley by a preoccupation in some circles with what might be dubbed the natural law theorist's "validity theorem". It is a familiar view that the legal positivist is prepared to recognize the validity of a legal norm quite apart from its moral defects, whereas the natural law theorist holds – here, the validity theorem – that moral defects of great magnitude may undermine the claim of legal validity. Thus understood, invoking the validity theorem is sufficient to draw a fundamental distinction between legal positivism and natural law theory. It is not at all clear, however, that the validity theorem figures necessarily in this distinction. That is, a theorist may hold a non-positivistic position while not endorsing the validity theorem. For example, Kant is correctly identified as defending a non-positivistic theory of law, but he does not defend the validity theorem.

To be sure, it may be argued that because Kant's concept of law is controversial, the use of Kant as an example here is less than persuasive. Aquinas's concept of law, however, is not controversial – not, at any rate, on the question of his standing *qua* natural law philosopher. And, as Finnis has shown, Aquinas does not appeal to the validity theorem either. In a word, the key in identifying these thinkers' positions lies not with the validity theorem but with their respective concepts of law. The point is that there is indeed work still to be done on the question of the nature of law.

What is the relationship between legal philosophy and legal practice? Should legal philosophers be more concerned about the effects of their scholarship on legal practice?

The question on the "relationship between legal philosophy and legal practice" is a tall order. There are any number of facets here – whether one is speaking solely about legal philosophy and not also about legal theory, whether the tie at issue is factual or normative, and so on. I shall limit myself to a single aspect of the general question, namely, how if at all legal philosophy has influenced legal practice. Certain examples from legal *theory* come to mind. A good bit of research makes it fairly clear that American legal realism, in its heyday, had an impact on the judiciary, and the same sort of claim can be made, *mutatis mutandis*, about Philipp Heck's interest theory, with its well-documented impact on practice in Germany. The rub, of course, is that neither view obviously belongs to legal philosophy. In the case of American legal realism, the overriding factor is empirical in nature, reflecting the legal realists' interest in applications of the social sciences to the law. In Heck's case, too, the empirical component looms large.

Pursuing the factual question of influence just a bit further, one might well suppose that Lon L. Fuller's work in an early article, "The Reliance Interest in Contract Damages" (*Yale Law Journal*, vol. 46, 1937–38, at pp. 52–96, 373–420), with its generous dose of Aristotle, does contain a philosophical component. If the supposition is correct, then we may have an interesting example of influence, for the contract lawyers in America report that this work of Fuller's did indeed have an impact on practice – both on the drafting of Section 90 of the *Restatement of Contracts 2d* (1981) and with respect to the conceptualization of the measures of recovery (expectancy, reliance) in civil actions for breach of contract. Still, the question remains open. For even granting that Fuller's paper contains a philosophical component, one would have to show that it was that very component, and not something else in the article, that had an impact on practice. The points in Fuller's paper that figured in the drafting of Section 90 are in fact technical, not philosophical.

One might conclude, cautiously, that if Fuller's article counts as an example of the influence of legal philosophy on practice, then it is surely the exception. That ought not be a cause for despair, however. Philosophical research is its own reward.

To which problem, issue or broad area of legal philosophy would you most like to see more attention paid in the future?

In answering this last question, on directions that future work in the field might take, I can be very brief. For I would want here to combine my plea – in question 2 – for more historico-critical research on major figures in the field, with the case I make – in question 3 – on behalf of the nature of law as the leading issue in the field. To wit: If people in the field were to engage in historico-critical research on the jurisprudential dimension of the work of, say, Francisco Suárez (1548–1617), Hugo Grotius (1583–1645), and Samuel von Pufendorf (1632–1694), we would all learn a good deal about the nature of law.

Representative recent publications

1. "The Theory of Public Law in Germany 1914–1945", in: *Oxford Journal of Legal Studies* 25 (2005), pp. 525–545.

2. "Some Issues in the Exchange between Hans Kelsen and Erich Kaufmann", in: *Scandinavian Studies in Law*, 48 (2005) (special number of the journal, ed. Peter Wahlgren, as a *Festschrift* in honour of Jes Bjarup), pp. 270–290.

3. "Zwei radikale Objektivierungsprogramme in der Rechtslehre Hans Kelsens", in: *Hans Kelsen. Staatsrechtslehrer und Rechtstheoretiker des 20. Jahrhunderts*, ed. Stanley L. Paulson and Michael Stolleis (Tubingen: Mohr Siebeck, 2005), pp. 191–220.

4. "Ralf Dreiers Kelsen", in: *Integratives Verstehen. Die Rechtsphilosophie Ralf Dreiers*, ed.Robert Alexy (Tubingen: Mohr Siebeck, 2005), pp. 59–97.

5. "Hugo Preuß und Hans Kelsen – Überraschende Parallelen", in: *Gemeinde, Stadt, Staat: Aspekte der Verfassungstheorie von Hugo Preuß*, ed. Christoph Müller (Baden-Baden: Nomos, 2005), pp. 65–83.

6. "Zum 'Formalismus' – Vorwurf im Weimarer verfassungsrechtlichen Richtungsstreit", in: *Argumentation im Verfassungsrecht*, ed. Jan Sieckmann (Baden-Baden: Nomos, 2005), pp. 33–50.

7. "On the Background and Significance of Gustav Radbruch's Post-War Papers", in: *Oxford Journal of Legal Studies* 26 (2006), pp. 17–40.

8. "Kelsen, Hans", in: *Encyclopedia of Philosophy*, 2nd edn., ed. Donald M. Borchert (successor to *The Encyclopedia of*

Philosophy, ed. Paul Edwards), 10 vols. (2006), vol. 5, pp. 49–50.

9. "J.W. Harris's Kelsen", in: *Properties of Law: Essays in Honour of Jim Harris*, ed. Timothy Endicott, Joshua Getzler, and Edwin Peel (Oxford: Oxford University Press, 2006), pp. 3–21.

10. "Der Normativismus Hans Kelsens", in: *Juristen-Zeitung* 61 (2006), pp. 529–536.

11. "Hans Kelsen's Ramified Concept of Law", in: *The Juridical Review*, 2006, pp. 291–307.

12. "Konstitutive und methodologische Formen: Zur Kantischen und neukantianischen Folie der Rechtslehre Hans Kelsens", in: *Kant im Neukantianismus*, ed. Marion Heinz and Christian Krijnen (Würzburg: Königshausen & Neumann, 2007), pp. 149–165.

15
Frederick Schauer

Frank Stanton Professor of the First Amendment
Harvard University, USA

Why were you initially drawn to the philosophy of law?
The path that drew me to the philosophy of law is an indirect one. In thinking and writing about freedom of expression, the subject of my initial academic specialization, I soon came to realize that the theoretical work on that topic was primarily philosophical. That realization in turn led me, even though I possessed no formal training in philosophy, to read and engage with the classical and contemporary philosophical work on freedom of speech and freedom of the press. But it soon became apparent that although much work on freedom of expression had been done by moral and political philosophers, virtually none of the philosophical literature on freedom of expression had drawn on epistemology, on the philosophy of science (with Popper's *The Open Society and Its Enemies* as the obvious exception), on the philosophy of language, or on various other philosophical areas outside of moral, political, and social philosophy. And thus my initial exposure to philosophy was through using philosophical methods and the philosophical literature, and in particular various branches of philosophy other than moral and political philosophy, to inform my own writing about freedom of expression.

When my academic interests eventually broadened so as to encompass constitutional law and constitutional interpretation, these same areas of philosophy turned out to be especially useful and turned out once again to have been widely, and surprisingly, neglected. Although moral and political philosophy were then and continue together to constitute a major presence in legal scholarship, especially in the United States, on constitutional theory and constitutional interpretation, few scholars had then, in the middle 1980s, drawn on the philosophy of language to inform an approach to questions of constitutional interpretation.

By then it was only a short step from using the philosophy of language as an approach to addressing questions of constitutional interpretation to using the same and related philosophical tools to study legal interpretation generally, and then it was only another short step to becoming interested in the nature of legal language, and thus in the nature of law itself. Because law is so dependent on language, because legal decision-making so often involves the interpretation of canonical language, and because language is the vehicle through which law exerts its power, it is impossible to focus on the interpretation and use of legal language without being drawn to thinking about the relationship between language and law generally, and thus to thinking directly about what law is, what law does, and how law does what it does. For me, therefore, I was drawn to the philosophy of law as the product of a long-standing and deep-seated interest in law and a newer but no less fundamental interest in language and what the philosophy of language could tell us about legal interpretation, legal reasoning, legal argument, legal decision-making, and thus of law itself.

Fortuitously, perhaps, an interest in the nature of law from the perspective of language pointed directly to the work of H.L.A. Hart (and indirectly to the speech act tradition from which Hart emerged and to which he contributed), and it was through Hart's work, including some of his early work on legal language, that my own interests expanded from an interest in the intersection of language and law to an interest in the philosophical dimensions of law itself. Through all of this I have been far less focused on moral, political, and social philosophy than have been many other legal philosophers, and instead I have tried to think philosophically about law and its mechanisms with the assistance of those areas of philosophy that have traditionally played less of a role in legal philosophy. Moral and political philosophy are, to be sure, important for all philosophers of law, but so too are epistemology, the philosophy of language, the philosophy of action, the philosophy of mind, the philosophy of science, and many others. I like to think that my work is characterized more by clarity and analytical precision than by substantive moral or political commitment, and I like to think that this feature of my scholarship is one that was fueled, initially, by my auto-didactic exposure to the rigors of analytic philosophy generally and to the insights of ordinary language philosophy and the philosophy of language more particularly.

For which of your contribution(s) to legal philosophy so far would you like to be remembered, and why?

If we define the philosophy of law very expansively, we might consider philosophical work about freedom of expression to be part of the broader topic, and in this respect I would like to be remembered, in part, for my contributions to the philosophical study of freedom of speech and freedom of the press. More particularly, I would like to be remembered partly for applying rigorous conceptual analysis, especially in *Free Speech: A Philosophical Enquiry*, in order to isolate the idea of a Free Speech Principle, and in order to distinguish that Principle from other moral and political principles, in particular the broader principle of liberty. And even more I would like to be remembered for casting an unfortunately rare skeptical (or at least critical) eye on the very idea of a Free Speech Principle and on the traditional arguments offered in support of it. Perhaps not surprisingly, theorists of freedom of expression have overwhelmingly been those who are drawn to the topic because of their own enthusiasm for the freedoms of free speech and press, and thus the field of freedom of expression scholarship remains dominated by celebrants, to the almost total (although less total now than several decades ago) exclusion of those who might be, in the characteristic and traditional spirit of philosophy, more skeptical and more critical. I will be pleased if my own critical attitude and skepticism not only advances our understanding of the idea of freedom of expression, but also encourages others to look at this vastly important topic as philosophers rather than as advocates or as cheerleaders.

Yet although I have been proud of my work on freedom of speech and heartened by its reception and influence, I would like mostly to be remembered within philosophy of law for two contributions to understanding the nature of law itself. First is my work on the analysis of rules in general, work embodied in *Playing By the Rules: A Philosophical Examination of Rule-Based Decision-Making in Law and in Life* and some number of articles, and more recently extended to questions of generalization, and to various contemporary policy issues, in *Profiles, Probabilities, and Stereotypes*. Although there had been interesting philosophical work on rules coming out of the debates between act- and rule-utilitarians in the 1950s and 1960s, little of that work addressed the very idea of rule-based decision-making in law, or, indeed, in and throughout the entire realm of human decisional practices. I hope that by a careful analysis of what rules are, what they do, and how they do it I have made an enduring contribution to understanding a vital component of individual (as well as institutional) thinking, reasoning, and decision-making. And by analyzing rules as entrenched prescriptive generalizations, I hope of helped people to see the way in which the generalizing and under- and over-inclusive character of rule-based decision-making distinguishes it from more case-specific, particularistic, or contextual approaches to decision-making. Moreover, by stressing the frequent (although hardly universal) virtues of rules, and pointing out the way in which those virtues might look different to rule-makers than to those whose best judgment would be constrained by rules, I would like to believe that I have provided a valuable counterbalance to the weight of a philosophical literature that has typically seen rule-following as irrational, and that has tended to castigate rules and their proponents as mechanical, formalistic, mindless, and guilty of the worst kind of rule-worship. All of these charges may at times be true, but if we come to understand rules as representing second-best strategies in a non-ideal world of imperfect decision-makers, we can understand, especially from the perspective of those who wish to constrain the sub-optimal decision-making of others, that rules can be a valuable device for channeling decision-making, even if imperfectly, in a world of limited time, limited resources, and even more imperfect decision-makers.

My other contribution is connected with but not congruent with my work on rules, and this is as part of an attempt, one shared in various ways by theorists such as Jeremy Waldron, Tom Campbell, Larry Alexander, and William Twining, to continue to develop a conception of legal positivism with roots in Jeremy Bentham and John Austin, and which may have been unfortunately obscured by debates between so-called exclusive and inclusive positivists about which conception of legal positivism best captures the very idea of the concept of law. Yet although these debates between the inclusive and exclusive positivists have had some value, they have tended to crowd out a historically and currently important conception of legal positivism (and one consistent with the understanding that of legal positivism that Ronald Dworkin takes as his primary foil) as a description of the way in which law might be understood as representing a domain of decision-making resources more limited than that generally available in the society in which a legal system exists. Moreover, and as Bentham most prominently advocated, legal positivism in this sense might be understood as the systemic analog of individual rules, in which restricting judges and other legal decision-makers to a limited domain of materials might prevent them from reaching optimally good decisions at times, but might also prevent them from making especially bad ones in the service of their own sometimes mistaken (or worse) conceptions of right decisions. From this perspective legal positivism can be seen as a dimension along which we might describe those legal systems that have this limited domain characteristic, and thus legal positivism emerges not as a conceptual description of what is necessarily true of all possible legal systems in all possible worlds, but instead as a characteristic of some but not all actual legal systems, and as a characteristic that may at times be an appropriate target for normative theorizing about how this or that legal system *ought* to be designed and ought to operate.

What are the most important issues in legal philosophy, and why are they distinctively issues of legal philosophy rather than some other discipline?

The most important issues in legal philosophy seem to me to be those invite the employing of philosophical tools to seek to explain (or deny) the distinctiveness of law itself, or to help us to understand law's characteristic methods and processes. Although law is without doubt the vehicle through which much of moral and political philosophy is put into practice, the issues of moral and political philosophy that are consequently embodied in law are not, at least to me, the primary issues of legal philosophy itself. This is not to chide those legal philosophers who have been concerned with such topics, but it is to say that at least such topics should not be considered as representing the central questions of legal philosophy. So, for example, it is plainly a matter of great moral and political importance whether the state should exercise a paternalistic role, and prohibit or otherwise control acts that harm no one other than the actor. But although it is of course true that paternalistic regulation would inevitably have to involve the making of laws and the interpretation and enforcement of them by the legal system, such issues are not to me the central and characteristic issues of legal philosophy as such. So too with questions of equality and discrimination, whose moral and political importance should be obvious, but whose importance pervades our public and private lives, rather than being the special or characteristic concern of law as such, legal institutions, or the processes of legal argument and legal reasoning.

By contrast, many issues of philosophical interest and importance are more focused on what the law is, what it does, and how it operates. Among those questions, and the ones of particular interest to me, are the nature of authority, the relationship of authority to law's pervasive use and citation of authorities, the nature of legal sources and their relationship to social sources, the role of rules in a legal system, the nature of common-law decision-making, the distinctiveness (or not) of legal reasoning and legal argument, the nature of precedent, the epistemological issues involved in law's fact-determining efforts, and a host of issues of procedural justice.

The foregoing list is hardly exhaustive of the important issues of legal philosophy that are about law as such, and the list is better understood as reflecting my own interests than as attempting to impose boundaries on a fluid and seamless field. So, for example, there are other theorists who are interested in using philosophical tools to understand areas of law such as tort, contract, and criminal law, or to understand concepts such as constitutionalism, and although these are not (with the exception of constitutionalism) significantly my own interests, these too are inquiries that are focused on law as such, and are thus central components of the philosophy of law.

Traditionally, of course, much of legal philosophy has been directed to the question of identifying the nature of law itself. This was the goal of traditional natural law theory, it was and is the goal of traditional positivist theory, and it is the goal of those who now debate the relative descriptive virtues of inclusive and exclusive legal positivism. Yet although it would be an error to question the collective insights that many of these debates have yielded, it is much less of an error to question whether these kinds of debates about the nature of law should have occupied as large a proportion of the field of philosophy of law as has been the case. Often with the assistance of the distinction between particular and general jurisprudence, those who train their philosophical tools on the trans-national, trans-systemic, and trans-temporal nature of the concept of law itself have too often explicitly or implicitly denigrated more contingent and less universal attempts to examine with philosophical methods and philosophical concepts the nature of legal reasoning, legal argument, and legal decision. Yet although general jurisprudence is interesting and important, and although many issues of general jurisprudence remain open for further analysis and argument, there is no reason why the somewhat more local issues of particular jurisprudence should not be understood as every bit as much a part of the philosophy of law "properly so called."

What is the relationship between legal philosophy and legal practice? Should legal philosophers be more concerned about the effects of their scholarship on legal practice?

Many dimensions of legal philosophy should attempt to explain, with philosophical tools, legal practice as it actually exists. Ronald Dworkin's analysis of legal argument and judicial decision-making is a very prominent example, but one sees the same thing in much of the philosophical analysis of precedent, of the nature of the common law, of authority, and of many other dimensions of the practice (in the Wittgensteinian sense) of law itself. Insofar as legal philosophy is, in part, a descriptive and explanatory enterprise, and insofar as one of the things being described and explained at a deep philosophical level is legal reasoning, legal argument, and legal decision-making, then good legal philosophy will inevitably strive to be as accurate as it can be about the phenomenon it seeks to describe, analyze, and explain.

I am less confident, however, that the reverse is or should be true. Not only philosophy, but also much of the best academic work more generally, seeks to step back from actual practice, and thus seeks to avoid being an active player in current issues precisely in order to achieve that degree of distance or detachment necessary to give academics and their enterprise a comparative advantage over what exists in day-to-day public discourse. Legal philosophy does and should influence legal practice by increasing understanding, and sometimes by making prescriptions that do or should be followed by participants in the legal system, but, like much of the best and most influential philosophy generally, this effect will not take place in the short term or even in the intermediate term. And not only is it rare for there to be short term or intermediate term influence, attempting to have such influence may distort the academic and philosophical enterprise. If legal philosophers are concerned with whether lawyers and judges and other legal actors read their work and follow their prescriptions, they may tailor those prescriptions to current realities or to the desire to have influence rather than to produce the right answer. This is of course appropriate for a political or practical enterprise, but the comparative advantage of philosophy may lie precisely in its depth, its abstraction, and its willingness to say things that are outside the realm of the currently possible. The philosopher who writes or thinks with an eye to relatively immediate influence may wind up impeding philosophical progress, and may as well, even if not completely consciously, attempt to cater to the very forces that the nature of the academic enterprise require to be kept at some distance.

To which problem, issue or broad area of legal philosophy would you most like to see more attention paid in the future?

In terms of the future, I wish there were more attention paid by legal philosophers to questions of legal procedure, in the largest sense of that idea. This attention would include the kinds of issues of legal epistemology that have been the subject of recent work by philosophers such as Susan Haack, Alvin Goldman, and Larry Laudan, but would also include addressing questions about the idea of a burden of proof, about the nature of the adversarial approach to legal decision-making, about the relationship between procedure and larger questions of fairness, and about much else. It remains surprising that there is so much very good philosophy about contract, tort, and the criminal law, but very little about evidence, and virtually nothing about other dimensions of legal procedure. Law is, in part, characterized by the procedures it employs, and it is law's procedures that, in large part, distinguish it from other policy-making and decision-making domains. Consequently, it would be a welcome development if the law's procedures, and indeed the idea of procedure itself, were subjected to the same kind of sustained philosophical attention that we have seen for various areas of substantive law.

Bibliography

Frederick Schauer, *Free Speech: A Philosophical Enquiry* (Cambridge: Cambridge University Press, 1982).

Frederick Schauer, *Playing By the Rules: A Philosophical Examination of Rule-Based Decision-Making in Law and in Life* (Oxford: Clarendon Press, 1991).

Frederick Schauer, *Profiles, Probabilities, and Stereotypes* (Cambridge, Massachusetts: Harvard University Press, 2003).

Frederick Schauer, "(Re)Taking Hart," *Harvard Law Review*, 119 (2006), 852–83.

Frederick Schauer, "Precedent," *Stanford Law Review*, 39 (1987), 575–605.

Frederick Schauer, "Formalism," *Yale Law Journal*, 97 (1988), 509–48.

Frederick Schauer, "Slippery Slopes," *Harvard Law Review*, 99 (1985), 361–83.

Frederick Schauer, "Exceptions," *University of Chicago Law Review*, 58 (1991), 871–99.

Frederick Schauer, "On the Supposed Defeasibility of Legal Rules," *Current Legal Problems 1998* (M.D.A. Freeman, ed., Oxford: Oxford University Press, 1998), 223–40.

Frederick Schauer, "Positivism as Pariah," in Robert George ed., *The Autonomy of Law: Essays on Legal Positivism* (Oxford: Clarendon Press, 1996), 31–56.

Frederick Schauer, "The Limited Domain of the Law," *Virginia Law Review*, 90 (2004), 1909–56.

Frederick Schauer, Positivism Through Thick and Thin," in Brian Bix ed., *Analyzing Law: New Essays in Legal Theory* (Oxford: Oxford University Press, 1998), 65–78.

Frederick Schauer, "The Social Construction of the Concept of Law: A Reply to Julie Dickson," *Oxford Journal of Legal Studies*, 25 (2005), 493–501.

Frederick Schauer, "Is the Common Law Law?," *California Law Review*, 77 (1989), 455–71.

Frederick Schauer, "Giving Reasons," *Stanford Law Review*, 47 (1995), 633–73.

Frederick Schauer, "Imposing Rules," *San Diego Law Review*, 42 (2005), 85–90.

Frederick Schauer, "Do Cases Make Bad Law,?" *University of Chicago Law Review*, 73 (2006), 883–918.

Frederick Schauer, "Fuller's Internal Point of View," *Law and Philosophy*, 12 (1994), 285–312.

Frederick Schauer, "The Phenomenology of Speech and Harm," *Ethics*, 103 (1993), 635–53.

Frederick Schauer, "A Comment on the Structure of Rights," *Georgia Law Review*, 27 (1992), 415–34.

Frederick Schauer, "Can Rights Be Abused,?" *Philosophical Quarterly*, 31 (1981), 225–30.

16
Scott J. Shapiro

Professor of Law and Professor of Philosophy
University of Michigan, Ann Arbor, USA

Why were you initially drawn to the philosophy of law?
For many people, jurisprudence is one of the drearier corners of philosophy. Someone's got to do it, they admit, but happily not them. I don't of course share this feeling but I do understand it. The law is a technical practice and many of the theoretical issues it raises are undeniably dry, even by the normal standards of analytical philosophy. It may also be true that we legal philosophers have a tendency to beat the life out our subject, unwilling as most of us are to let even the most insignificant issue drop. And, of course the name "jurisprudence" doesn't help either. Still I have always been drawn to the field from the moment I encountered it, and have remained enthralled ever since. I believe that this fascination reflects the intrinsic interest of the field; although they may not always be addressed in most graceful or accessible ways, the questions that legal philosophers confront – about the nature of law, how to interpret legal texts, whether legal authority can ever be legitimate and, if so, under which circumstances – are clearly as central and as they are difficult. But my immediate attraction to jurisprudence probably has a lot to do the peculiarities of my background. I think that the law mirrored certain puzzling aspects of my own upbringing and that legal philosophy offered, among other things, a way of making sense of it all.

Although I did not grow up in a religious home, I went to an orthodox Jewish *yeshiva* from elementary school through high school. I lived at that time in Paterson, New Jersey, a dying industrial town with a failing public school system, and my parents felt that the *yeshiva* was the best option to be had. My teachers were largely orthodox rabbis (or their wives) and half of the curriculum was devoted to Jewish law and literature. Since the Talmud was regarded as the pinnacle of Jewish learning, we started studying it from 5th grade on, and spent several hours a day poring over the ancient Babylonian texts. I was taught that I was extremely lucky to have been born a Jew because, despite enduring thousands of years of persecution, we at least have the Law. According to my teachers, the Law is God's greatest gift to mankind and our highest obligation is to learn it.

Jewish law has a lot of rules and I spent a shocking portion of my youth studying them. There are rules about what one is allowed to eat, how long a woman's shirt sleeve must be, how much interest one is permitted to charge a fellow Jew, what blessing one must say upon seeing a rainbow, how one is supposed to put on their shoes (answer: left shoe first, then right shoe, then tie left shoe, then tie right shoe), how to tear toilet paper on the Sabbath if one has no other recourse (answer: not along the perforations), and so on. I was taught that if a rule requires someone to perform, or not perform, some action, then that is the end of the story. You are required to listen to it. A rule is ... a rule. Correspondingly, if an action is permitted by a rule, then one is free to engage in it. This is so regardless of whether the action permitted appears to be as bad as the action forbidden. One of my favorite examples of this phenomenon is the rule requiring married women to cover their hair – the rationale being that a woman's hair is sexually arousing. Many rabbinical authorities have interpreted this rule to permit women to don wigs made from other women's hair. The point of human hair wigs, of course, is to hide the fact that one is wearing a wig and, given advances in wig technology, it is often impossible to tell whether an orthodox married woman is wearing one or not. As my grandmother would say, "Oy Gevalt!"

The same zealous respect for rules was preached at home as well, although the rules were not God's. My father liked everything in the house to be a certain way – he worked as a quality control engineer (enough said) – and he made lots of rules in order to bring his vision of the perfect household into being. My personal favorite had to do with ice cube disposal. If you drank anything with sugar, you had to dispose of the ice cubes that came in contact with the liquid in the right sink. The reason? Because that sink didn't have a garbage disposal, and my father swore that sugar had a corrosive effect on gears. Time after time, I found myself on the wrong side of this particular injunction, having absentmindedly emptied the last dregs of a glass of orange juice on the wrong side. At the time, I did not think that a lot of these rules made sense but my father's perspective was that I had to follow his rules because he is my father and, after all, rules are rules.

Growing up, then, I was surrounded by a mind-set that I referred to in my dissertation as "rule-think." Here is how I described this outlook then:

> One who engages in rule-think always looks, in the first instance, to a rule in order to determine whether a given action is justifiable. The rule-thinker doesn't consider whether the act is justifiable by virtue of its consequences; nor does he ask whether the action is intrinsically good or bad. When a rule prohibits an action, that action is deemed unjustifiable. But if a rule can be found which permits it, then that action suddenly becomes acceptable. In the curious logic of rule-think, the mere fact that a rule governs in any case is of paramount importance.
>
> People often look foolish when they engage in rule-think. They don't appear to care about the questions that seem most relevant to those who are not steeped in their culture, i.e., they don't ask whether the public will be better off if others are allowed to engage in the activity under consideration. Rule-thinkers argue about whether Rule A, Rule B or Rule C actually governs in the given case. They scour legislative codes, administrative regulations and judicial opinions looking for some "loophole" which will justify the behavior they want to justify. And they all agree that an action is justified, even if completely absurd, if a rule can be produced which credibly sanctions that action.

This description of rule-think in the law might just as well be a description of my childhood. When I asked about the rationality of being guided by legal rules, there is a sense in which I was really inquiring into the reasonableness of my teachers and parents. Is rule-think a proper way to conduct oneself or does it represent a throw-back to a primitive and irrational way of life? How could Jewish Law be God's ultimate gift if it permits women to wear wigs made out of women's hair while at the same time deeming the very same hair sexually arousing? And can sugar really break a garbage disposal?

This is not of course to say that my interest in jurisprudence is reducible to these childhood issues, or that there aren't plenty of good intellectual reasons for studying jurisprudence which have nothing to do with getting over a rule-dominated upbringing, whether it be religious or not. It is simply by way of saying that my own experience of rules probably explains why jurisprudential issues resonated for me so immediately and strongly.

For which of your contribution(s) to legal philosophy so far would you most like to be remembered, and why?

The question presupposes that I have made a contribution to legal philosophy—definitely a shaky premise. I have worked on several different issues since I finished graduate school in 1996 – the problem of rule-think has been a particularly major though by no means exclusive, preoccupation. But I honestly can't say that I feel like I have solved these problems to my own (or to anyone else's) satisfaction.

Like many academics, I tend to feel that finished work is hopelessly inadequate while any in progress teeters on the edge of brilliance. So, in keeping with that (possibly occupational) quirk, I would like to be remembered for the theory I am currently working on, which I have no doubt will revolutionize the field. But before I briefly describe this theory – which I call the "planning theory of law" – it would probably help to say a few words about my jurisprudential orientation in general and why I think that we need a new account of law.

As far as I can remember, I have been a confirmed, dyed-in-the-wool, (and to steal a phrase from Peter Railton) stark-raving-mad legal positivist. On my view, morality and law are governed by very different ground rules. In morality, the only way to establish the existence of its rules is to engage in moral argument. It is never enough simply to say: "That's what we do around here." Convention might be relevant, of course, but if this is so, it is due to the fact that some moral rule requires that conventions be given significance in such circumstances. In law, by contrast, rules must pass the system-specific tests for legal validity, criteria which can never be discovered through moral inquiry. One must first know what certain members of the legal community think, intend, claim and do and, only based on this sociological assessment, can one divine how one legally ought to act. It is simply irrelevant to point out that these tests of validity are not morally sound. Worthy or not, the law is just what we do around here.

Like many other legal positivists, I have been drawn to this picture of law for a very simple reason: it seems to me an obvious truth about the nature of law that regimes that are morally illegitimate may still have law. I say this because it is easy for me to imagine legal systems that are evil. In fact, human history is a sad tale of such systems. The past century provides a long list of wicked regimes that had law: the Soviet Union, the Third Reich, the Khmer Rouge, the Taliban, the Iraqi Baathists, the Burmese Junta, etc. If the concept of law required that the tests of validity be morally sound, then it would seem that none of these regimes had law. Not only does it seem to me that the Nazis had law, but what made the Nazis so dangerous is precisely that they had it.

While I think that allowing for unjust legal systems is an excellent reason to be a legal positivist, it would be unsatisfying if it were the only one. For starters, not everyone agrees with these intuitions. Some deny that the Nazis, the Soviets, the Taliban, etc. had law—they claim that these regimes merely had "law-like" systems. Now I find these reactions idiosyncratic, but the fact that many people that I respect have them means that I cannot dismiss them out-of-hand. If legal theory is to be interesting, it can't just be a game of "he intuits-she intuits."

Secondly, and more importantly, it is open to the natural lawyer to concede that we sometimes impute law to wicked regimes, but that this attribution represents a mistake on our part. They can claim, in other words, that our grasp of the concept of law is imperfect and that the role of philosophy is to correct this confusion. One way for a positivist to rebut such a response, then, is to stop relying on a bare intuition and instead provide more theoretically robust grounds for thinking that law ultimately rests on social, not moral, facts.

In my opinion, legal positivists have failed to provide such an explanation. For example, consider H.L.A. Hart's theory in *The Concept of Law*. As is well-known, Hart thought that all legal systems rest on a social rule, which he called the "rule of recognition." The rule of recognition is a social rule practiced by legal officials that sets out the tests of validity in that legal system.

Hart claimed that the rule of recognition can only be generated by social practice because social rules *are* practices. When men regularly take off their hats in church because they take the pattern of behavior as a standard of conduct, the behavior is itself a rule. Likewise, the practice of officials deferring to certain sources of norms generates the rule of recognition because the rule of recognition is nothing but the practice of recognition. Hart's positivism, therefore, is predicated on his theory of social rules: law is ultimately grounded in social practice because it rests on a social rule and a social rule is nothing but a social practice.

With all due respect to Hart, this account appears to commit a category mistake. Rules are abstract objects. They are like games, numbers, plots, propositions and concepts – they are objects of thought, not entities that exist within space and time. Practices, on the other hand, are concrete events. They take place within the natural world and causally interact with other physical events. Social rules cannot be social practices because they occupy different ontological categories.

Surprisingly, not even Joseph Raz, clearly the greatest living legal positivist, has produced an argument purporting to show that the law ultimately rests on social facts. Raz has, of course, developed an incredibly interesting and influential argument attempting to show that the tests of legal validity must refer only to a norm's social source, never its moral properties (the so-called "Argument from Authority" for the "Sources Thesis.") This argument, however, does not prove, nor does it claim to prove, that the tests of validity setting out the sources of law must themselves have social sources. It does not show that, at bottom, the law is simply what we do around here.

In my recent work, I have tried to offer such an argument. My strategy is to show that there is another normative realm in which the same ground rules apply, namely, the realm of *planning*. The proper way to establish the existence of plans, I argue, is to point to the fact of their adoption. Whether I have a plan to go to the store today depends on whether I adopted such a plan and have not yet rejected it. Likewise, whether we have a plan to paint the house depends on whether we adopted such a plan and have not repudiated it. As far as their existence is concerned, it is simply irrelevant to point out that the plans in question are good plans for us to follow. These plans exist only if we have made them our plans.

I want to be clear here that I am not simply offering an analogy – I am drawing an implication. The existence conditions for law are the same as those for plans because the fundamental rules of legal systems *are* plans. Their function is to structure legal activity so that participants can work together and thereby achieve the political objectives of the practice. As a result, whether someone has legal authority in a particular system depends on whether the officials in that system plan to defer to this person in the relevant circumstances and not whether they morally ought to do so.

The picture of law that emerges is one in which the creation and persistence of the fundamental legal rules are grounded in the ability that groups possess to formulate and adopt plans. This power is not conferred on us by morality. Rather, we have the capacity to create plans for ourselves because, as Michael Bratman has emphasized in his groundbreaking work on intention and action, human beings have a special kind of psychology, namely, we are *planning* creatures. We not only have desires to achieve complex ends, but we also have the ability to settle on such goals and to organize behavior over time and between one another to achieve our purposes. That the law is founded upon plans in large part explains how groups are able to accomplish the immensely complex and sophisticated ends they characteristically perform, e.g., maintaining order, redistributing wealth, protecting the rights of at least some parties, providing facilities for private ordering, settling disputes and so on.

In my view, then, the philosophy of law can helpfully be seen as a form of applied philosophy of action. To understand the law, we have to understand our special psychology and the complex forms of agency that it enables. Fortunately, in recent years philosophers of action such as Bratman have made important advances developing a rich theory of planning. We now have a pretty good understanding of the process of planning, the structure of plans, the motivation for creating plans and the rationality constraints that attend such an activity. Legal philosophers have at their disposal a whole new set of tools for analyzing legal institutions and activity.

Indeed, one need not accept my planning theory in order to see a tight connection between the philosophies of law and action. The law, after all, not only regulates human activity, it results from human activity. If we want to understand the nature of legal activity, then, we should look to the branch of philosophy that concerns itself with individual and shared agency.

What are the most important issues in legal philosophy, and why are they distinctively issues of legal philosophy rather than some other discipline?

Traditionally, legal philosophy is divided into two parts: normative and analytical. Normative legal philosophy deals with the moral foundations of the law and may itself be sub-divided into two branches. The positive side of normative legal philosophy aims to describe the actual moral underpinnings of current law. It asks, for example, why our criminal law punishes criminals. Is it to deter others from committing crimes or to rehabilitate them? Do we punish in order to incapacitate offenders for a while or so that they get their just deserts? The positive theorist is also interested in why the law holds contractual parties liable when they make certain contracts. Is it because they promised? Or is it because economic efficiency demands that we hold people to their bargains? And so on.

The second branch of normative legal philosophy – call it the reformist side – asks a different question. Instead of attempting to describe the actual moral foundations of current law, it asks what, from a moral point of view, current law should be. Regardless of why the criminal law we have punishes criminals, should criminals be punished? Is property theft? Should abortions be legal? Do people have the moral right to die? Is there an obligation to obey the law?

Analytical legal philosophy, by contrast, concerns the philosophical analysis of the law and it also consists of two sub-branches. The first part seeks to analyze basic legal concepts such as "responsibility," "rule," "authority," "obligation," "validity," "cause," "property," "agency," "crime" and the like. It asks, for example, whether the legal concept of cause is the same as our ordinary concept of cause, whether every legal right implies a legal remedy, whether property is best understood as a bundle of rights and so on. Admittedly, the line between this branch of analytical legal philosophy and the positive side of normative legal philosophy is not always so clear. Is it possible, for example, to understand the concept of a tort, and how it differs from, say, crime, without understanding why we hold people liable for the torts that they commit? In these cases at least, it would appear that one couldn't do analytical jurisprudence without also engaging in normative jurisprudence.

The second branch of analytical jurisprudence seeks to analyze the nature of law and legal systems. It asks, in the traditional formulation: "What is law?" Because my recent work has concentrated on this question, as well as being the focus of so much philosophical attention in the last several centuries, I would like to take a moment to dwell on it. As I will suggest, philosophers have not been particularly clear about what they mean by the question "What is law?" and that once we are clear about the question, we can get a better sense about why legal philosophers have asked it and should continue to do so.

Legal philosophers usually say that the question "What is law?" concerns the nature of law. "What is law," then, is shorthand for "What is the nature of law?" But what is this latter question asking? What does it mean to ask about the nature of something?

Here it is important to distinguish between two possibilities. One option is that when we ask for the nature of something we are asking about the thing's *identity*, namely, what it is to be that thing. For example, philosophers who study epistemology inquire into the nature of knowledge. To ask "What is knowledge" – where the question is understood as the search for the identity of knowledge – is to ask what it is about knowledge that makes it *knowledge* and not some other thing.

In general, to ask about the identity of X is to ask what it is about X that makes it X and not Y or Z or any other such thing. I call this the "Identity Question." A correct answer to the Identity Question must supply the set of properties that make (possible or actual) instances of X the things that they are. To take another example, the identity of water is $H_2 0$ because water is just $H_2 0$. Being $H_2 0$ is what makes water *water*. With respect to law, therefore, to answer the question "What is law?" understood as a search for the law's identity is to discover what makes all and only instances of law instance of *law* and not something else. It is to ask for its essence, or its essential properties.

Another possibility is that when we inquiry into the nature of an entity, we care about something other than its identity. We are not so much interested in what makes the object the thing that it is, but rather what *necessarily follows from* the fact that it is what it is and not something else. I call this the "Implication Question." It is to ask for the thing's necessary, not its essential, properties.

To see how these questions are different, consider the number 3. What makes the number 3 the number 3 is that it is the number that comes after 2. The identity of 3, therefore, is being the successor of 2. Clearly, however, when mathematicians study the number 3, they are interested in more than its identity. Mathematicians want to know all of its mathematical properties. They want to know, in other words, what follows from the fact that a certain number is the number 3 and not some other number. To take a trivial finding, mathematicians have discovered that 3 is a prime number. While being a prime number is not part of the number 3's identity (being the successor of 2 is), we might still say that it is part of the nature of 3 because being 3 necessarily entails being prime. Put in another way, being prime is part of the nature of 3 because if a number is not prime, then it is impossible for it to be 3.

So when we ask "What is law?", we can either mean to ask about the law's identity – what makes law *law* – or about the implications of something being law – namely, what necessary follows from the fact that something is law and not something else.

It is very easy to confuse these two questions. Consider the notorious "Separability Thesis," which is usually formulated as the claim that "there is no necessary connection between law and morality." Tradition tells us that legal positivists accept the Separability Thesis whereas natural lawyers deny it. Recently, a number of philosophers have questioned whether the Separability Thesis is an issue between these two schools of thought. For example, Joseph Raz has argued that no legal positivist can plausibly deny that there is a necessary connection between law and morality. As Raz points out, surely the social order that law necessarily brings about is morally desirable. It follows that all legal systems have some morally desirable aspects to them, even if on balance the harm created outweighs that good, and hence law and morality are necessarily connected.

Raz is certainly right that no one can plausibly deny the Separability Thesis as it is traditionally formulated. But I think that the Separability Thesis is best seen as a claim about the identity of law, not its necessary implications. The positivist, in other words, concedes that law and morality may share some necessary properties in common. They maintain, nonetheless, that law and morality are not *essentially* connected, that the properties that make law what it is are non-moral in nature. The natural lawyer, on the other hand, insists that a social institution is a legal institution because it possesses some desirable moral properties. He believes that morality is part of the identity of law. Understood in this manner, then, the Separability Thesis is a point of contention between legal positivists and natural lawyers.

What is the relationship between legal philosophy and legal practice? Should legal philosophers be more concerned about the effect of their scholarship on legal practice?

In one obvious sense, legal philosophy is connected to legal practice. Since law is a social practice, legal philosophy has no choice but to attend to the way it is practiced. Legal practice, in other words, is the object of legal philosophy. For this reason, most, if not all, legal philosophers have assumed that the law must be studied from the "internal" perspective, namely, from the point of view of the legal participant. The philosopher is supposed to listen to the claims that participants themselves use to defend and justify their actions so as to determine the practice's nature. As it is sometimes said, the philosophical study of the law is a "hermeneutic" inquiry.

The question posed might be understood, however, in a very different sense: must legal philosophy have some impact on legal practice if it is to be a worthwhile human activity? Many have thought so. Consider the following quote from Richard Posner from the opening of his Clarendon Lectures: "I have nothing against philosophical speculation. But one would like it to have some pay-off; *something* ought to turn on the answer to the question 'What is law?' if the question is to be worth asking by people who could use their time in other socially productive ways. Nothing does turn on it."

Unsurprisingly, I do not share Posner's attitude about analytical jurisprudence. First, I have little sympathy for the instrumentalist conception of philosophy that Posner is implicitly assuming. I am not sure why philosophical speculation must have a practical payoff while other forms of human activity need not. Surely watching a movie, playing with one's kids, eating dinner or proving a theorem in set theory about the existence of large cardinals are worthwhile activities even if they don't have any socially productive consequences (they might, of course, but that is not what makes them valuable).

But I also reject the idea that legal philosophy is irrelevant to legal practice. *Pace* Posner, something extremely important does turn on the question "What is law?" For it seems to me that it is not possible to address many of the most pressing practical matters that concern lawyers – such as who has legal authority to do what and how to interpret legal texts – without also addressing the analytical questions that have preoccupied philosophers of law. The answer to what the law is in any particular case, in other words, depends in important ways on the answer to what law is in general.

An example will help make the point. Consider the debate

about the constitutionality of the death penalty. Some claim that when the Eighth Amendment prohibits "cruel and unusual punishments," it should be read as barring punishments that are cruel and unusual. "Cruel" means cruel. And since many of the same people think that the death penalty offends human dignity, they believe it to be morally cruel and unusual and, hence, unconstitutional.

Others maintain that the constitutional provision should be read so as to prohibit only those punishments that the framers considered cruel and unusual. Since it is clear that the framers did not think that the death penalty was cruel, those who support this originalist reading of the Eighth Amendment conclude that the death penalty is constitutional.

Here we have a simple disagreement about the law. One side claims that the Eighth Amendment bars cruel and unusual punishments, while the other maintains that it only prohibits punishments that the Framers deemed cruel and unusual. How are we supposed to resolve this disagreement? Which facts are we supposed to look for in order to settle whether the Eighth Amendment ought to be interpreted in one way rather than another?

In truth, the only way to know how to answer this question is to know which facts ultimately determine the content of the law. And the only way to know that is to be in possession of the correct theory of law. This is so because, as I argued earlier, theories of law attempt to answer the Implication question. They purport to specify those truths that necessarily follow from the fact that something is law. That the content of the law is ultimately determined by certain types of facts is a truth that necessarily follows from the fact that something is law. Theories of law, then, will purport to specify what those ultimate determinants of the law are. Hence, if you want to answer questions like "is the death penalty constitutional?" one has to know what necessarily follows from the fact that something is law, which is precisely what a correct theory of law will tell you.

Legal positivists, for example, argue that the content of the law is ultimately determined by social facts. Hart thought, for example, that the content of the law is determined by the social rule of recognition. If the positivist is right, the answer to the question about the Eighth Amendment is to collect social facts. There is no other way to do it. On the other hand, if the natural lawyer is right, then collecting social facts is not enough. One must also engage in moral deliberation as well because the content of the law ultimately depends on moral facts as well. One can't know whether to read the constitution according to plain meaning or original understanding unless one engages in moral philosophy.

It turns out, then, that legal philosophy is anything but irrelevant to legal practice. But several words of caution are in order. Firstly, I am not suggesting that one cannot answer a legal question correctly unless one is also fully in possession of a correct philosophical theory about the nature of law. Most legal questions can be answered by asking a lawyer, reading a law book or typing the query into Google. Moreover, even when there is no expert to consult, it is likely that the answer will not depend on any particular view about the nature of law. It is probable, in other words, that both positivism and natural law theory will give the same answer to the question. The claim, rather, is that the answer to some questions do depend on which view about the nature of law is correct. When this is the case, knowing the nature of the law is invaluable.

To which problem, issue or broad area of legal philosophy would you most like to see more attention paid in the future?

There is one grievance that lawyers have towards legal philosophy which, I think, is entirely valid. The objection often voiced is that jurisprudence as it is currently practiced is too removed from the real world activity of lawyers and judges. The idea here is not so much that legal philosophy is irrelevant to practice but that the theories of law expounded by philosophers do not seem to reflect the activity of actual legal institutions. In particular, lawyers often complain that legal philosophers ignore considerations of institutional competence in developing their accounts of law, especially their theories of legal interpretation. In this respect I think that lawyers are absolutely right.

The disconnect(ion?) between lawyers and philosophers can best be seen by considering the way that interpretive debates proceed in the "real" world. When judges, lawyers and law professors argue for one interpretive methodology over another, they routinely justify themselves by reference to the degree to which certain members of the group can be trusted to act competently and in good faith. Textualists like Justice Antonin Scalia, for example, believe that judges should be constrained to follow the plain meaning of the statute because they do not trust judges to look beyond the text. They fear that judges will insert their own personal political views in the name of effectuating legislative purpose. Other textualists such as Judge Frank Easterbrook reject the search for purpose because they do not trust legislators to fashion public-interest legislation. Statutes, on this view, are built on compromises between opposing interest groups, not unified visions of the general welfare developed by altruistic public servants that can be extended to unanticipated cases. Purposivists such as Henry Hart and Albert Saks, on the other hand, generally presume legal officials to be "reasonable people pursuing reasonable ends reasonably" and thus accord judges broad powers to delve into the "spirit" of the statute when its letter produces results that they find objectionable.

But despite the importance that practicing lawyers attribute to trust relations when determining interpretive method, the concept of trust almost never arises when philosophers discuss the nature of legal interpretation. Ronald Dworkin's theory of interpretation is a case in point. Dworkin argues that interpreters should always interpret texts in a way that will present them in their best moral light. Dworkin never considers, however, whether such a methodology is appropriate for participants with normal cognitive and moral capacities. On the contrary, Dworkinian interpretation presupposes a tremendous trust in the philosophical abilities of group members and in their good will for carrying out such rigorous intellectual exercises. If, as is reasonable to suppose, most individuals are not particularly adept at, or unlikely to engage in, philosophical analysis, it would be especially imprudent to allow them to interpret the practice in accordance with the principles that they strike them as portraying it in the morally best light.

Dworkin's disregard for considerations of trustworthiness is not unique, but is rather a pervasive feature of modern analytical jurisprudence. Jurisprudential theorists have tended to approach issues of legal interpretation through the lens of traditional philosophical concerns, such as linguistic meaning, political morality and conceptual analysis. In keeping with this, their work evinces a notable enthusiasm for debates about the proper semantics of words like "vehicle" and "cruel," the relation of justice to fairness and the conceptual preconditions of law's claim to legitimate authority.

This indifference to considerations of trust is not only irritating to lawyers but deeply ironic, given that it flies in the face of a core assumption to which we earlier saw philosophers of law subscribe. Although the hermeneutic orientation of legal philosophy constitutes part of the shared understanding of legal theorists, the accounts that these theorists propose generally fail to live up to this standard. This is so because these theories do not reflect the actual structure of legal argumentation. Legal participants take questions of competence and character very seriously and legal philosophers unfortunately do not. And because legal philosophers don't take trust seriously, legal participants don't take legal philosophers seriously.

In my own work, I have tried to rectify this failing. My aim has been to develop a theory of law in which considerations of competence and character are central to the understanding of legal institutions and the structure of legal reasoning and argumentation. Here, very briefly, is how I do so.

As I mentioned before, the planning theory of law claims that legal activity is at bottom premised on plans. Legal institutions are structured by plans developed for officials so as to enable them work together in order to achieve the political objectives of the system. But the planning theory not only maintains that legal activity result *from* social planning, but also that it results *in* social planning. Legal institutions plan for the communities over whom they claim authority, both in the sense of telling their members what they may or may not do, as well as providing them with the facilities for realizing their own plans. On this account, legal rules are generalized plans issued by those with the authority to plan for others and adjudication involves the application of these plans to those to whom they apply. The function of legal plans is to organize both individual and collective behavior so that members of the community can bring about moral goods that could not have been achieved, or achieved as well, without them.

Because the law is a planning institution, the need to discriminate between the trustworthy and the untrustworthy will always be a central and pressing concern of legal systems. Insofar as legal institutions must rely on their own members and others to execute its goals, it is perpetually vulnerable to exploitation, ineptitude and negligence. When legal authorities assign rights and responsibilities to the technically incompetent or morally unsavory, they threaten the legal enterprise by placing vital tasks in the hands of those who are unable or unwilling to live up to their responsibilities.

Trust matters in law, then, because the law depends on others to satisfy its political objectives and reliance creates vulnerability and opportunities for exploitation. In large part, legal systems derive their character from the various ways in which they decide to manage their vulnerability – how much they are willing to trust others, whom they trust and what they trust them to do. The distribution of trust and distrust manifested in the institutional design represents what I have called in other work the system's "economy of trust."

When one reflects on the importance of assessing competence and character in allocating legal rights and duties it becomes quickly apparent that such considerations are crucial to determining interpretive methodology as well. Roughly speaking, interpretive discretion must track systemic judgments of trustworthiness: those who do not receive the benefit of the doubt in a system's economy of trust are entitled to little discretion in interpretation, whereas those deemed to be more trustworthy people are legally permitted to exercise greater discretion.

To see this, suppose that a system holds a very distrustful view of the competence and character of officials, an outlook manifested in its institutional design: authority is widely dispersed throughout the system, executive and judicial officers are forbidden from legislating, lengthy waiting times are set up before legislation can be passed, there are severe sanctions for abuse of discretion, ..., etc. Now imagine that the proper interpretive methodology for this distrustful system accords officials a great deal of interpretive discretion. This methodology does not require them to hew too closely to the plain meaning of legal texts but allows them to deviate from them when they think that the texts has been poorly drafted or give unreasonable results. When reading statutes, therefore, officials tend to interpret grants of power broadly, constraints narrowly, ignore legislative texts when it gives a result with which they mildly disagree, refuse to defer to the interpretation of regulations by the appropriate administrative agencies, etc. All of this is permitted according to the proper interpretive methodology.

The obvious difficulty with this mode of proceeding, however, is that the interpretive methodology in question creates too much vulnerability from a systemic perspective. By according officials a large degree of interpretive discretion, the methodology provides them the opportunity to expand their powers, reduce restrictions and further increase their discretion beyond that which had been contemplated. The resulting distribution of power and authority is one that could not be justified by the distrustful views of the regime. From the systemic point of view, the interpretive methodology in question is far too risky, in that it can be rationalized only by attitudes that are more optimistic than the system happens to be.

Likewise, a system that does take a more optimistic attitude towards human nature and cognition is ill served by a highly restrictive interpretive methodology. While such a methodology diminishes the vulnerability of the law, from the point of view of the system it reduces the exposure too much. By curtailing the degree to which officials can exercise interpretive discretion, officials are precluded from pursuing the objectives that they were entrusted to serve.

To be sure, the argument just presented is incomplete, in that it does not tell us *whose* judgments constitute the systemic point of view. Nor does it tell us how exactly interpretive methodology ought to track these judgments. It was simply meant to give one a sense of how a theory of law might try to account for the lawyerly preoccupation with considerations of trust and why they are right to be so concerned.

Bibliography

"Fear of Theory," 64 University of Chicago Law Review 389 (1997)

"The Difference That Rules Make," *Analyzing Law: New Essays in Legal Theory*, B. Bix, ed. (Oxford: Clarendon Press, 1998)

"Rule-Guided Behavior," *The New Palgrave Dictionary of Economics and the Law*, P. Newman ed. (with E. McClennan) (1998)

"On Hart's Way Out," *4 Legal Theory* 454 (1999) and, with minor revisions, in *Hart's Postscript*, J. Coleman ed. (Oxford: Clarendon Press, 2001)

"Law, Morality and the Guidance of Conduct," *6 Legal Theory* 127 (2000)

"The Bad Man and the Internal Point of View", *The Path of the Law and Its Influence: The Legacy of Oliver Wendell Holmes, Jr.*, S. Burton ed. (Cambridge: Cambridge University Press, 2000)

"Judicial Can't," 35 *Nous* 530 (2001)

"Law, Plans and Practical Reason," *8 Legal Theory* 387 (2002)

"Authority," *Oxford Handbook of Jurisprudence and Philosophy of Law*, J. Coleman and S. Shapiro eds. (Oxford: Clarendon Press, 2002)

"Ulysses Rebound," 16 Economics and Philosophy 157 (2002)

"What is the Internal Point of View?" 75 Fordham Law Review 1157 (2006)

"The 'Hart-Dworkin' Debate: A Short Guide for the Perplexed," *Ronald Dworkin*, ed. A. Ripstein (Cambridge: Cambridge University Press, 2007)

About the Editor

Morten Ebbe Juul Nielsen, PhD, MA (phil), BA (psych). Currently Post Doc at Roskilde University. Awarded Copenhagen University's Gold Medal for Master's Dissertation on Communitarianism, 1999. PhD at Copenhagen and Oxford Universities 2004, *Liberalism, Neutrality, and Perfectionism*. Several publications, mainly in political philosophy. Reviewer for *Synthese*, *Filosofisk Årbog*. Editor of *Political Questions* and *Legal Philosophy*. Commentator for Danish main intellectual Broadsheet *Weekendavisen*.

About Legal Philosophy

Legal Philosophy: 5 Questions is an excellent introduction to contemporary Jurisprudence, showing the broad range of work being done in the field. Many of the best scholars in the area summarize their ideas in their own words, in accessible short essays. The collection shows how legal philosophy can be a calling, a fulfilling path, whether to truth or to justice. The book also displays the richness and variety of Jurisprudence today.

—**Brian H. Bix**, Frederick W. Thomas Professor of Law and Philosophy University of Minnesota

The importance of this invaluable collection of essays is that they are not only concerned with current issues in the philosophy of law. The collection also gives us a fascinating view both forwards - to new philosophical questions likely to preoccupy thinkers in the future - and backwards, to the influences that led these leading scholars on to their chosen path. It is an intellectual goldmine for those working in philosophy of law today.

—**Jeremy Horder**, Professor, Law Commission for England and Wales; University of Oxford

Who are these philosophers of law? Their disputes resonate far beyond the academy, and for half a century now they have enjoyed a collective prominence greater than that of philosophers of any other specialty. Is it good that our "public intellectuals" are likelier to be philosophers of law than mere philosophers, or mere lawyers? Five questions are put to each of 16 leading-edge figures in the field, which is itself understood as a "quest for identity." What drew you into philosophy of law?...What have you contributed to it? ... Where is it headed? ... The answers are surprising, intimately personal, enlightening, witty, and – in some instances – even inspiring. Best of all, the questions and answers gently force the reader to engage in his or her own reflection and reminiscence. It is impossible to over-praise this wonderful collection.

—**William A. Edmundson**, Professor of Law and of Philosophy, Georgia State University

Index

Aarnio, A., 177
abortion, 14
adjudication, 61, 68
Adler, R., 2, 177
agency, 132, 216
Alexander, L., 40, 202
Alexy, R., 1, 177
American Legal Realists, 144
American Model Penal Code, 137
annulment, 35
apology, 55
Aquinas, T., 195
argumentation, 2
Aristotle, 41, 81, 196
Ashworth, A., 91, 129
Austin, J.L., 60, 89, 126, 131, 150, 172, 202
authority, 77, 216
Ayer, A.J., 75

Bankowski, Z., 179
Bayles, M., 27
beauty, 195
being, 195
Beiser, F.C., 190
Bell, J., 129
Bennett, J., 190
Bentham, J., 76, 102, 118, 126, 161, 202
Bentley, D., 173
bioethics, 15, 147
Birks, P., 128
Brooklyn College, 28
Burge, T., 31
Buxton, R., 173

Calabresi, G., 32
Campbell, T., 13, 202
Canada, 75
Cane, P., 129
case-law, 23
cause, 216
Cawkwell, G., 127
Chomsky, N., 76
Church of Scotland, 13
Civil War, 168
Clinton, B., 184
Cohen, G.A., 84
Cohen, J., 46, 127
Cohen, M., 30
Coleman, J., 27
Collins, H., 126, 129
compensation, 35
constitutional theory, 147
constitutionalism, 61
Cornell University, 160, 179
correctness, 10
correctness thesis, 7
Cotterrell, R., 134
court, 61
crime, 216
criminalization, 91, 96, 132
Critical Legal Studies, 178
Cross, R., 128
Crow, J., 168

D'Estaing, G., 179
Davidson, D., 30
death penalty, 220
decision-making, 202
demarcation problem, 145
democracy, 9, 62, 157, 189

Democratic National Convention, 28
discourse theory, 3
Downie, R., 15, 172
Dreier, R., 1, 179
dual-nature thesis, 6
Duff, A., 15, 47
duty, 34
Dworkin, G., 114
Dworkin, R., 21, 37, 51, 60, 76, 126, 147, 166, 173, 176, 202, 222

Earman, J., 29
Easterbrook, F., 222
economic analysis of law, 147
economy, 184
Edwards, J., 190
Eekelaar, J., 129
Eighth Amendment, 220
empowerment, 194
equality, 4, 14, 79, 203
'ethical positivism', 16
ethics, 61, 106
European Free Alliance, 179
European Parliament, 179
Evans, G., 173
explanation, 55

FBI, 157
Feinberg, J., 30, 37, 92, 96
feminist theory, 135
Finnis, J., 46, 60, 76, 77, 126, 173, 177, 190
Fletcher, G., 115
Floud, J., 173
Frank, J., 68, 149
Frankfurt, H., 30, 173
Frazer, E., 135
free speech, 14
Free Speech Principle, 201
freedom of expression, 199
Frege, G., 1, 192

Freud, S., 150
Friedman, M., 190
Fuller, L., 15, 20, 76, 196

Galligan, D., 126
Gandhi, M., 167
Gardner, J., 45
Gavison, R., 59
Gaza, 69
Glover, J., 46, 76
Goldman, A., 206
Göttingen, 1
government, 107
Green, L., 75, 127
Grotius, H., 197
Group of the Greens, 179
Guest, S., 126

Haack, S., 206
Hampshire, S., 89
Hare, R.M., 89, 172
Harm Principle, 96
Harriman, A., 160
Harris, D.R., 172
Harris, J., 129
Hart, H.L.A., 15, 37, 59, 76, 102, 130, 136, 145, 158, 171, 188, 200, 213
Hart, J., 174
Harvard Law School, 89, 187
Harvard University, 28
Heck, P., 196
Hegel, G.W.F., 76
Heginbotham, C., 19
Hirsch, A.v., 89
Honoré, T., 46, 76, 77, 101, 128, 129
Horder, J., 49
Hornsby, J., 135
Horsburgh, H., 172
human rights, 4, 62, 63, 71, 107, 127

Hume, D., 14, 89, 172
Husak, D., 98, 113
Husserl, E., 192

incorporationism, 38
Indiana University, 115
injustice, 7, 21, 118, 163
intentionalism, 164
interests, 69
interpretive methodology, 224
intersubjectivity, 10
intuition, 148
Israel, 69
Israel's Association for Civil Rights, 61

Jareborg, N., 94
Jellinek, G., 191
Jhering, R.v. , 188
judgement, 104
judicial activism, 20, 62
jurisprudence, 27, 37, 42, 126, 134, 147, 187, 209, 216, 221
   general, 48
   realist, 144
justice, 8, 14, 18, 32, 163, 183
   corrective, 35
   retributive, 33
justification, 10

Kant, I., 49, 190
Kaufmann, W., 143
Kavka, G., 29
Kelsen, H., 60, 76, 126, 145, 172, 188, 189
Kim, J., 29
knowledge, 10, 195
Krier, J., 144
Külpe, O., 192

Lacey, N., 45, 103, 125, 148, 174, 178

Lamont, W.D., 172
language, 42, 104
language game, 130
Laudan, L., 206
law, 3, 15, 20, 61, 64, 106, 107, 114, 131, 163, 183, 184, 195, 203, 205, 216, 222
   anti-discrimination, 48
   as social practices, 138
   criminal, 48, 116, 127, 136
   natural, 126
   nature of, 79, 82, 87, 115, 120, 195, 197, 200, 201, 204, 209, 213, 216, 217
   'of normativity', 194
   of torts, 48
   philosophy of, 65
   positive, 21
   theory of, 85
lawyer vs. philosopher, 221
legal
   argumentation, 2, 8, 223
   constitutionalism, 24
   discourse, 2, 18
   institution, 175
   language, 200
   obligation, 16
   philosophers, 116
   philosophy, 8, 15, 22, 50, 64, 122, 146, 150, 187, 195, 205, 219
      analytical, 215
      normative, 215
   positivism, 15, 16, 38, 40, 64, 145, 202, 212
      prescriptive, PCP, 16
   practice, 9, 16, 22, 42, 80, 184, 195, 219
   procedure, 206
   realism, 144

reasoning, 2, 16, 144
rule, 131
scholarship, 147
science, 193, 194
system, 131
legalization, 61
legislation, 23
Leiter, B., 83, 143
Lewis, P., 173
liability, 35, 194
liberal social democracy, 180
liberalism, 62
liberty, 201
litigation, 109
Litschewski Paulson, B., 6
logic, 59
Lovibond, S., 135
Luhmann, N., 133
Luther King, Jr., M., 167
Lyons, D., 153

MacCormick, N., 2, 15, 60, 171
MacDowell, J., 76
Mackie, J., 127
Macklem, T., 49
Maclagan, W.G., 13, 172
Marcus Aurelius, 77
Marx, K., 54, 150
Marxism, 178
McCarthyism, 154
McDowell, J., 127
McMahan, J., 34
Mill, J.S., 102, 161, 172
mischief, 34
misfortune, 34
Moor, A. de, 129
Moore, G.E., 188
Moore, T., 40
morality, 108
Morris, J., 128
Münsterberg, H., 192

National Endowment for the Humanities, 68
naturalism, 83, 192, 194
naturalistic revolution, 150
New York University, 32
Nietzsche, F., 143, 150
Nonet, P., 173
norm, 175, 189
  -creator, 183
  -giver, 183
  -user, 183
'normative positivism', 16
Nozick, R., 29
Nuremberg Trials, 69

objectivity, 10
obligation, 118, 216
Offence Principle, 96
Ohio State University, 113
optimization, 5
ordinary language philosophy, 18, 101, 150, 172
ought implies can, 149

Parfit, D., 46, 76, 127
Patzig, G., 1
Paulson, S.L., 6, 187
Peczenik, A., 177
penal theory, 91
Perry, S., 35
Philip Randolph, A., 143
philosophy, 114, 192
  experimental, 148
  moral, 146, 199
  of science, 29
  political, 51, 75
philosophy of
  constitutional law, 27
  contract, 27
  criminal law, 27
  property, 27
  tort law, 27
Pinkard, T., 190

Plamenatz, J., 60
Plato, 89
Podgorecki, A., 173
political constitutionalism, 24
political obligation, 14
political philosophy of law, 27
politics, 61, 153, 168
Popper, K., 199
Posner, R., 68, 219
Postema, J., 34
practical reasoning, 145
Princeton University, 143
principle theory, 5
privacy, 61
proof, 146
property, 216
proportionality, 5, 91, 93
    cardinal, 93
    ordinal, 93
proportionality analysis, 5
psychology, 192
Puchta, G.F., 188
Pufendorf, S.v., 197
punishment, 31, 92, 95, 115, 118
punishment-as-blaming thesis, 92
Pure Theory of Law, 189
purpose, 165
purpositivism, 222

Radbruch, G., 7
Railton, P., 144, 212
Raphael, D.D., 14
rationality, 10
Rawls, J., 14, 18, 162, 178
Raz, J., 21, 46, 59, 60, 76, 126, 128, 132, 145, 173, 188, 218
Reagan, R., 143
reality, 10
Réaume, D., 76, 127
reconceptualization, 18, 91

Regan, D., 29
Reid, T., 172
religion, 61
reparation, 55
responsibility, 101, 105, 116, 132, 136, 145, 216
retributivism, 92
Rickert, H., 192
rights, 10, 14, 19, 69
Rivers, J., 5
Roberts, S., 134
Rockefeller University, 29, 30, 37
Rorty, R., 143
Ross, H., 134
Ross, W.D., 172
Rousseau, J.J., 75
rule, 210, 216
Russell, J.J., 172
Rutgers University, 90, 115
Ryle, G., 101

Saks, A., 222
Sartre, J.P., 143
Scalia, J.A., 221
Scandinavian realism, 148
Schauer, F., 21, 40, 144, 199
Schönfeld, M., 190
science, 190
Scottish Enlightenment, 14, 179
Scottish National Party, 179
Selznick, P., 173
Sen, A., 46, 76, 127
sentencing theory, 91
Separability Thesis, 218
Shapiro, B., 28
Shapiro, S.J., 209
Shute, S., 49
Simpson, B., 173
Sklar, L., 29
slavery, 168
Smith, A., 14, 172

social change, 61
society, 20, 107, 178
solidarity, 63
special case thesis, 2
St Andrews University, 172
Strawson, P.F., 89, 127, 190
Suárez, F., 197
Summers, B., 179

Tamanaha, B., 133
Tapper, C., 129
Taylor, C., 76
Taylor, P., 28
Teasdale, A., 77
Telfer, E., 15
Teubner, G., 133
textualism, 221
The Australian National University, 15
The Mental Welfare Commission for Scotland, 19
Thoreau, H.D., 167
Titchener, E.B., 192
trust, 164, 222, 223
truth, 59, 65, 85, 146
Turnbull, R., 114
Twining, W., 129, 173, 177, 202

understanding, 146
University of Cambridge, 90
University of Edinburgh, 171
University of Glasgow, 13, 171
University of Michigan, 113, 143
University of Oxford, 13, 77, 89, 101, 171
University of Stirling, 15
University of the Saarland, 177
utalitarianism, 158
    act, 158

validity, 216

Vienna School of Legal Theory, 188
Vietnam War, 17, 28, 69, 113

Waldron, J., 21, 76, 127, 202
Waluchow, W., 38
war on terror, 24
Weber, M., 188
Weinberger, O., 175, 176
welfare, 14, 158
White, J.J., 144
Williams, B., 47
Willock, I., 176
Windelband, W., 191
Wittgenstein, L., 130, 131, 172
Wolff, R.P., 75, 190
Wootton, B., 125
Woozley, T., 101
World War II, 153
Wundt, W., 192

Young Communist League, 154
Young Progressives of America, 154

www.ingramcontent.com/pod-product-compliance
Lightning Source LLC
Chambersburg PA
CBHW031311150426
43191CB00005B/174